This book is dedicated to you …

… to you from failing hands we throw the torch;
be yours to hold it high.

From *In Flanders Fields*
John Mcrae
May 1915

19. The Miscellaneous Pile..............................138
20. Hand-Held Mini Metal Detectors......................146
21. Pavlova Politics (and the Man on the Roof)..............188
22. Mr Majestic 201
23. No Moon Shift 204
24. The Victim Culture Part III...........................233

Preface

I arrive in a Transit van, which I seem to do rather a lot. Before me is a scene of utter devastation. It's like the aftermath of a Tourettes sufferers' beer festival. To my left is PC Flower, leaning against a battered pick-up truck and yelling in agony, an extensive trail of snot leaking from his nose and smearing on his neatly creased trousers. To my right is the portly figure of PC Kidney, having what first appears to be an almighty seizure, until I realise he is also screaming in pain, whirling his arms blindly around in a windmill-like motion (the first proper exercise he's done in years) and scattering the local drunks like skittles.

From the nearby Day Centre come howls of anguish and the sound of breaking furniture. Drunken jeers mixing with forceful commands to *stop resisting*! Amidst the hubbub of disorder and chaos a familiar voice yells from an unseen room, 'I'VE FUCKING HAD ENOUGH OF THIS SHIT!' I begin to run towards the Day Centre. This wasn't good. This could only mean one thing, and that was enough to make me sprint. PC Butch was inside. He was cross, and he was fighting. And he'd used his Captor ... again.

The situation could only get worse ...

Introduction – Part I

Hello and welcome to *This Victorian Playground Part II; Arriving in the Van.* The reasons for this title are simple. Firstly, in Britain, we live in a Victorian playground – a pink and fluffy utopian fantasy. Secondly, I'm a police officer (still), and I tend to arrive at situations in a Transit van quite a lot. For the police are very good at reacting and arriving, and departing of course. One could write a book of stories about the times we have received the call, turned up and buggered off. The bigger picture, of course, is *why*.

Why do we turn up? Why do we do what we do when we turn up? What difference does it all make? Only when we begin to understand the futility of it all will we fully appreciate just how fucked Britain is at the moment. We might also begin to understand how mentally degenerated we have become and how weak we really are. When we realise where we've come from and compare it to the morass we're in now, it might come as something of a shock. Or, it might not.

For we might like where we are at the moment. We might think it's great. Nevertheless, it would be very foolish to assume that we're moving on up and reaching for the stars. I rather think we're scrabbling around on the floor picking up the crumbs from beneath the table.

It's the wrong kind of humility. It's embarrassing. We British weren't born to be such mentally subservient dolts. There's nothing wrong with bowing or kneeling down, but it's got to be done in the right place for the right reasons. At the moment we have given up and given in. As a nation we have traded our dignity for counterfeit truths and insubstantial ideologies, and squandered our destiny in favour of short-term plans and fragile hopes. We've opted out of chiselling our names and deeds in blocks of granite, and opted in for degradable memories on plastic plaques.

I think we could all do with a trip to a war cemetery and kneel down, as one, in a field full of crosses. As hands are tightly held, and private prayers whispered, we might begin to remember our past and the future it promised; a future now blighted by crass, callous and tasteless behaviour, and dogged by sweet-talking liars in high, distant towers; while society begs, yields and crumbles, and readily forsakes a destiny built upon the eternal sacrifice of our own dearly beloved relatives.

We shall fight on the beaches. Ha, what the fuck happened to that kind of political attitude? Nowadays it's, "We will let them do whatever they want to do because we just don't have the gumption to do anything about anything any more. In fact, come on over and take what you want …"

The sovereignty of Britain is being slowly but surely eroded away and very soon there will be nothing left to be grateful for. Nothing left to celebrate about the nation at all. Nothing to preserve. Britain should be moving from strength to strength, but we're not. What are we producing now that you'd want to see in a museum in 200 years' time? Anything? What's so great or permanent about our culture nowadays that will stand the test of time? Absolutely fuck all. We have a decaying society and nothing of any permanence whatsoever, except that which was built in ages past.

Thus in this book we will take a further and deeper look at the discordant state of this nation through the eyes of a police officer, with tales to back up the claims – a look at where we've arrived and where it's all going horribly wrong!

For now, though, how about this for an insult …

Introduction – Part II

The other day some chap called me a 'bald ginger c**t'.

PC Snipper looked at me and shook his head. A *bald ginger c**t?*[1] This charming gentleman, who really put the idiot back into oxymoron, was handcuffed after a rather impressive struggle and then shoved into the back of a police car.

Unfortunately, we didn't have a van. That's because I'd run out of the door without one. I'd heard PC Grin and PC Snipper over the radio requesting some form of assistance, and fortunately they were just around the corner from the station. By the time I arrived the situation was somewhat under control, although drugged-up topless males who smash windows and scream blood-curdling abuse at 2am generally don't come quietly, and tend to have significant problems understanding the basic requirement to '*Shut the fuck up.*'

I think it was this dismissive command of mine that inspired my favourite insult of all time – the one about being bald *and* ginger. Ironically enough I am neither bald nor ginger, but I might be a bit of a C-word sometimes. Irrespective of this, our delightful prisoner continued to hurl the most bizarre abuse at all of us and then tried to kick the window in the back of the police car …

Not a good move. *We shall fight on the beaches.* Please sir, please stop doing that. Please don't do that sir. Oh please. Come on sir, I'm asking you nicely. Am I not being reasonable with you sir? Now come on sir, that's just unnecessary. Can we not just *talk* about it sir?

---

1   I'm not sure which of these three words was the more insulting … but said *together*… sheesh. It was like being hit by a spell from three wands.

PC Michael Pinkstone

I didn't say any of this really. My grandfather didn't earn war medals for valour to have a grandson who takes that kind of crap from a drugged-up scumbag. People like that don't deserve *conversation*.

Instead he got dragged from the back of the car and pummelled with legal and proportionate force, while I yelled into his face exactly what I thought of him, and told him in no uncertain terms that he was an arsehole. Of course, I didn't really call him an arsehole. I called him something far, far worse. Now *that's* quality of service.

As I was kindly admonishing this gentleman about his lack of compliance I heard a yell. From an upstairs window of a nearby flat came an angry voice. 'That's gotta be the worst bit of policing I have *ever* seen!' PC Snipper, who was also helping me, looked up. My goodness, if stares could kill. So under the watchful gaze of a pillock with a camera on his mobile phone (which twit invented that application?) my exhausted colleague and I managed to "assist" our prisoner back into the car, with me "controlling" him in the back.

Meanwhile his brother is also kicking off. They often work in pairs. It's like a tag team from hell. PC Fresh, PC Latvia and PC Grin are trying to fend him off from saving his sibling, and he's hurling equally insulting abuse at me for being too rough. Oh please sir, please. Oh don't call me that sir. Please don't say such nasty things to me sir – I find it all very upsetting. I'm just doing my job sir, but I'm transparent and open to criticism sir. After all, it's the worst bit of policing I've *ever* done sir. Perhaps you would like to make a complaint? Are you a *victim* sir? I'm ever so sorry, sir ...

The last I saw of our prisoner's brother was him being pushed all the way down the road and out of sight. The only reason he didn't get arrested was due to the usual story. Not enough cell space. Not enough resources to deal with him properly anyway. The end of a gruelling twelve-hour shift and the all-important question: *What's the fucking point?*

* * *

We arrive. We deal. And we've got the arriving down to a "T". Sometimes we're a bit late, owing to a distinct lack of frontline staff and an enormous amount of shit to shovel, but we do try. Once we're on scene we deal with things as best we can and then depart to the station to make our pointless updates.

This is the pattern. The method. The process. As discussed in *This Victorian Playground Part 1*, the circumstances are often irrelevant and some itchy-fingered civilian sitting at a desk is gagging to record any incident onto CRAPPIES[2] as soon as possible, which is the most important thing in the world. This is where the police are stranded at the moment.

You call, we respond. You tell us, we record. You demand, we yield. Sod any form of context. Sometimes we have to take a bit of initiative and maintain the Queen's Peace by doing something physical and active, but that's clearly the *worst* bit of policing we can do, so we'd prefer to sit down with you and just talk about it for a while. Perhaps take a statement. Give you a reference number. Treat you like that poor little victim. Build bridges. A bridge too fucking far.

You are calling the shots at the moment, by the way. We are policing by *your* consent. The other day I was having a few drinks with PC Latvia and we were watching a "reality" TV show about the police. Not generally my favourite kind of programme, but it passed the time. There was a scene of some incarcerated baddies in an Australian detention centre. Now these guys were *mean*. I've wrestled with some scumbags, but these ones were beyond aggressive. They had viciousness oozing from every pore. Unfortunately they were causing something of a riot and had armed themselves with big pieces of metal. The prison guards and police went in en-masse with riot shields, batons and all manner of appropriate equipment and comprehensively subdued these males. The incident was filmed, aired and the public complained about police brutality. *That's the worst bit of policing I've ever seen ...*

The public are always complaining. Police brutality! Nasty, nasty police! In fact, they don't complain about police brutality in Britain very much. Probably because we're so fucking soft and squelchy. Instead, they moan about extraordinarily pathetic things. We are, after all, a buzzword for blame and failure. Responsibility for everything lies with us. And we're not allowed to do anything that undermines your falsely promoted perceptions of us.

---

2 The police computer database, known privately as the 'Crime Recording and Analysis Portal: Police Investigation and Evaluation System'.

PC Michael Pinkstone

I've even received a complaint for *eating*. There I am, sitting in a police car, trying to shove a sandwich down my face as quickly as possible – the first food I've had for seven hours and the only food I'll have for a further six hours, and some old bitch walks past and tuts with annoyance. Shouldn't I be out catching murderers and rapists? Shouldn't I be stopping those youths in hoodies from damaging that phone box? I pay your wages, filth. So she complained.

I guess she felt she was a victim. A victim of some kind of betrayal. She *pays* my wages after all. She employs me. I answer to her. In fact, I need her to check my PDR,[3] but she'll probably only give me "Satisfactory". Still, I'll just grin and bear it.

Public perception is very important to the police, you see. It's all about how we present ourselves and how we appear. An image; an icon. A semblance. A representation of stability, safety and security in the form of a uniformed constable grinning and bearing it. Or, as the case may be, not grinning.

Not long ago, PC Peas was doing a "scene watch". This basically meant that she was standing by some railings after someone had fallen into a nearby subway, with a goodly length of police barrier tape wrapped randomly around various nearby lamp posts.[4] Unlike some American films or programmes concerning crime scenes, we don't have a whole load of clinical-looking, suited individuals who turn up straight away and get immediate DNA hits from random objects or check wine glasses for two types of lipstick – one belonging to the dead person and the other belonging to the outstanding witness who managed to miraculously escape by leaping thirty-eight floors into a swimming pool (just put her on CRAPPIES as "anonymous" at the moment).

No, we're not quite so lucky. We have the odd scenes of crime officer, who will turn up and do a pretty good job under the circumstances (those circumstances being lack of staff, lack of decent wages, lack of resources and lack of pretty much everything). Of course, if it's been a really serious incident that makes it onto the national news then you can be assured that things will *look* pretty darn efficient. There will be police barrier

---

[3] Performance Development Review.
[4] This is what barrier tape *was* designed for. Not turning psycho-bitches into interactive mummies.

This Victorian Playground - Part 2

tape wrapped around just about everything of some fixed permanence; perhaps even tents covering the crime scene to protect it. There will be individuals kitted up in white full-on suits walking slowly around with technical-looking equipment, and in the foreground a journalist will be explaining exactly what it is they don't know about the circumstances, and postulating wildly on the bits they do know. One thing you can be assured of, though, is the smart uniformed constable standing near the entrance to the crime scene wearing their helmet and their high visibility jacket is busting for a piss and bored out of their fucking mind.

But for the majority of "crime scenes" we don't have that kind of attention or context. PC Tall once spent a whole night guarding a bone at a building site, by himself, without light or a chair. The bone turned out to belong to a mid-sized mammal.[5] And now PC Peas was guarding – well, not even she knew what the fuck she was guarding. She was guarding a *crime scene*, which basically meant standing in the sun for seven hours while no-one did much about anything and even when they did turn up, they didn't find anything because it was obvious that nothing sinister had happened, and even if something *had* happened, there was nothing blowing around the filthy subway to suggest that it had happened in the first place. Yet we have to do it, just in case.

Anyway, I'm somewhat getting off the point. *Public perception.* So PC Peas is standing there feeling quite fucked off and an important police officer drives past on his way to the station. The following day in our briefing meeting we have an email read out to us by the Sergeant. Basically the important police officer was disappointed to drive past PC Peas and find that she wasn't *smiling*. What kind of an image does a non-smiling officer present to the public? So we all got told off, and told to smile.

Fucking political prick. I can't stand people like that. Public perception my arse. So now we can create victims if we don't *smile*. OK, so we're not allowed to eat, we have to grin permanently, and always parade ourselves in a wishy-washy manner that dares not undermine this fantasy so desperately promoted by pathetic morons without any clue

---

5 PC Tall has also guarded a dead pigeon and some squirrel blood. Lots of hours and lots of money are spent protecting expired wildlife. Quality of service has never been so thorough.

whatsoever. We mustn't do anything that shatters the image or illusions of this child's game; this victim culture in all of its sickly-sweet glory; this Victorian playground. My goodness, the situation has gone beyond the pale.

Thus in the following chapters we will attempt to add some further context to this shambolic state of affairs, and offer some more insight on just how buggered up everything really is. From crime scenes to scene watches; from days out in court to days in ticking boxes; from statements to withdrawals; from prickly fruit to pointless policies; from something to nothing; from modernism to postmodernism; from Transit van to calamity – this book is about where we've arrived, and the resulting confusion and chaos. In other words, we're here – now what the fuck are we doing?

Enjoy.
Well, try to.
PC Michael Pinkstone
October 2007

www.michaelpinkstone.wordpress.com

1. My Brain Hurts

Who are these people? Where do they live? What do they eat? Where do they shop? What cars do they drive? *Who* are they?

I've never seen them, or spoken to them on the phone. In many respects, it's hard to believe they actually exist. Yet I've seen the results of their surveys and read the recommendations from their studies. I've perused their reports. Pondered their findings. Puzzled over their summaries.

Their conclusions have made me frown. Made me gasp. Made me shake my head in despair. A hopeless shrug. A heartfelt sigh. A shadow cast upon an already despondent face. Yet obey I must.

I've breathed the suffocating air of their indifference, and walked upon the fragile pathways of their unconcern. I've gagged on the bitter aftertaste of their ruinous designs, and choked on the incredulity of their proposals.

I've wallowed in the slough of their indiscretions, and staggered up the steep hills of their vain ambitions. I've snarled at the viciousness of their pointless directives and bowed beneath the weight of their hollow enterprises.

I've listened with knowing ears to their empty rhetoric. Sat and stared at their shallow posturing; their vacuous displays of magnificence.

I've waited in line for their specious generosities, only to stare, again, at the meagreness of their promised munificence. Never failed to be shocked at the depths of their dishonour, yet somehow still find myself bound by their contemptible judgements. Wondering, questioning, challenging, yet never quite finding the truth.

Who *are* they?

PC Michael Pinkstone

Who the *hell* are they?

The voice of the people? The mouthpiece of this generation? They are the knowing ones. The all-seeing eye. The builders of the tower. The ones to gather us in, and gather us up, and bring us all together. The uniting ones. The blenders. The stirrers of this melting pot. The ones with the plans; the blueprints; the designs for life. Our sentinels in their citadels. Our protectors in their watchtowers. Our role models and mentors. Chiefs and cardinals. Our captains and commanders. They know best. Nanny knows best. Come to us. We hold the keys to this city.

* * *

Yesterday I read a report that a Government think-tank had suggested *playing down* Christmas in an effort to appease people from other faiths, who may find themselves "upset" by the festive season.

Just out of interest, I've *never, ever* met anyone in my entire *life*, who is "upset" by Christmas, or who feels alienated by it because it isn't part of their faith. I've certainly never met anyone who finds it offensive.

And talking of offence, I was reading recently that a story based on "The Three Little Pigs" had been turned down from a Government agency's annual awards because the subject matter could "offend Muslims".

Apparently the agency judges stated that they had "*concerns about the Asian community and the use of pigs raises cultural issues*".

Now let's just cast aside this sycophantic, pandering bollocks and consider a pertinent point: Jews have similar prohibitions regarding pork.

Let me just repeat that in case you missed it. In case it whipped past you like a Saab on the M4. (After all, they own the whole fucking motorway.)

Jews have similar prohibitions regarding pork.

So, if this is true, why not worry about offending Jews? Do they not matter? Does our Jewish community not breathe the same air? If we prick them, do they not bleed? Why are we concerning ourselves purely with Muslims in this little political ritual of grovelling to certain communities? Do these idiots ever hear what they sound like, and do they know what effect they are having?

This Victorian Playground - Part 2

I can only assume that the Jews would not be offended, and the Muslims would be ready to rise up in some kind of revolt against this heinous and deliberate attack on their religious sensibilities in the form of a classic children's tale. My goodness, how subversive. I can only but guess at the chaos those Anchor butter adverts are causing within the Hindu community.

So, to cut a long story short, who the fuck are these people who suggest such things? *The use of pigs raises cultural issues.* My good God. Hello? HELLO? WHERE ARE YOU? CAN YOU SHOW YOURSELVES PLEASE? CAN YOU AT LEAST PUT UP YOUR FUCKING HAND SO I CAN SEE WHO YOU ARE?

Do these people truly exist? Did that Government think-tank really exist? Where did they get their information from? Why do we have to suffer the indignities of their fucking ludicrous suggestions time and time and time again? Suggestions usually starting with one, or more, of these kinds of phrases:

Research has shown ...
A recent study has suggested ...
A Government think-tank has proposed ...
The findings of a report published today conclude that ...
Recommendations from the inquiry indicate ...

Now wouldn't it be great if tomorrow, in the newspaper, you were to read something like this:

Research has shown ... that Britain is currently pretty fucked and that's about it really.

I think this would be quite a refreshing read. However, we never have anything as exciting as that. Instead we get things like this:

Research has shown that eating is entirely damaging to your health and you simply shouldn't do it.

PC Michael Pinkstone

A Government think-tank has proposed that Christmas should be replaced with any other religious festival that is more diverse than, er, Christmas. And The Three Little Pigs is racist, in case you weren't aware.

The findings of a report published today conclude that serious questions need to be asked regarding the handling of domestic incidents by police. Evidence suggests that they are not doing their job properly and should, in fact, face even more blame when they don't arrest someone for having had a verbal argument about the salad with their partner. After all, if he murders her in twenty-seven years' time, their inaction will be called into account.

Recommendations from the inquiry indicate that all victims of crime, no matter what the context, should be contacted by police following the conclusion of their case to ensure that they have received a good quality of service. There should be targets for this as well.

A recent study has suggested that victims of burglary are not bothered about getting their stuff back and really don't give a shit if the offender is caught. They just want the police to treat their diversity with respect, and tell them what their self-defined ethnicity is, from a little chart.

A Government think-tank has suggested that everything is absolutely fine in the country and that the police service is well-resourced, full of morale and ready to face the next few challenging years ahead ...

Are we fuck.

* * *

This Victorian Playground - Part 2

So, just when we thought it couldn't get any more pathetic – it did. On a daily basis.

Sergeant Chelsea was slumped over the printer in the office, his face a picture of complete resignation. 'Listen to this, Pinkstone,' he said, in a voice that was incredulous, yet somehow not surprised.

'New guidelines for Sergeants regarding the Victim Codes of Practice.' He paused, as if trying to piece together the shattered remnants of his will. 'From the 1st November Sergeants will be required to carry out dip checks in relation to crime reports concerning the Victim Codes of Practice.'

Another pause. The effort was enormous. 'Sergeants will now have to contact victims of crime to establish whether or not they have received decent assistance from their police service. Sergeants will be phoning victims once the crime report has been filed, to gauge their victim satisfaction in line with the current performance indicators.'

Hopefully by the end of the year we'll have an improvement from 48% satisfaction to 54.839% satisfaction and, therefore, guarantee some form of sycophantic bollocks at some point. Perhaps a congratulatory email or two from someone without numbers on their epaulettes. And something about your PDR, and quality of service and stuff.

The email went on. And on. It was like listening to the verbal equivalent of golden syrup – a cloying, thick, sickeningly sweet, altogether puke-inducing load of sludge. Not that I've got anything against golden syrup.

Yet the best part was still to come. 'Listen to this,' he said again, wide-eyed with amazement, as he thumbed to page 378. He paused anew, as if not fully believing what he was seeing. 'If you phone someone who is driving, please ask them whether or not they are using hands-free. If not, please instruct them to pull over to the side of the road and talk to you safely there ...'

I stared back, my head shaking numbly from side to side. Recent exhortations ringing in my ears from newly appointed prime ministers. *Getting tough on crime. New laws to combat disorder. Hand-held mini metal detectors to tackle gun crime.*

And here, a Sergeant, almost collapsing under the weight of bollocks being showered upon him from above. It was a horrible sight. I've never

PC Michael Pinkstone

seen anyone quite so defeated. He slouched back to his office, a mere shadow of his former self. A wraith. Covered in testicles.

A few minutes later during the briefing meeting, Acting Sergeant Luton added his input. 'Yeah,' he said, 'if they don't want to talk to us we have to go through a list of about twenty questions to establish *why* they don't want to talk to us …'

At this point I tuned out and switched off. Saved my electricity. From stand-by to stand-down. I closed my eyes and began to dream.

* * *

It all started in 2003 when I went through the various stages of becoming a police officer. I was supply teaching at the time, just to pay the bills of course, and looking forward to the change of scenery. Not that I hated teaching – I just didn't want to do it any more. I could see myself … fifty-five years old, wearing a cream cardigan, sitting in a staffroom, eating Ryvita with cottage cheese. This was my future. My own little purgatory. So I filled in some forms, ticked some random boxes and sent my application off in the post.

Miraculously, I managed to get past the paper sift. This was the first hurdle. I guess my application didn't contain too many spelling mistakes or other glaring errors, and was sufficiently low-key to warrant taking further. Fantastic.

After this I did some random role-plays and ran up and down a tennis court a few times. I only remember one of the role-plays, which was a scenario involving a dissatisfied customer. How ironic. I think the gist of it was that the customer wasn't happy about a bus tour that she had been on and subsequently complained to me – quite vociferously I might add – that she wasn't happy.

So I listened with theoretical sympathy to her whingeing and whining, little realising that this was a perfect induction to the world of policing. I'd worked in retail before becoming a teacher, so was quite used to "customer dissatisfaction", and my response to her story was the usual diplomatic bollocks, gleaned from a few years' experience. Neither a "yes" nor a "no". A fobbing-off. A deflection. A smoothing-over. A squaring-up. Ideal for my forthcoming career.

This Victorian Playground - Part 2

Remarkably, the assessors thought that I passed the various role-plays, and subsequently invited me back on a later date for more questioning, in the form of The Interview.

This took place in late November. I arrived in my suit, feeling slightly nervous. My hair was trim and my shoes were shiny. I walked into the room to face a panel of three, and sat down.

'So, Michael,' said the important chap sitting in the middle. 'Why do you want to be a police officer?'

'Hmmm,' said I. 'Well, I really want to *help* people. Make a difference. Support victims. You know, that kind of thing.'

'Are you a racist?' They stared impassively.

I blinked. 'No!' I spluttered. 'I value *everyone*!'

'Good,' said the chap on the left. 'Welcome to the police service.'

It wasn't long, however, before the cynicism began to set in. Training school was quite good fun and by my own admission I tried very hard and did OK. There were exams and tests and swimming and marching and lots of things about diversity. I came away after fifteen weeks not having a fucking clue about policing whatsoever. The *real* training would take place on the streets and in the station. The only thing I really learned was "Watch Your Back". No-one else will.

If you can spend the next thirty years of your life somehow avoiding anything that may be considered racist, sexist or homophobic, criminal, or lacking in honesty and integrity, then you will be fine and you'll get your pension. If, however, you knock any of those hurdles over (in fact, make any of them wobble slightly) – you're fucked and you don't stand a chance. No-one will help you. No-one will back you up. You'll be on your own. So good luck and enjoy the Job.

After two months I was jaded. After eleven months I had a relapse and enjoyed things for a while following my driving course. This didn't last long. After a year and a half I was emotionally and physically drained, lurching from one job to the next in a kind of detached stupor.

Two and a half years passed and things were getting worse. The Government was killing us all. I never thought I'd ever hear myself say something like, 'This job is fucked,' especially after such a short space of time (8.3% of my service, to be fairly precise). But I said it on

PC Michael Pinkstone

a daily basis, along with vocalising the same kind of sentiment about the country in general.

Three and a half years passed and I was on the edge. 11.6% of my service completed and things were looking bleak. *Think of the pension.* Fuck that! What about the here and now? Every time I loaded up my emails there seemed to be messages about retired officers who had died somewhat early. All this "thinking of the pension" malarkey seemed rather cruel, for many officers didn't seem to stick around long enough to enjoy it. Why should I spend thirty years of my life thinking about my fucking pension?

Then, of course, you get emails about the Government fucking around with that fucking pension anyway, or generally abusing our pay in some form or other. So the pension I allegedly have to look forward to may, or may not, exist in the future. In which case, why am I expected to spend three decades desperately anticipating something that may not end up being what I anticipate it to be?

Then, of course, you've got the fact that if you make one tiny, irrelevant, completely insubstantial faux-pas – you could lose your pension anyway. Think of the fun in that! Think that if you spend twenty-four years of your life being a brilliant police officer, but one day you get caught out having sent an allegedly "racist" text message – you'll most likely get fired and lose your pension as a result! Think of the pension? Fuck that shit.

Not long ago in my police service our local coroner was fired for sending an allegedly racist "joke" text message. The content of the text was considered entirely inappropriate and, as such, an agreeable decision would appear to have been made. Jokes or comments that malign certain races are clearly evidence of very bad character, and would indicate that people who indulge in these malicious forms of communication should, at the very least, be sacked. An example should be made of them and their otherwise impeccable work record must be expunged from existence. None of us should *ever* behave in such a fashion, and *every* joke or ostensibly "racist"-sounding remark that we make clearly means that we are hateful, hurtful bastards who need to be struck off the list, just like that coroner. He was obviously a vicious, racist scumbag and we should never have employed him in

This Victorian Playground - Part 2

the first place. SUCH BEHAVIOUR WILL NOT BE TOLERATED. Blah, blah, blah. So I would just like to say, for now, that *firing* someone for sending a *text message* is an absolute fucking disgrace. It's like arresting someone for sending a text message.[6] It is a travesty and a tragedy. It is beyond words. How typical of an organisation that is so desperate to appear nice and precious, to behave in a manner that is so subversively dictatorial. It makes me twitch. While true racism is unacceptable, dismissing someone for sending a joke text message is even more unacceptable. How fucking dare they. What a shambles of ghastly proportions.

* * *

This victim culture affects everything. Absolutely everything. As stated before, it can hardly be summed up. Everywhere you look, things are deteriorating, although they are supposed to be getting better. Surely as we march inexorably forwards in time, civilisations are supposed to improve? Surely we have ironed out all of the problems by now? Surely we are heading towards organisational perfection? Surely our tower will reach the skies?

Surely I need to stop complaining? Perhaps I'm just tired and grumpy. Perhaps it's the nature of my job that's getting me down. Are all coppers the same? I wonder. Is our world view now so tarnished that we make things sound much worse than they really are? Surely things aren't *that* bad?

Actually, they *are* that bad. In fact, things are shit. It's somewhat difficult to put your finger on it at times, but admitting that things are fucked up is a start.

The more you dig the worse it gets. This onion is rotten from the core. Every layer reveals even more decay.

Somewhere, somehow, we lost sight of something. We lost our innocence, some people say. But were we ever really that innocent to

---

[6] See how everything is linked together? If we arrest someone for doing something so minor, it only goes to prove that we have to fire one of our own for doing something equally minor. Talk about a self-fulfilling prophecy of quite hideous dimensions.

start with? Who knows. But we must know one thing – society *has* changed. And changed for the worse.

What has happened in the past couple of decades, and in particular the last few years, to really bring this shambolic state of affairs to the fore?

Perhaps things have always been the way they are, and in the past decade I grew up slightly, thus appreciating what was going on. Not that "appreciating" is a good choice of words, but you get my drift.

Perhaps becoming a police officer fucked me up. Perhaps dealing with so many fuckwits fucked me up. Perhaps seeing just how much leniency bad people get is wearing me down. Perhaps I don't really know. Perhaps, perhaps, perhaps. I guess it's just a matter of perspective.

So many views and so many opinions. Perhaps I should just get on with the next chapter because my brain hurts.

2. Anti-Social Behaviour?

Anti-social behaviour has evolved. In bygone years that heinous crime of scrumping apples has become almost a symbol of a lost innocence; an innocence where youths were little rascals, but not criminals. A clip round the earhole and a stern word of advice was enough to put a grubby little scoundrel back on the straight and narrow; enough to leave him reeling from the robust intervention of "The Law" and, no doubt, aching from some physical admonition at the hands, or the belt, of his father. Nowadays groups of youths don't scrump apples. They form large, unruly gangs and kick people to death for no reason, and film it all on their mobile phones for fun. A soulless generation of mindless, evil, violent scrotes that all need locking up, after having the shit whacked out of them first. No, I shouldn't say that. I don't advocate violence. But I do advocate common sense and justice ... I seem to recall writing that somewhere before.

Our streets are being ruled not only by foolish and mindless scumbags, but by callous and indifferent thugs. We already know that the police are ineffective and powerless and that the Government would rather we deal with irrelevant crap than with stuff that needs desperate – and forceful – intervention, so it should come as no surprise when you read horrific stories about deaths brought about by apparently unprovoked acts of extreme violence on our streets. Acts of downright aggression and disorder carried out by *kids.*

Of course, the police aren't really powerless. We can ask these youths for their names and addresses. We can move them on. We can direct them to leave the locality. If applied for, we can impose a "dispersal order".[7] Wow, super. They really work. They really combat the heart of the problem. They create *fear*.

Pah, what a load of fucking wishy-washy crap. This *isn't* anti-social behaviour – it's gone way beyond that. We've entered into the realms of gang warfare; of tribal allegiances and vicious social rebellion. When parents feel they need to buy stab-proof vests for their children then you know there's a problem. When groups of youths roam the streets tooled up with blades and other items intended for the sole purpose of causing pain, then you know the situation has got somewhat out of control.

My colleague and I – think it was PC Fresh – recently got asked to respond to an incident reported by a member of the public where several youths were sitting on the top of a garage block behind some flats and pelting pedestrians with various missiles.

Little rascals. I'd never get cross with anyone for sitting on a garage block but throwing things at people is taking things a little bit too far. This would be ideal for some "local resolution" – taking each one of those children home to speak to their parents, who in turn would suitably admonish their child, ground them for a week, and everything would be hunky-dory.[8]

However, by the time PC Fresh and I arrived at the scene there were only three young children left – two boys and a girl – and they were kicking a football against the garage block. They were clearly not the ones we were looking for.

I walked up to them and said, 'Hi guys.' One of the young lads, who was about nine, picked up his football and said, 'Hello officer.' Meanwhile the other little lad was already poking my handcuffs and simultaneously asking me what my Captor spray was. I told him to ask PC Butch – he's the expert on that shit. I didn't really say that, but I did say, 'Have any of you seen anyone up on that garage roof?'

The lad with the football pointed in a random direction behind him and said, 'Yeah, they all ran that way about five minutes ago. They were gangstas.'

---

[7] As stated in *This Victorian Playground Part 1* – we don't really "solve" problems. We tend to move them elsewhere. In this case, *disperse* them ...

[8] Theories and ideas sound great on paper don't they?

This Victorian Playground - Part 2

I stared at him, suddenly feeling old and out of touch. There's me, an ex-primary school teacher – a relatively recent ex-primary school teacher – and in all my years of teaching I'd never heard any child use the word 'gangstas', *ever*. Perhaps I wasn't very good at listening, or perhaps I'd misheard.

'I'm sorry, did you say *gangsters*?' The lad nodded solemnly. 'Yeah, they were all wearing gangsta clothes too.' He said this with a touch of reverence, looking with disgust at his own sensible football shirt.

Gangster clothes? Now I felt *completely* out of touch. 'How old were they?' The lad threw me the football and I headed it back straight into his hands – ha, not out of touch at all – 'Oh they were about thirteen, some of them were older. One of them is called Luke.'

Aha, now the penny drops. Every Luke I've ever dealt with has been a little shit. Apologies if you're called Luke and you're not a little shit, but you can't argue with the statistics. Teachers used to discuss things like this: did your name have any impact on your behaviour or skills? The general consensus was: *yes*.

When I was teaching, the top three boys' names for being little shites were: *Jordan* (they were always in the remedial "Green Group"); *Ryan* (not *every* Ryan was a scrote, but the general feeling was that despite the odd anomaly, they were all awful); and *Luke* (complete pains in the arse).

I remember once sitting in a Year 5 class in Cambridge with about ten minutes to go until the end of lunch break when the door burst open and a breathless child came running in, closely followed by another equally exhausted and excitable looking friend. 'Mr Pinkstone, Mr Pinkstone!' The poor little thing was positively hyperventilating. 'Luke hasn't taken his medicine!'

I looked with some bewilderment at my bearer of bizarre news. 'OK,' I said slowly. 'Is that a good or a bad thing?' The little girl just stared back at me. 'He's going to be very angry,' she said at last. 'Mrs Latcham from the office has already rung his mum and she's on the way.'

I blinked, trying to remember which one of the delightful children I'd been teaching all morning was called "Luke". That's because I was covering as a supply teacher and couldn't really be bothered to learn names. The only name that mattered was *mine*. As in, 'Yes, Mr Pinkstone.

I'll sit quietly and not throw a desk at your face Mr Pinkstone ...'

So I thanked the fretful little girl for her worrying news and started to build barricades. By the time I'd finished there was no way that anyone, not even angry Luke, was going to be able to break through my defences. This isn't true really. Instead, I walked to the office, and made enquiries about this problem child. The receptionist told me that mum was on the way, and just to have Luke in the classroom "as normal" until she arrived with his medication. She looked apprehensive as she told me. 'Good luck,' she whispered, as I turned and began the slow, heavy walk back to my inevitable demise. Fuck me, what was wrong with Luke and what the fuck was his mother bringing – a tranquilliser gun? I half expected someone to sneak through the classroom door and fire a lethal looking dart into Luke's neck and then do some complicated hand signal to the rest of his camouflaged comrades, before melting back into the corridors and using a radio to update HQ. *'Broadsword calling Danny Boy, Broadsword calling Danny Boy – the target has been eliminated; I repeat, the target has been eliminated.'*

So I walked back into the classroom with three minutes to go and prepared a strategy. As soon as the children walked in I'd have them sitting at their desks reading books in silence, which would hopefully allow me to see which one Luke was, as I was sure he wouldn't do anything in silence. I'd then decide what to do with him on the spot, as there are no real strategies you can prepare for children who haven't "taken their medicine". You just have to be reactionary and trust to luck. A bit like the police.

Well, let's just say that it took Luke about half a second to make his presence known. He swaggered in through the door and toppled a small bookcase before viciously kicking various children at their desks and throwing several classroom objects at the window, including a couple of prized items from the technology shelf and a cardboard monster truck that had taken about eighteen years to construct. He then turned on me ...

My mind wandered back to the present, and the lad with the football. 'Luke? You say his name was *Luke*?' The lad nodded and I felt a cold chill down my spine. 'Thanks guys,' I said. 'Which way did they go?' The little girl, who hadn't said anything up until now, suddenly piped up. 'They all went that way! I know Luke, he lives at number 4! He's

This Victorian Playground - Part 2

a gangsta!' I turned to face her. I didn't actually want to know where Luke lived, but asked her anyway.

Two minutes later, PC Fresh and I, armed with relevant local information, made our merry way several streets away to look for Luke the "gangsta" and his gang of ... gangstas.

We never did find them of course. Far too clever and subversive a gang to be tracked down by two police officers, one of whom was actually terrified at meeting anyone nasty called Luke ever again.

* * *

The sad fact, of course, is that society is fucked. When you have mere children revelling in the title of "gangster" and other children treating them with solemn respect then you have a rather grave predicament. In the past several years youth behaviour has deteriorated rapidly. It's never been perfect, but it's now reaching the stage of the totally grim.

What kind of social meltdown leads to crews of teenagers *killing* people and filming it on their phones? What kind of fucked up cultural melting pot leads to youth gangs shooting and stabbing each other on pretty much a daily basis? And what kind of degraded societal shambles leads to nine year olds wishing they were "gangsters"?

This isn't *anti-social behaviour.* It's adolescent anarchy. It's kids playing wargames. It's teenagers playing with fire and wielding weapons and spilling blood ... without remorse and without fear of consequence.

Hi, I'm PC Pinkstone and I require you to provide me with your name and address because it is believed you have been acting in an anti-social manner ...

Does this Government have *any* idea whatsoever about *anything?*

3. 82%

In a variety of contexts, 82% could be seen as a rather splendid figure. For example, if I got 82% in my Sergeants exam, I would have been in the "top bracket" (or whatever they call it), and I would have had an invite from the Chief to get a winning smile and a firm handshake. As it was, I didn't.

And If I'd got 82% in my degree, I may have walked away with a First, but yet again I was knocking on the door of 70% and ended up with a particularly solid 2:1. Shame. I think, though, that one of the reasons for this was an incredibly annoying tutor at my university, who never gave anyone a percentage above 65% when marking their assignments. After providing him with an awesome essay regarding gymnosperms and angiosperms (the content of which I neither comprehended nor appreciated, seeing as I was doing a fucking primary school teaching degree, and he wanted us to complete the science element of that degree to a level of understanding that would baffle Einstein), which only got me 63%, I kind of resigned myself to my fate. Still, I ended up with a Bachelor of Arts in Teacher Education with Qualified Teacher Status with Science. Bit of a mouthful, but it sounds pretty darn good on paper.

David Blunkett then welcomed me to the glorious teaching profession with a wonderful letter outlining how valued and appreciated we all were and blah, blah, blah. Nothing changes eh?

Anyway, 82%. Another context in which this could be a favourable amount would be if you took home 82% of your salary. How nice would that be? I look at my wage packet these days and think that it would probably be more beneficial to jack it all in and throw myself upon the

This Victorian Playground - Part 2

mercy of the welfare state, but I guess I'm a touch too honest to claim more than I need and deserve.

82% is, therefore, quite a decent figure. Obtaining this amount as a pass mark in any exam would be pretty darn good, and in a variety of other situations one could appreciate how marvellous getting 82% would be.

However, there's another side to the fence. Imagine, if you will, someone coming up to you before you board a plane, and saying, 'Hey, you've got an 82% chance of surviving that flight.'

Or, on a more bizarre level, how about if someone popped their head around your bedroom door one morning and said lightly, 'Hey, you're going to lose 82% of your body today.'

I'm sure you can now think of a variety of situations where 82% would actually be quite negative. It all depends on the context. As a percentage all by itself, 82% means absolutely nothing, of course. It needs an environment in which to be presented and, depending on the circumstances, may be either a good or a bad thing ...

* * *

Recently a freshly inducted colleague of mine, PC Trooper, shared with me his "results" from his assessment day at the police training centre in 2007.

Now, you would think that PC Trooper would have shared some solid facts and figures like, 'Hey, Pinkstone, I got 82% in my numeracy exam.' Or, 'Hey, Pinkstone, I got 82% in my spatial awareness test.'

This would be quite objective and I would nod my head in appreciation at the sensibility of it all. Nice, firm, decisive, reasonable assessment. Measurable, quantifiable and generic enough not to be too biased.

Follow this up with a decent interview with a panel of police officers and you could say that the recruitment process would be pretty thorough. Who could argue with a few tests of numeracy and literacy skills, as well as a rigorous fitness test and an interview to examine a candidate's background and experience? Maybe even a couple of role-plays to at least elicit some small appreciation of how that person interacts and communicates. Keep it all nice and balanced and objective. Try not to place too much emphasis on any particular element of this process and you end up with something about as fair and appropriate as you can get.

Hmm. Unfortunately, of course, the system has gone rather downhill in recent months. It's all become a bit too fucking precious. This nicey-nice, pink and fluffy, insipid organisational bollocks we all have to face every single day, has led to a dampening down of all things gritty and relevant, and inspired some quite frankly perplexing methods of recruitment.

The interview has become prescribed and formulaic. Certain questions are not allowed to be asked, and most of the remaining questions are immaterial anyway. The role-plays are focused on precious things like quality of service, community focus and, of course, the most important thing in the world – diversity. It's become all sugar-frosted and puke-worthy, which really shouldn't come as any form of surprise. Now, all you have to do as a potential recruit, is ensure you aren't racist; and demonstrate that you value, respect and love everyone equally. Of course, it's quite difficult to do this during an interview or set of role plays, but don't worry – you'll still be *graded.* You'll get your "results" in the post and they will inform you of where the gaps are …

PC Trooper, for his part, is a damn fine fellow. I think I need to say this now, just in case he reads this and feels upset all over again. However, he's only 82% competent in Respecting Race and Diversity.

Please allow me to repeat that whilst pinching myself somewhere excruciating because I need to make sure I haven't died and gone to some kind of precious purgatory: *PC Trooper, for his part, is a damn fine fellow. However, he's only 82% competent in Respecting Race and Diversity.*

He looked at me, almost pleadingly, and said, 'Does that mean I'm 18% racist?'

I was driving at the time and nearly swerved off the road. That familiar bubble of rage was rising to the surface yet again and my eyes were wide and bloodshot with uncontrolled emotion. 82% COMPETENT IN RESPECTING RACE AND DIVERSITY?! How the fuck has it come to this? How on earth has it got to the stage whereby we are *grading* people on their level of "respect"?

And what was the cut-off point? Did those in charge have a little chart that instructed them to give the nod to anyone with a "respect

This Victorian Playground - Part 2

level" above 70%, but encouraged them to cast into the fiery furnace those poor souls who didn't quite cut the mustard? How on earth does the system work? What the fuck are the criteria? Who on earth dreamed this shit up? Where's my sanity?

I can only guess that those in charge will be keeping a very close eye on PC Trooper in the future, just to make sure that he bucks his ideas up and increases his "respect level" by 18%. But, the crucial point here, is what exactly does this deficit in "respect" equate to, in the eyes of the management?

In real terms I guess it means that PC Trooper has a slight attitude problem he needs to address, or he'll undoubtedly lose his job. He's clearly an accident waiting to happen. *The Secret Policeman Part II,* perhaps?

It can only mean that for every fifty people he deals with, nine will find themselves disrespected and badly treated. I can only assume, therefore, that PC Trooper will single out those folks displaying obvious cultural differences and malign them in some way for their ethnicity – seeing as he is somewhat defective in his esteem for race and diversity issues. Imagine this for a PDR entry:

"Today I dealt with fifty people. Forty-one of them I smiled at, and respected, and treated nicely. They were all white British. The other nine consisted of a Turk, a Pole, a Frenchie, a Pakistani, a Yank, a Jap, a Hun, an Aussie and a blind chap from the Yemen. I stamped on all of their shins and batoned several of them really hard about the face, especially the Frenchie. Fucking bald ginger c**t. That's because I'm only 82% competent in Respecting Race and Diversity, so what did you fucking expect? The End. Love from PC Trooper."

Please don't try and get your head around the situation because it will explode, or implode. Either way, your head won't work especially well after trying to comprehend just how we could have got ourselves into this state. How we ended being so fucking yukky. I'm clenching my fists and gritting my teeth as I write this, because it's such a travesty I can hardly find the words.

4. Statements

CJ Act 1967, s.9; MC Act 1980, ss.5A(3) (a) and 5B; Criminal Procedure Rules 2005, Rule 27.1

> *This statement (consisting of __ Page(s) each signed by me) is true to the best of my knowledge and belief and I make it knowing that, if it is tendered in evidence, I shall be liable to prosecution if I have wilfully stated in it, anything which I know to be false, or do not believe to be true.*
> Denise MALHONEY
> Full Time Mother

I am the above named person and I live at an address known to the police. For the past three years I have been going out with a male called Jason DICKENS. I would describe Jason as about 31 years old, 5' 11" tall, with short brown hair. He has a tattoo of "*Chantelle*" on his right upper arm, which belonged to his previous girlfriend's best friend's friend, who he was secretly shagging.

Jason and I met whilst drinking around a mutual friend's house several years ago. We started going out with each other at the end of 2004. From the beginning, our relationship was rocky and we used to argue a lot. Jason has a drink problem and would often come home from the pub drunk and be verbally abusive to me. After the birth of our triplets – Orlando, Keira and Johnny

This Victorian Playground - Part 2

– in 2006, Jason began to get physically abusive.
He used to hit me lots of times but I would never report this to the police. One day he fractured my jaw, bust my leg, imploded my spleen, ripped out one of my kidneys and beat me repeatedly with a mace until I fainted. A neighbour called police while this was happening, but I declined ambulance.

After this attack I told Jason that it was all over and he left me for 2 weeks until he came back again and I let him in. Everything was OK for a few months and he kept telling me that he'd changed, but he started drinking heavily again because he wasn't working, and started getting verbally and physically aggressive towards me on a daily basis.

At the beginning of this year I split up with Jason again and he went to stay at his dad's house for an hour and a half before he came back to me again and I let him in. However, he became instantly abusive towards me, and at this stage I called the police myself, creating a lot of paperwork for the 2 police officers who attended and I got given a CRAPPIES reference number, filled out a Domestic Risk Assessment Form and got contacted by a concerned person working in a Domestic Violence Unit, a letter, a follow-up call, and the equivalent of several hundred pounds spent on me.

For the past several months Jason has been staying with me on and off – he has contact with the children and is a really good dad, but we just don't get on very well. I've had the police out on a number of occasions and have had Jason arrested twice for commonly assaulting me but he denied it and I didn't really want to support police proceedings once I'd sobered up anyway.

However, 3 months ago, I told Jason that it really was over, even though he was still sleeping with me. He left and came back and then left and came back again an indeterminate amount of times in between then and now, but I really can't remember how many.

PC Michael Pinkstone

Last week he sent me a threatening text, from his mobile phone; number 07177 777244. I deleted it but it said something like 'U BITCH U FUK U SLAG U KNOW I GUNA GET U.'

This week I have had 8 more text messages from him which I wrote down and then deleted:

'FUK U DENISE U FINK U CAN DO THIS 2 ME U FUK?'
'SORRY'
'U CNT U FUK I WANTED TO C ORLANDO THATS AL U R A CRP MUTHA'
'SORRY BABE'
'FUK U BITCH U FUKING WIV MY HED'
'I DIDNT MEAN THAT'
'IM GUNA FUK U UP AND URE BROTHER THE CNT, HE IS DEAD U FUK'
'SORRY SWEET HART'

These messages really upset me and have caused me to worry a lot. I haven't barred his number from my phone or done anything else to sort my own problems out, but called you so that he could get arrested for harassment. Perhaps if he admits sending them, you might get a detection.

I did not give Jason permission to harass me, and Orlando, Keira and Johnny aren't sleeping properly due to the stress it's causing. Jason is coming round tomorrow and we're going out for a few drinks to talk about us and the children but I want him arrested and charged anyway.

This statement is being made of my own free will and I have only drunk 9 alcopops this evening. That screaming noise you can hear in the background is Orlando taking after his father and the disgusting smell is commonplace. Sorry if you had to write all of this with the television on in the background and apologies that the Log was created 3 days ago and I couldn't

This Victorian Playground - Part 2

get to see you, but I was round a friend's house with Jason and then seeing my new boyfriend Luke REARDEN – you may have heard of him too.

I am willing to support police proceedings this time because it really is all over between me and Jason. I am not happy about going to court and would require a screen because I am terrified of him and what he might do to me.

***

Now assuming that part of my target readership would be police officers, then there are certain elements in that statement that will ring true for them, even if it is a little bit unrealistic. However I am hoping that anyone would be able to spot the unrealistic parts.

Statements. We write a hell of a lot of statements. And in these strange and bewildering times we have written a lot of very strange and bewildering statements. The above example, minus the sarcasm, is pretty much your bread-and-butter domestic statement nowadays. All you need to do is change the names, the dates and the order of the text messages, and hey presto! A full scale domestic harassment – Log number 345 and already on CRAPPIES awaiting an OIC.[9]

It's something of a tragedy that a nation once tough, resilient and stoic has lowered itself to not only behaving in such a manner, but is also being forced – from a police point of view – to treat it seriously! Yet considering the dissonant social themes and often antipathetic cultural issues present in our nation, it is hardly surprising that we are simply trying to make sense of it all. And what better way to make sense of it than to treat it with thorough and earnest attention? Surely it would be unkind of us as police to ignore such a cry for help in a world gone mad? Welcome to the victim culture!

So we write it down in its pure, unadulterated form. We boil it down to scrutinised simplicity. We get it on paper – old-fashioned and trustworthy. There's something scholarly; something erudite about a police officer with a pen and a new, crisp sheet of statement paper. Something aloof.

---

[9] Officer In Case

PC Michael Pinkstone

Something tangible in a wildly unpredictable world.

The statement format itself reeks of this stable and studious approach to social problem-solving; this authenticated and industrious form of intervention. In a world overrun with computerised and synthesised information, the hand-written police statement stands out as a true bastion of unchanged, unflinching, tried-and-tested procedure. It's almost primal.

We arrive, we take a statement. That's what we do. If we don't take a statement there has to be a very good reason why. We even take statements when something wasn't witnessed or nothing has really happened – just in case. But we never really get to discover what that "just in case" is, because there isn't really anything to worry about a lot of the time. Our paranoia breeds paranoia, which spawns loads more statements – and the problem becomes self-perpetuating.

If I had a pound for the amount of times I've written a statement in the past few years, I'd have ... a few hundred pounds. Now if I had a pound for the amount of times I've written a *pointless* statement in the past few years, I'd have ... a few hundred pounds.

For there's a rather crucial phrase in the first paragraph of this chapter – namely *"tendered in evidence"* – that implies statements are for a specific purpose, and that purpose is for use in criminal proceedings, particularly in court.

Unfortunately, most of the statements police officers write never see the light of day in a courtroom. Most of that lovely, juicy, time-consuming, hand-written "evidence" is now stapled to a copy of the CRAPPIES report and a filing sheet in some dusty archive – arriving straight there from the police station. In fact, it's got so bad, that for much of the time we can't "file" a job without having some form of a statement in the first place.

Why? you ask. *Why* do you need a statement just to file something? Don't fucking ask me – I've just got to do as I'm told, or someone with a sense of self-importance who looks at CRAPPIES all day will tell me off.

This statement (consisting of __ Page(s) each signed by me) is true to the best of my knowledge and belief and I make it knowing

This Victorian Playground - Part 2

that the police officer writing down what I'm saying shall be liable to an administrative form of buggery if he doesn't waste his time doing what he's doing now.

To help you appreciate even further just how stupid it is – and I really hope that by the time you read this book, obviously several months after it's been written, it will have all changed – so I'll be able to say 'to help you appreciate even further how stupid it all *was*' – here's another example:

One day in the not-too-distant past I sat down in front of CRAPPIES, as is my bread-and-butter, and looked at my allocated crime. It was an "attempted snatch theft" and already four days old by the time I'd been given it. The crime report contained all the essential details, beginning with the name, ethnicity and date of birth of the victim, whether or not she wanted victim support and whether all the various codes of practice had been adhered to, and then there were some small updates about what had happened, which were kind of irrelevant I suppose.

Basically the person who had taken the call from the "victim" had written down, allegedly, what the victim had said – namely that an unknown male had come up to her after she had parked her car and tried to snatch her handbag. So on the face of it this poor woman truly appeared to be a victim of an unpleasant crime and had been allocated her necessary crime reference number and OIC – yours truly.

I arrived on her doorstep a few minutes after reading through CRAPPIES and getting all my statement paper ready because, after all, this chapter is about statements, and after a few moments the door was answered by a female in her twenties. This is the following conversation as best as I can remember it:

Hello Rachel?
Yes.
PC Pinkstone from the police station. I'm here about the attempted robbery you reported to us.
(Pause)
Robbery? I haven't reported a robbery ...
(I check my copy of the crime report)

25

PC Michael Pinkstone

You are Miss Lataya?
(Confused look)
Yes, I'm Rachel Lataya, but I didn't report a robbery ...
Er, you called us on the 15th about a male trying to snatch your handbag?
(A small chuckle)
No! Oh, hang on, is it about Jackson?
(My turn to look confused)
Jackson?
Yeah, you know – the local piss-head. He's always hanging around these streets asking for a pound.
(Frown)
I'm sorry, may I come in?
(30 seconds later, settled in the lounge)
Sorry, madam, I think we may be getting some wires crossed here. Could you please tell me what happened and why you called us because I get the feeling there's been something of a misunderstanding ...[10]
Yeah, well, there's this old guy called Jackson who hangs around the streets – he lives just around the corner. He's always pissed and asking passers-by for a pound. I've given him a pound in the past – he's harmless really. Anyway, the other night I got out of my car and he suddenly loomed up out of the darkness and scared the shit out of me so I told him to 'fuck off' and he did. He usually does leave when you get aggressive with him.
Oh, I see. I thought he'd tried to rob you.
(Laugh)
No, who said that?
(Internal struggle to stay calm ...)
Well, like I say, I think there was some misunderstanding. So did he say anything to you?
No.
How close to you was he when you saw him?
Oh, about 2-3 metres.

---

10 It was no fucking misunderstanding – it was those pillocks creating crime reports *prior* to officer attendance. But I didn't show any of this frustration to my "victim"...

This Victorian Playground - Part 2

How close did he get to you?
He didn't come any closer than that – he just scared me.
Did he gesture to you in any way?
No.
Did he make any attempt to come closer towards you?
No.
Did he try and snatch your handbag?
(Incredulous look)
What?
Never mind. Anyway, so he scared you. Is that why you called us?
Yeah I called you just to make you aware. He's harmless but you never know. I was on my own and although I can handle myself I was just a bit concerned in case he scared anyone else.
OK. So do you feel that you have been the victim of a crime?
No – I didn't even report that I was the victim of a crime ...

I looked at the female and shook my head, feeling rather deflated. Then guess what I did? That's right. I took a statement. I pre-empted what I'd most likely be asked to do if I *didn't* take a statement. I took a statement detailing the fact that this woman felt that she wasn't the victim of a crime, otherwise – from my point of view – this "investigation" was not going to be "filed". *Ever.*

So someone rings the police and *we* decide that they are victims of a crime even when they are clearly not, even if *they* feel that they are. (We saw that in *This Victorian Playground Part 1.*) So here's the latest angle – someone rings the police even when they *don't* feel that they are victims of a crime, and we decide that they *are,* even though they haven't said anything that would suggest that they are, because we're so keen for them to be victims and so keen to crime stuff. After that, we have to go round their house and ask them, bizarrely, to confirm that they are *not* victims of a crime by taking a statement from them to that effect.

Sometimes we are able to get away with not taking a *whole* statement, but can write down some form of distilled account in our Pocket Note Books instead. Nevertheless, it is a statement of sorts, signed and sealed by the person making the report, so it's all the same crap. So if someone reports that they *think* a crime has taken place, and we turn up

PC Michael Pinkstone

to discover that it *hasn't* taken place – we have to jot down some form of statement, somewhere, that the person who reported it feels that they, or anyone else, are not victims of a crime. This is also true for someone who *hasn't* reported a crime but we assume they have.

Are you about as confused as I am, because I just want to jump off a fucking cliff. So regardless of whether this debacle of a situation has been resolved in the time between me writing this very paragraph and you reading it hot off the shelf in a few months' time, I hope you can see just how fucked up it all is/was, and at least it will provide you (and me, in later years) with a small memento of what the Government did to policing in and around 2007. If nothing else, *This Victorian Playground* is my little window on the here-and-now, but I hope to fuck it all changes for the better.

So the bottom line is that if you are absolutely determined that you are a victim of a crime, irrespective of *any* opposing facts whatsoever – and if you *don't* feel that you're a victim of a crime but have rung the police about something completely different – then you will most likely have a police officer turn up at your doorstep with a pen and some nice, fresh statement paper, and write it all down anyway. They'll write down what *has* happened, what *could have* happened, and even why you think you might not be a victim of a crime even if something *hasn't* happened. Whatever the case – you're going to make that officer write some shit down.

Of course, this isn't the end of the charade – let's not forget the whole issue of "first accounts". Now, after a few years in the job I think I am at the stage where I *just* about understand the requirements for a first account.

They are basically micro-statements taken from someone who is practically unable to do anything except tell you a couple of things about what has happened to them. For example, if someone has been run over by a car and they are lying there in a hospital bed half mangled, and they say to you, 'It was a green Rover and a white guy was driving it. I think he had brown hair' – this would be a first account. It may also end up being a dying declaration, but let's not go there.

If, however, the person is able to tell you more than, say, half a page worth of information – you need to take a statement. In other words,

This Victorian Playground - Part 2

the criteria for a first account are that the person really is incapable, for whatever reason, of hardly telling you anything at all – and most likely unable to sign whatever it is you are writing on.

Ah, *whatever it is you are writing on.* Because here's me rambling on about "first accounts" as if you are at a police training centre (I mean at college) – but there's a very good reason for this. And that reason is because I have *only* just begun to grasp what a first account really is, and that is after a relatively decent time doing frontline policing. I may, of course, be completely wrong.

For in the past few years we have had a bit of, er, conflicting advice from different people of different ranks and departments about first accounts and I have decided to distil that advice down into the following points:

1. They must not be written in a Pocket Note Book.
2. They must be written in a Pocket Note Book.
3. It is not advisable to write them in a Pocket Note Book.
4. If it is written in a Pocket Note Book it must be photocopied and exhibited, but not necessarily either, but certainly both. Or either. Or neither.
5. The first account must be signed.
6. The first account must not be signed.
7. If it is a juvenile making a first account, it must not be signed by anyone.
8. If it is a juvenile making a first account, it must be signed.
9. If it is a juvenile making a first account, only an appropriate adult should sign it.
10. A juvenile cannot give a first account.
11. A first account must be written in an Incident Report Book.
12. All officers are now to ensure they carry an Incident Report Book around with them.
13. The Incident Report Book is to be used so that the statement part at the top can be signed, otherwise there is no point using the Incident Report Book. You might as well use your Pocket Note Book, which you are allowed to do anyway,

PC Michael Pinkstone

and not.
14. It is much more advisable for a first account to be written on regular statement paper than anywhere else.
15. You must write a first account on regular statement paper.
16. You do not necessarily have to use regular statement paper if there is none to hand, but it is preferable to use an Incident Report Book so long as it is signed, photocopied, exhibited and unsigned, and a full record is made in your Pocket Note Book, along with an attached duty statement on regular statement paper, that fully accounts for the first account and any subsequent accounts made before, after or during the incident, to which the first account or any related accounts relate.
17. You can write a first account on a tissue.

So, as you can see, there has been a general remit of confusion with this particular kind of "statement" and I have to say that this overwhelming mystification applies to pretty much every statement that we write.

The whole system is all at once so arcane and so bewildering that the circumstances almost play no part in the proceedings whatsoever. I turn up at incidents so preoccupied with *where* I'm supposed to write something, and in what format, and in what style, that I almost forget to ask what has actually happened.

One day I may begin to fully understand the why's and wherefore's of the "system" and appreciate with a knowing nod why we had to write so much shit down and why we were told so many conflicting things by so many different people. Not that it all fucking matters anyway.

I need a beer.

* * *

Of course, the *real* reason why we need statements is for evidence. And that evidence will most likely be tendered in court. So if there is absolutely no chance that something is going to court, or if it's so trivial it shouldn't even be dignified with a police officer attending in the first place, then please, let's stop writing so many fucking statements!

CONTEXT, PLEASE!

Think of all that wasted paper! Think of all those groaning rainforests and bulging archives where this nation's crappy and insignificant affairs reside in hand-written form ...

I've got a great idea for November 5th ... anyone care to join me?

5. Of the Courts and of Fear

PC Bean, OIC for that serious robbery case involving Gooboo and Buglfob, has been to court well over twenty times. She hasn't given evidence once. Now, according to Acting Sergeant Luton, police officers are going to court less and less nowadays. This may very well be true because Sgt Luton has been in longer than me and he used to be in CID, so he gets respect, innit.

Regardless of any statistics, though, going to court as a police officer can be a complete and utter waste of time – but I suppose it's a day out. My own experiences of court have been quite varied, although I would suggest that for some really interesting tales you should speak to some old sweats who have been in the job for years, especially the grizzled-looking ones in CID. They have some cracking stories, including ones where the Judge has screamed at them, as well as thrown random items of stationery in their direction, before ordering them out of the courtroom immediately.

However, I'm not that lucky. Yet in the couple of dozen or so times that I have been to court so far, I've given evidence a few times in the Magistrates Court and a few times in the Crown Court, which isn't bad going. Some officers, like PC Bean, have just been spare parts, it would seem. Or it might have something to do with crap investigations that I've carried out, or other mistakes or ambiguities that need clearing up by the defence or prosecution. Either way it seems pretty irrelevant whether I'm there or not.

Going to court is also supposed to be a solemn and serious occasion. In many respects it is. In others, it's not. For me, it's a game. The whole

This Victorian Playground - Part 2

of the English legal system is a game. This shouldn't come as any kind of shock because we all know it's true. Because it isn't about "truth" or "justice" – it's about the standard of proof, amongst other official-sounding things. If something can be proved *beyond all reasonable doubt* – which is the criminal standard of proof – then that looks pretty good if you're on the side of the prosecution. Up to the point when the sanction is imposed.

For if a person is convicted, based upon the evidence weighed against him, then he will receive some kind of court-induced sanction. Obviously the police and the victim would be hoping for some kind of custodial sentence if the offence were serious enough to warrant such a sanction.

Nowadays, of course, criminals run the show. Thus the attendance of a police officer at court is pretty fucking irrelevant. We might as well not bother. I don't give a damn if I go to court or not because the whole system is fucked from top to bottom and bottom to top, so what difference does it make? If it wasn't fucked then I wouldn't have to arrest the same criminals over and over again for the same offences, and deal with so many real victims of these regular criminals as a result of this.

One day, quite early on in my career, I had the pleasure of arresting a shoplifter. He was seventeen years old and cried when I nicked him. Ah, poor little mite. The fact he'd been arrested several times before was entirely by the by. The fact that he was one of the town's nastiest up-and-coming scumbags was also irrelevant. And the fact that the little shit is now in prison for a very serious GBH is, I guess, quite ironic. At the time, of course, none of this mattered. The only thing to be considered was whether or not he had dishonestly appropriated property belonging to another with the intention of permanently depriving the other of it. In other words, could I prove that he'd stolen some stuff without suitable excuse?

Well, I did my best. He was duly taken to custody and interviewed. During this little chat[11] he gave a heartrending account of how some nasty boys had bullied him into stealing the computer games, and how it was all their fault.

---

11 We don't really *interview* criminals any more. We sit them down, give them a cup of tea, and be all pink and fluffy with them, in the hope they might give us a detection or three.

PC Michael Pinkstone

Ah, that's right. I remember those "nasty boys". They were the ones laughing and joking with him from outside the shop when I led him away, saying things like, 'Text u later bruv,' and 'Unlucky bruv – we is gonna be like waitin' for u round Ismael's later innit.'

Whatever it was they were indeed saying, it was clear that they were all in cahoots with each other. "Bruvvaz" until the end. A true example of teeth-sucking, knuckle-knocking respect. I swear down. Furthermore, after conducting some pertinent enquiries back at the station, I discovered that the males were all certainly associates of each other, and had committed a string of offences together up and down the area. Such blessed little children.

Anyway, the case eventually went to the Magistrates Court, and I took my place in the stand and introduced myself. 'My name is Michael Pinkstone, a police constable employed by (insert name of police service), currently fulfilling the duties of a uniformed shift officer, your Worships.' A short, but respectful, bout of genuflecting followed, and I waited with rigid professionalism for my first question.

'So, PC Pinkstone. I notice from your statement that you arrested my client at 2.15 pm on the 17th November. Is that correct?' The defence barrister had that lazy, pompous air about him. It's all a game.

I look at the Bench. 'Yes, that is correct.'

'What did you arrest him for, and where?' He was going somewhere with this. *Damn, he was good!*

'Your Worships, I arrested Mr Scrote on suspicion of shoplifting some video games from HMV.'

The barrister almost sniggered. 'Thank you PC Pinkstone. And may I ask – did my client *say* anything to you upon his arrest?'

I paused for a moment, as if I'm thinking carefully about the question. It also presented the illusion that I gave a fuck. 'Hmm,' I said. 'I don't recall him *saying* anything in particular. He was just a bit upset.'

At this, the barrister leaped into action. 'Upset! I should say he was upset, PC Pinkstone! That's because he had been coerced, or rather viciously *forced*, into stealing the video games by the large group of males waiting for him outside the shop. My client was, in fact, an innocent party facing a severe beating from these males if he didn't do what they demanded. That's why he was upset, PC Pinkstone!'

This Victorian Playground - Part 2

I felt my heart sink. Goodness, I could never have foreseen this coming. I thought that Mr Scrote was bang to rights and that the defence would crumble before the weight of evidence in front of them! Oh my dear God. How can I rescue the case now?

'I put it to you, PC Pinkstone, that you did *not* carry out a thorough investigation into the actions of those males. In fact, you did not carry out an investigation into those males at all! My client stated to you, as you led him away in handcuffs through a crowded shopping centre – which was certainly very distressing for him in itself – that those males were the ones who had made him do it. But you ignored him, didn't you PC Pinkstone?'

I frowned in the stand. My heart racing. My credibility ebbing away like a globule of phlegm about to finally slip through the plughole, with a helpful blast of water from the cold tap.

'Hmm,' I said. 'Well, your Worships, I was on my own and that's why I handcuffed Mr Scrote. Furthermore, the males were laughing and joking with him, leading me to believe that they were all in it together.'

The barrister pounced, like a cat spotting a mouse. 'But you didn't check it out at all did you PC Pinkstone? You didn't make any enquiries *whatsoever!* My client did not know any of those males and was, in fact, terrified of them. He even said this during his interview, but still no action was taken. You just assumed my client was in the wrong and charged him forthwith. What do you have to say about that?'

I shifted my weight slightly onto my left foot, contemplating my answer. It was up to me to save the day. Not that I had much hope, of course.

'Your Worships, I did not make any enquiries into these males because I did not consider it to be necessary or proportionate. I believed them to be friends of Mr Scrote and, as such, felt it impracticable to waste my time chasing after them.'

The defence barrister sat down with a satisfied look. 'No further questions,' he said.

The prosecutor – a bumbling bumblefuck if ever there was one – peered at some random sheets of paper and then said, 'I have no questions your Worships.'

PC Michael Pinkstone

The female sitting in the middle of the trio on the Bench took off her glasses and said with received pronunciation, 'Thank you, PC Pinkstone. You may leave.'

I left the stand, ignoring Mr Scrote sitting at the desk. He was looking all young and forlorn and browbeaten. Poor little thing. Perhaps he really was innocent after all?

Shortly afterwards I received a phone call from the court stating that Mr Scrote had been let off scot-free because the Bench believed his sob story and that the case had not been sufficiently investigated to warrant a conviction of any description. I just sighed. It was the first of many such phone calls. Perhaps I'm just a really shit police officer. Perhaps not. I might not be perfect, but I know pink and fluffy crap when I see it.

Perhaps the court system is so utterly pathetic and pandering nowadays that it is entirely incapable. There is no other way to look at it.

At other times, it is bizarre beyond words and frustrating to the point of self-harm. Usual procedure for a police officer regarding the court system nowadays is thus:

1. Assist your colleagues in Paxton Court one day by arriving in a Transit van to transport a prisoner to custody. You haven't arrested him. You don't interview him, and you are *not* the OIC. Your only involvement is to have your name and shoulder number mentioned in a statement by the OIC, who simply notes that you "conveyed the male to custody, where his detention was authorised".
2. Six months later you receive an email from Witness Care stating that you are required to attend Fucklebum Magistrates Court at 9.30 am on the 23rd July.
3. You shake your head and swear copiously, firing off an email to Witness Care stating that you are *not* the OIC and had no evidential involvement with the case whatsoever. You state that there is simply no evidence that you can give, save that you are a police officer and saw the Defendant very briefly in the back of a van one morning, ages ago.
4. Witness Care ignore your email.
5. You email them again a week later.

This Victorian Playground - Part 2

6. Witness Care ignore your email, again.
7. You phone Witness Care a few days after this.
8. You are told, in no uncertain terms, that if you have been called to court, you need to go to court. You tell them that not only is the 23rd of July one of your Rest Days, but it's also in the middle of a block of leave that you have taken to have a holiday. There's nothing that anyone can do about that, so you are told to phone the CPS.
9. You phone the CPS. There's no reply.
10. You phone the CPS again. No reply. You leave a message.
11. Your message is not returned. So you phone them again. You miraculously get through to someone called "Steve" who is only working there part-time (don't they all?) and he will try to contact the prosecutor of the case you have mentioned, and leave them a message.
12. A week passes with no response, so you phone the CPS again. You have no luck with getting hold of anyone, not even Steve.
13. A month later, after several emails, voicemail messages and mounting stress levels, you are told – in no uncertain terms – that you are required at court. You have been called, and that's that.
14. The 23rd July arrives and you have rescheduled your holiday just to be here. You get to the court at 9.30 am, along with PC Bean, who is the true OIC for this case. She can't understand why you're here either.
15. At 10.28 am a middle-aged woman with a clipboard wanders into the waiting area and wanders out again.
16. At 10.56 am the same woman pops her head around the door, as if looking for someone specific. All of you unlucky bastards who are in the waiting room look at her with hopeful expectation, but she disappears without a word.
17. At 11.09 am the woman comes back into the room again and asks everyone who they are, telling various people things like, 'The prosecutor is late,' and 'Mr Poo hasn't shown up yet,' or 'The case may be adjourned until the next millennium

PC Michael Pinkstone

because the Defendant's brother's dog has got a cold.' She tells you nothing.

18. At 11.22 am you are informed that your case won't be heard until after lunch. So, together with PC Bean, you wander around Fucklebum for two hours and come back just after 1.30 pm.
19. At 2.23 pm you are told that the relevant people are back from lunch and are discussing a particular case. Not yours, of course.
20. At 3.12 pm the OIC is spoken to by the woman with the clipboard. She states that she will try to have a word with the prosecutor to find out what is going on.
21. At 3.41 pm the woman comes back and says that she has had a word with the prosecutor and that she will be in "shortly".
22. At 4.06 pm another woman comes in and says, 'Who's here for Mr Scum?'
23. The OIC, and yourself, look up with hearts beating eagerly.
24. The prosecutor says some wholly irrelevant things that basically result in her telling you that the case is going to be adjourned for another five months. You take this opportunity to ask her why you have been called and she says, 'I don't know.'
25. Five months later you come back to court and do all of this again – on a Rest Day, of course – to be finally stared at by the woman with the clipboard at 4.12 pm, who says, 'Why are you here PC Pinkstone? You were de-warned a year ago. Did no-one tell you?'

Of course, even when we do get called to court for a genuine need to give vital evidence, and we do take the stand – it's all pointless anyway. I once went to Crown Court for several days in a row and on the last day of sitting in the waiting room doing fuck all, I was finally called into the courtroom. This is how it went:

Prosecutor: So, PC Pinkstone. On the 23rd April 2005 you attended an address – let me see – (rustles paper) er, it was, er – one moment

This Victorian Playground - Part 2

– er, yes, it was number 39 Bogey Drive. Once you were there you saw several males at that address, one of whom was a Mr Swine. You later arrested Mr Swine on suspicion of Grievous Bodily Harm with Intent and took him to custody. PC Pinkstone, could you please tell me: was Mr Swine wearing a white coloured traditional outer garment?

Me: Yes.

Prosecutor: Thank you. No further questions.

I then left the court and went home – forty-five miles away. Now multiply that kind of bollocks by the amount of police officers in the country and you will arrive at a rather significant number. A rather large pile of wasted time and money, with plenty of related stress and frustration. It wouldn't be so bad, of course, if real criminals actually got some kind of half-decent sanction to make it all seem worthwhile. Maybe one day there will be a teeny-weeny bit of real justice meted out to those who truly deserve a more fearsome approach to dealing with their crime.

I relish the day when I turn up at court for a "regular" criminal – let's say a burglar because they are all fuckers – and, following a successful prosecution case with all the necessary elements conducted in accordance with the "system", the Judge says something like this:

'Hmm, Mr Rutton. I see this is the fifteenth time you've been arrested and charged for burglary and related offences. You've done some time in prison, although I notice for no more than a few months – and you've had numerous opportunities to come off the drugs, which you haven't. In fact, thousands of pounds have been spent on you in an effort to "rehabilitate" you. However, we can see that you are beyond rehabilitating. You are taking the piss. How many more warnings or chances do you need? You have a house provided for you and paid for by other people, yet you still continue to ruin the lives of dozens of others on a daily basis.

'I know, Mr Rutton, that you will have committed many, many burglaries before you were caught, and I don't give a jolly roger about TICs.[12] For me, one burglary is enough, Mr Rutton, but I'm bound by

---

[12] Taken into Consideration. It's a chance to have a reduction in your prison sentence if you admit to committing lots of other crimes and pretend you're really, really sorry for your behaviour.

PC Michael Pinkstone

what the Home Secretary tells me. Nevertheless, I'm going to make your case somewhat different. I'm going to make sure it acts as a deterrent for others. Let me also tell you that your drug habit isn't an excuse, or an illness – it's a reason. For there are no mitigating circumstances here, save one: you are a pitiable excuse for a human being, Mr Rutton, and no amount of human rights bollocks or civil libertarian input is going to sway me here. You are a *bad* person Mr Rutton, a *bad* person, because you do *bad* things. It's what we *do*, Mr Rutton, that makes us bad. And what you do, Mr Rutton, is *bad.* Not only bad, but it's against the law. It undermines the constitution of this country and flies in the face of what is decent, just and honourable. Therefore I have no option but to sentence you for five years. You will not be out after two years, or after three years. You will stay in prison for five years. Get this fucker out of my courtroom and out of my sight …'

Now wouldn't that make a grand day out? I'd fucking cheer from the back row. I'd turn up without even being paid just to hear a Judge say that. I'd grab the hands of all of the victims and dance around the fucking courtroom. I'd then send a letter to every well-known burglar in the police area and tell them that if they carry on being such bastards then they'll go to prison for half a decade – and actually *stay* in prison for that long. I know this sounds harsh, but I don't care. We *must* toughen up.

Please allow me to quote a couple of things from the first volume of *This Victorian Playground*:

> *Most police officers and I dare say most citizens would like to see real criminals locked up for longer and pay back towards the economic and emotional damage they have caused. This isn't some kind of "lock em up and throw away the key" mentality – rather it is a heartfelt cry to get those bastards off the streets for longer and instil some much needed fear back into the criminal justice system.*

And also:

> *There is something slightly worrying about full prisons. Perhaps it's the fact that even with full prisons, we still have a fucked up*

*country. Perhaps there's not enough prisons. My feelings are
that criminals don't spend long enough in prison after committing heinous crimes and, therefore, it's hardly a punishment for
them. If they received decent sentences and actually got punished
properly for their crimes, it might act as a deterrent for other
people. Without fear of re-offending, you are always going to
have full prisons. Without fear in the justice system, it's always
going to be overcrowded. It's that carousel.*

There is one important word repeated in both of those paragraphs: *fear*. Sadly, at the moment, all the fear seems to be in the wrong place. Police officers are afraid of giving evidence when they are the ones trying to stand up for fucking justice; or else they are afraid that some small, insignificant technicality is going to fuck the whole case up. How many stupid, pointless, trivial, crappy little particulars have blown cases apart when the rest of the evidence is overwhelming? That's because the justice system protects criminals and lets them go, and police officers get treated like the bad guys in the courtroom.

Instead, I'd like to see some proper fear reinstated. I'd like to see some real criminals quaking in their fucking shoes when they stand before the Judge. They may do this now of course, but it needs to quadruple in its intensity. I'd consider it a day out better than Alton Towers when some regular scrote was handed down a sentence that made him faint. Some wretch in human form that deserves nothing less than to be locked up for a goodly length of time. Then watch him call me "Bruv" on the streets after that and spit in my direction. He just *wouldn't*.

Fear. There *is* no fear. And the scrotes love it. I don't advocate throwing away the key any more than I advocate beating people up, but I do advocate sentences that actually work. All we're doing now is advertising how long the scrotes *don't* have to spend in prison. We're *bargaining* with the little shits:

1. Admit the offence during interview and we'll give you a third off your sentence! (A third off a sentence that was nowhere near long enough anyway.)

2. Admit the offence a bit later on and we'll give you a quarter off your sentence!
3. Admit the offence a bit later than that and we'll do something else nice for you!
4. Admit hundreds of TIC's and you might as well not bother going to prison at all, because this is a clear signal of your intent to "Turn Your Life Around" and "Wipe The Slate Clean".[13]

What the fuck is going on? Who is calling the shots here? Who's in charge? Where has all the fear gone? The baddies are having a fucking ball. They need to start feeling afraid.

If I saw a regular criminal on the street I'd want him to crap himself, not because he's seen me and thinks I'll hurt him, but because he knows that if he fucks up on his last chance, he's going to get a proper prison sentence, and I would represent the first stages of that process. Yet at present there is simply no dread left in the law or in the legal system. There is no fear of the police because we represent that wishy-washy, namby-pamby first stage of the criminal justice system.

By the time we've spent hundreds of man-hours and thousands of pounds on our "investigation", the criminal smiles at us in court and walks out the door practically a free man, possibly with some poxy term to serve first. Fuck that. Full prisons my arse – we're just locking up more people for less time, when what we need to do is lock up fewer people for more time. And of course the population of Britain is expanding rapidly as well, so we might need some more prisons anyway just in case, but not if we're going to carry on doing what we're doing. It's perhaps not really a question of needing more prisons – it's a question of using the ones we already have much more effectively. The real issue isn't about lack of space – it's about lack of fear. If people aren't afraid of the penitentiaries we have now, what difference will a few new ones make? And if there's still a problem with space – let's try deportation. Not just promise we will, in some hollow political speech, but actually get on and do it. We've got enough home-grown shit without the hassle of housing the worst of other nations as well.

---

13 All of these are real initiatives, of course.

This Victorian Playground - Part 2

The minute this country grows a spine and finds its balls again then I propose that the prisons perhaps aren't going to be nearly as rammed as they are now. They'll be busy, no doubt, but they won't be packed out and needing police custody suites to cope with the overspill. I'm talking in terms of *regular* offenders here. People who have squandered their chances. For at the moment they have as many chances as they want, and even when it would appear they've used up their *final* chance, they get a sentence of something like two years and they'll be out after eight months. Wow! What a deterrent!

And for all those people who commit one-off, heinous crimes without reasonable excuse or mitigation – they should also receive hefty sentences without fear of how they "feel". How about the poor fucking victims for once? *We shall fight on the beaches?* Nah, we won't fight for justice or goodness at all. We'll let the fuckers rule the roost. We'll let them take over.

What the fuck are we playing at? Where did we go wrong? Who the fuck put these pink and fluffy pillocks in charge? *Fight on the beaches.* We're not fighting at all. There is no resistance to malfeasance in any way, shape or form. We've completely given up. Drowning in our own fucking political incompetence. We've let some pathetic, wretched, fucked up, so-called human rights dolts and spineless civil libertarians tell us that we can't *punish* people; that we can't *penalise* them for doing wrong. Fuck that crap. If they want to stand up for their impotent and insipid ideologies then let them. Let them fucking drown in their own cesspool of weakness and inaction. But for the rest of us who have the opportunity and guts to actually punish people for their crimes, then let us do so.

I don't advocate revenge. I don't advocate hurting people. I don't advocate any form of vigilante groups or social anarchy. I don't advocate making a bad person cry from me or anyone else inflicting upon them physical pain. I don't promote hanging, flogging or beating. *We* are better than that, no matter what *they* have done. But if what they have done is so bad, then they should be locked up and removed from society immediately. Incarcerated. Separated. Taken away and put in a cell. Not thrown in a cell. Not abused. Just removed, and removed for a decent and lengthy time. For this is about the only thing that we have left!

PC Michael Pinkstone

I don't present myself as an expert on this whole fuck-up of a "system", but I do know that whatever we're doing now simply isn't working. I have no faith whatsoever in British criminal justice.

For it's high time that some fear – some proper *fear* – was instilled back into this pathetic and irresolute so-called "justice system". At present I am looking to the courts for this, because the police have no powers to do that whatsoever. I look to the Government, pathetic as they are. I look to them and say, '*We* fight on the beaches, now what the fuck are *you* doing …?'

6. People of Substance

I arrived at the pub, along with PC Tank, one foggy Saturday evening in December. We ordered a pint of beer each and sat down at a free table. We were both on duty.

It felt rather bizarre to be sitting there, swigging back pints of delicious brew, wearing smart casual clothing, and chatting about the good old days, whilst there for a remit-related reason.

PC Tank and I joined the Job at the same time and were in the same class together at training college, and classmates at our local police training centre. Having spent several nights out on the piss together in bygone years (off duty) and being of like-minded humour, it was rather fun to lean back in our chairs and muse on the situation we now found ourselves in.

Looking back to those paranoid days of training school, it seemed utterly inconceivable that we would one day find ourselves crewed together in a pub, getting merry, on duty. And it was even more unimaginable that our mission was being funded by the Home Office, who clearly wanted some kind of an insight into the now escalated-beyond-control problem of alcohol-fuelled violence and disorder in Britain.

For that is why we were there. Not to contribute to the violence and disorder, I might add, but to cast an undercover beady eye on the serving of alcohol to drunk people within licensed premises, and to make a note of any booze-related disturbances.

Well, for the next hour or so, as we sat chatting, it became apparent that alcohol seemed to be the least of anyone's problems. How ironic. It could only be a Home Office-inspired plan to investigate incidents of alcohol abuse that would lead to uncovering abuses of a much more widespread and worrying nature.

So while PC Tank and I sat there quite happily getting tanked up ourselves, we spotted the first of our little problems.

It was a small group of males – three of them, in fact. Standing by the bar in the first pub we went to, and all acting like fools. We stared at them and realised that they weren't even particularly pissed. For there's a subtle difference between how alcohol makes you behave, and what being a person of substance really means nowadays.

That substance is, of course, Charlie. Not Charlie Brown, but Charlie Powdery White. That short, sharp snort of pleasure in a little wrap. A little packet of happiness. Ah bless.

The eldest of the males – he looked to be about forty-ish – was loud, obnoxious and clearly smacked off his face. I've met him before – not *him* specifically, I've met many like him, you see. And so have you. They're everywhere. Charlie has many fans, and they come in all shapes and sizes.

PC Tank looked at me and said, 'He's all Charlied up.'

'Yep,' I replied. 'Without a doubt.'

Soon enough the three men left the pub, and my colleague and I ordered another pint, while the rest of the patrons sat happily and quietly sipping on their own. So much for the alcohol-fuelled violence and disorder. It happens of course – don't get me wrong – but oh the irony that it wasn't happening tonight.

Our next watering hole was a local on the west side of town, in a large and well-established residential area – a little town in its own right. Shops and schools and bits and bobs. Typical suburban Britain. And a typical local pub.

We walked in and stopped short of walking straight out again. Karaoke night. And oh my word was it horrific. My eardrums have never been so violated.

If cheese graters could sing – it would be the heavily tattooed woman with the microphone. I think her name was Lynne and she couldn't sing for toffee. It was like listening to a cat falling down a lift shaft. She had the musical grace of a timpani rolling down a spiral staircase. By the time PC Tank and I had ordered our next pint and sat down, cringing,

This Victorian Playground - Part 2

we were being treated to a hearty rendition of "I Will Survive", at which point I thought quite seriously that I wouldn't.

So I popped to the toilet to enhance my observations and found it to be empty. While I was doing the necessaries at a urinal, a chap walked in and went straight into the cubicle.

Now, some blokes are a bit like that. I often have a wee in a locked booth, even if there's room at the little white altars, purely because I find it easier to concentrate. There's nothing worse than someone sparking up a conversation with you when you are trying to wee. I can't say that it happens to everyone, but my bladder refuses to comply when this happens.

Anyway, the chap who locked himself in the sanctuary of the cubicle didn't have a wee, or a number two. He walked out twenty seconds later, sniffing and blowing his nose. I think he had a cold. Poor thing.

So I washed my hands, exited the toilets, and wandered back to my table, accompanied by an ecstatic version of a popular love song blasting discordantly out of the speakers. It moved me in a special way, and I sat down next to my colleague, shaking my head at the uniqueness of the moment.

"Bohemian Rhapsody" soon followed, with screeches of "Let me go!" resounding in our ears. PC Tank and I were, by now, resigned to our fate, and wetting ourselves with laughter. We were also getting quite merry, and all the dear locals were having a fantastic time too. So much for alcohol-fuelled violence and disorder. It happens of course, don't get me wrong.

Just then PC Tank's phone rang, interrupting our enjoyment. It was our co-ordinator, and he was ready to take us to our next licensed premises. Having recently broken the seal, I decided to pop to the toilets again, just to be on the safe side. For once my seal breaks, nothing can hold back the torrents.

I pushed open the wooden outer door and made my way into the inner sanctum. Being a fairly beady-eyed person I saw a male standing directly in front of me, facing the door, whom I would describe as white, about 5' 10" tall, wearing a coat. I can't remember the colour, or anything else about him, except that he was certainly carrying something in his hands – a little wrap. Ah bless.

PC Michael Pinkstone

It was then that I noticed the toilet was full of men – about seven in all, and only one of them was having a leak. He was doing so whilst having a raucous conversation with the guy behind him, and the other chaps were at various poses around the room, each with their own private powdery enjoyment.

Taking my place at the corner wee-wee receptacle, I tried to unleash the mighty fury of my bladder. It didn't work. Someone was talking. Technically they weren't talking to me, but it didn't matter. I steadied my nerves and tried again. About ten seconds passed and eventually my internal valves got themselves into gear, and about £5.50 worth of beer exited my body, never to be seen or enjoyed again.

Unfortunately, I'd been there for too long, and the chap behind me just couldn't wait any longer. Leaning over my left shoulder, he put his face to the window sill and snorted a line of cocaine straight up his nose – right in front of my little eyes, and I was still peeing. How ironic.

I stepped back and washed my hands, while the male made some apologetic comment about not meaning to, er, 'look at my pecker'. I told him that it was fine. No harm intended. I don't think he could see it anyway – I employ a special technique that shields it from prying eyes whilst doing the necessaries.

Now you may wonder why I didn't intervene. Why I didn't flash my badge and save the day. Some kind of vigilante hero with my metal shield of justice.

The fact of the matter is that we weren't allowed – and rightly so. We were there purely to observe, so observe we did. What difference would it have made anyway? The evidence was already halfway around someone's bloodstream.

I wandered outside and relayed my little story to PC Tank. He burst out laughing, and so did I, as we hopped in the undercover car and got transported to our next destination – a nightclub.

Aha. A *nightclub*. Surely here we would find some decent examples of alcohol-fuelled violence and disorder, and various heinous breaches of the Licensing Act? Surely here we might even be *forced* to intervene if the shit really hit the fan?

The previous night had been quite interesting, you see. PC Tank

This Victorian Playground - Part 2

and I weren't working, but we'd heard the story from one of the chaps who was in the nightclub in question.

He'd sat in there, along with his undercover colleague, getting merrily pissed, when a rather raucous disturbance caught his attention.

It turned out that although the club was open until 1.30 am, it officially closed its doors at 11.30 pm – but the door staff were somewhat lax about the rules. They were quite happy to let friends and acquaintances into the club after closing, but not the large group of Albanian males looking for an evening of fun and friendship. I mention the word "Albanian" purely because they were. It's not a metaphor.

Anyway the Albanian group – or should I say "gang", which is actually what they were – soon cottoned on to the fact that the door staff were being a little bit underhand and selective with the opening of the doors. So they decided to act on instinct and write a letter of complaint to the management of the club like true Brits.

Actually, they didn't. What they did do, however, was to kick their way through a reinforced glass door and brutally assault one of the bouncers. Then they all ran off and disappeared into the shadows, never to be seen or recognised again. Certainly never to be acknowledged by the Home Office that groups and gangs of all different cultures are gradually becoming more and more prominent, and dangerous, in this nation. Integration is such a precious thing.

Apologies, I'm getting a bit ahead of myself. So PC Tank and I paid our entrance fee and wandered into the club. Aside from being part of the tiny minority of English people in there, we were about the only people in there anyway. From the moment we entered to the time we left, the club only entertained a maximum of about fifty people, which is pretty dismal for a Saturday night.

So it would be unkind of me to suggest that the mission was a failure, because if that club was packed to the rafters there would undoubtedly have been some incidents of alcohol-fuelled violence and disorder. Or would there?

Is it only alcohol that is causing the problems? Is it Charlie? What is making this society collapse and crumble around us – leading the Home Office to pay good money to coppers like me and PC Tank to sit inside licensed venues and try to ascertain where the predicaments are?

PC Michael Pinkstone

Hmm, let me see. Well, let's just pop back into the club for the moment. There may have only been a few dozen folks in there, but what a story that told. If you knew what you were looking for, of course. Something the Home Office either doesn't understand, or doesn't want to know about ...

* * *

We took a window seat first of all. PC Tank looked around and eyed up the chav girls in the corner. They were all tarted up for a good night out, but we both decided it wasn't going to be a particularly successful one, owing to a number of mitigating factors.

Next to us at the adjacent table sat two middle aged Asian males in jumpers and jeans. They were perched in silence, without drinks, staring at various people around the club.

'What the fuck are *they* doing in here?' PC Tank was incredulous.

I said nothing because I didn't want to appear racist.

Soon enough the males left. There wasn't really anything too fitting to ogle at. The chav girls clearly weren't giving off the right vibes. It was at this moment that PC Tank and I realised we were the only ones sitting by the window, and that most of the people were at the back end of the club near the dance floor and outside smoking area.

So we gathered our drinks and made our way to another table, which afforded us a good view of practically everyone inside.

In the corner by the fire escape were about ten Polish people – a good mix of male and female. One of the chaps – who turned out to be fantastically entertaining – didn't stop dancing like a maniac for the whole two hours we were there. It wasn't really dancing in the strictly traditional sense – more like a Space Invader on Prozac, but at least he appeared to be enjoying himself. And his female companion didn't seem overly concerned that she was dancing with a complete nutter. Interestingly enough, this particular club used to be quite popular with, er, the "locals", but they soon abandoned it to due to another race of people practically taking it over. Even the Polish living in the town said things like, 'There's too many Polish people here!'

Standing by the dance floor were a group of about eight Albanian

This Victorian Playground - Part 2

males, one of whom was wearing very long, white pointed shoes. PC Tank stared and sniggered.

'Do you think that by the end of the night they will be all curled up?' He giggled into his beer and I did the same. By this stage of the night, anything was funny.

Shortly after that, two more Polish males entered. One of them, who was completely bald, was wearing a large, black leather jacket, and he strutted in, casting a vengeful eye on his surroundings.

'Polish Mafia,' I whispered fearfully to PC Tank.

'Yep,' he replied. 'Without a doubt.'

Standing just behind the Albanian gang were some Asian drug dealers. This may sound a bit nasty – why can't they just be a gang? Why do I have to make them the drug dealers?

Well, they were. I recognised a couple of them. Drug dealers. And they were part of a gang too, so put that on your credit card and snort it.

They were standing, almost motionless, for a couple of hours, and didn't really appear to be doing anything else, except loitering and looking nonchalant. Obviously business wasn't booming on this particular night. And like the rest of the males in the club – along with a drooling PC Tank – they were captivated by the young girl on the dance floor, who was wearing a revealing pink dress. She writhed and wriggled and inspired many an inappropriate thought, no doubt.

Meanwhile, the two Polish girls to our right weren't having much luck with male attention – at least not from anyone they found agreeable. They were quite pretty, and nicely dressed – not quite as brazenly as the girl in pink – but certainly not getting the testosterone-charged advances of the male sex they craved, which is really what clubs are all about – getting pissed and trying to pull. I'd hate to sweep aside the whole nightclub culture in one sentence, but most of them are meat markets, wherein it's too dark to see; too noisy to hear, too expensive to bother, and nowhere near as good as a decent pub. Either that or I'm getting too old.

Anyway, the Polish girls did get a bit of male regard, from a slightly pissed young Asian lad who was dancing like his hands weighed about two tonnes each (this was how PC Tank described him anyway, and I can't think of anything more appropriate). It was an exhausted-looking routine and it definitely did not impress the girls, who pushed him out of their space with gusto, as they glanced angrily and jealously at the wanton young trollop on the dance floor, who was gyrating with lavish abandon to some shit song designed exclusively for promoting one's raw sensuality and universal availability, all in one go. Kind of takes the fun out of life, if you ask me. And the bloke who had joined her on the floor was clearly a good choice of mate. What an extraordinary coincidence that he should meet the love of his life under such strange circumstances:

Here, look at me. I'm thrusting my hips forwards in a subtle and sensitive rhythmic motion in front of some tart I've never met, whilst pissed out of my tree, and smacked off my tits, while the music plays so loud I can hardly hear my lone brain cell operate, let alone hear anyone else talk. Then I'm going to shout something senseless in her ear, but she still won't be able to hear me, then maybe, just maybe, she'll fancy me enough – or get sufficiently wankered – to be of some small pleasure to me later on. Then we'll get married and have lots of kids and stuff. Don't worry about my septum – it's still hanging on in there. For now. Have you seen this move? It's called "The Electrocuted Testicle". All part of my well-rehearsed clubbing routine. Pulled many a fit bird with that one, even though the risks of serious injury are high. That's what the beer jacket is for. But nothing beats the coat that Charlie gave me.

My wandering mind returned with a jolt as I realised just how much I detested being in nightclubs, and I turned my head away in disgust – with an almost Puritanical huff – from the lascivious displays of human sexual impetuosity evident on the dance floor before me.

Then, suddenly – without so much as a 'do you mind?' – the bald-headed Polish Mafioso strutted past the Albanian gang, giving them evils. This was more like it – some proper undercover shit. The look was venomously returned and then heads went together furtively to discuss this impudent visual attack. They'd get him later. No way was any Polish heavy going to impede on their turf.

Clearly the Asian lads in the background felt the same, although they didn't want either the Polish *or* the Albanians on their patch, and whispered amongst themselves regarding the possibility of reprisals. It was war, and all the gangs were involved. Innit. So much for our remit.

This Victorian Playground - Part 2

Ironically enough, very few people in the club seemed particularly pissed, and there were no overt displays of disorder to make any note of. PC Tank finished his fifth pint and stated that very soon *we* would be the most rowdy which, given our previous, wasn't that far out of the question.

Any disorder you see, while certainly often fuelled by alcohol, doesn't really need the demon drink to make it happen a lot of the time. And if someone has been served a drink in a pub when they are so paralytic they can hardly stand up – this is clearly a breach of the Licensing Act, but that person is only going to be a danger to themselves.

The danger, here, of course, was the underlying tension between the conspiratorial gangs, clearly evident in the room, even though there were just a few representatives out flying their various cultural and ideological flags. The delegates from all the other various Eastern European countries, plus the Turkish and Somalians, and the Jamaican Yardies, among many others, as well as the travelling fraternity, and the Sikh gangs, and the Muslim boys who hate the Sikhs – and vice-versa – and the Hindu lads who complete this tripartite committee of mutual disdain, along with all the other multiform British, immigration-hating, popular-culture subdued muppets, and all the rest who simply don't know what to think; and every other little group, gang, alliance, company, mob and crew – religious or otherwise – well they weren't in the club at all. Imagine what a festival that would have been?

Alcohol-fuelled violence and disorder? *Alcohol?* Barely! A few months back we had a serious assault in the town centre. Some Asian lads had bottled a couple of males from another country, and then kicked one of them in the head. The CCTV was so horrific that the main offender got remanded without any fuss, which was quite amazing considering the CPS were involved. He's obviously not in prison now though. On another night, a group of males from a particular part of Europe went around the town asking white people if they were English. If the answer was, 'Yes,' then the locals would get beaten up.

These attacks weren't alcohol-fuelled, and neither was the Albanian nightclub-door-kicking antics of the previous evening. And neither are many of the problems this nation faces, although alcohol often acts as a handy lubricant. It would thus appear that drink, in many cases, merely

PC Michael Pinkstone

acts as a catalyst for highlighting much more serious social issues. Therefore placing much of our focus on the drinking side of things does not adequately address what truly needs to be addressed.

Take a look back at Victorian times and you will discover that alcohol abuse was very prominent. Even more so than now. So why are we focusing so much on booze? – as if it holds the keys to the fucked up state we find ourselves in. Perhaps another Prohibition is the answer. Or is it that the Government simply doesn't want to admit the real reasons why this country is simply getting worse and worse?

The pertinent issues nowadays are much more insidious and worrying than the dangers of booze, even though the alcohol problem is big enough in its own right. So if we clamp down on this binge drinking culture we will undoubtedly save a few livers perhaps – and potentially salvage a few relationships from the fires of indiscretion and abuse. We may even save some lives and prevent some altercations here and there. In some instances we will negate large scale fights and nasty assaults. Perhaps even reduce our detection rate for Section 5 of the Public Order Act 1986 at the same time. How ironic. Alcohol-related violence and disorder is, of course, a major problem, and we must continue to tackle it as best we can. This is a given.

But it could only be a Home Office-funded operation into examining potential breaches of the Licensing Act, that would lead to PC Tank and I – among others – exposing the merest, tiniest tip of the iceberg: the drugs, gangs and malignant cultural cults, who strut around the various towns "defending" their turf – dealing out narcotics and violence with impunity; displaying exactly the kinds of destructive behaviours, and other shambolic displays of social ignorance, that I have come to expect from various people in Britain these days.

But the Home Office wouldn't pay me to tell them that.

7. Making a Scene

PC Snipper – that guy should write his own bloody book – has commented on a number of occasions that police jargon has infiltrated his everyday life. For example, when he has finished making love to his girlfriend, he rolls over and says 'much obliged'. He also has a trouble saying 'yes' once – it always comes out as 'yes, yes'. Furthermore, his classic saying has to be, 'Morale making off … yeah, total loss.'

We police love our jargon, and one policing word we use perhaps more than any other is the word *"scene"*. Whatever has happened, and wherever it's happened – it's a scene. We love to make a scene. PC Shrimp once stood all night at a "scene watch". Now a scene watch is basically where something allegedly serious has happened and it needs "watching". So we stand there and watch it … for fucking hours and hours and hours. Then CID turn up, smoke some cigarettes and leave after eight seconds (yes, they smoke that quickly) and then several hours after that, Scenes of Crime turn up. They spend a few moments poking around the area and, if it's inside, cover every surface with a fine layer of grey dust, and then leave pretty sharpish too. The barrier tape is then removed and the exhausted officer collapses to the floor, the "scene log" still in his hand. This is prised from his cold, dead fingers and the body is disposed of in a vacant locker on the third floor of the station, and his outstanding investigations on CRAPPIES are allocated to the rest of the team. It is then decided, after all, that the whole thing was a load of shit and didn't need such attention, and the associated "job" is filed straight away.

So if you are a frontline police officer, you can be assured that a *lot* of your time will be spent at scenes – and your role? It's to fucking *watch*

PC Michael Pinkstone

it. No more, no less. You just have to stand there like a moron (smiling, wherever possible) and … just stand there. And … stand there some more. Then, when it appears that someone might actually do something about something else … no … it's a false alarm – you carry on standing there. Standing and watching. Watching and standing. And making occasional notes in the scene log that you're still there and haven't moved, eaten, drunk or pissed for nine and a half hours. It really is a fantastic part of being a police officer.

Oh, sorry, I forgot about PC Shrimp – which is ironic, because that's what everyone else did. He *stood*, *all night*, in the rain, near some random bush. Then, when 7 am came and he was supposed to be relieved by another officer who would also have to stand by the bush for hours and hours – he wasn't. Legend has it that at about 9 am a small voice piped up on the radio, 'Er, is anyone gonna come and relieve me, cos I've been standing here for eleven hours …'

One day, I was standing at a scene – the purpose of which escapes me now (and escaped me then too) and suddenly my radio beeped in my ear. The lovely radios we use allow for personal messages to be transmitted by typing in a code and you can talk directly to whoever you want to, which often helps to relieve boredom at a scene watch, or any other kind of "watch" that we have to do. Unfortunately the number flashing up on my radio wasn't one of my friends – it was the Inspector.

(Beep, beep)
Hello Sir.
Pinkstone, you look like a sack of shit. Put your fucking hat on.
(Pause)
Yes Sir.

This was because I was standing, in *public* view, at a scene watch – *without my hat.* Oh my good God. The scene was compromised! The courts would rip this case to shreds! I'd have to fill in an embarrassing MG6B for the rest of my career! It's all over!

However, despite my swearing at the Inspector (obviously without him hearing) he was right. We *are* a professional body, allegedly, and we *should* try to impress upon the public that we are professionals, but

This Victorian Playground - Part 2

my hat made my head hurt and I just couldn't be fucked on this particular day. But I did as I was told because, despite my internal feelings, I still obey orders from higher ranks. If he told me to jump off a cliff, I would. I'd push the fucker over the edge first, but I'd still jump nonetheless. Now *that's* dedication to a cause.

Anyway, apologies. I'm writing this chapter after a few sherbets so it might be a little bit incoherent or bizarre in places. There's a good reason for that – I want it to be a celebration – a champagne toast, in fact, to thousands of hours wasted at scenes by frontline guys and gals like me (guy, in my case), which was all done for the greater good. And that good would be for ...? Now there's a good question.

In all seriousness, the "good" is pretty much for the preservation of evidence. In fact, it is *solely* for the preservation of evidence that we have scene watches. If something has happened that warrants a scene watch being started then you can be assured that there is potential evidence at that particular scene that needs "preserving". As PC Tall from Introduction Part II will tell you – it is all about the preservation of wildlife. In his case, expunged vertebrates. Yet, again in his case, the *greater good* was proving that a slightly worse-for-wear pigeon (in fact, the crushed remains of a very dead pigeon) was not, in fact, the scene of a serious criminal offence. *Tango Zulu, Mike Bravo Nine One?* Nine One, go ahead. *Er, Nine One, could you please clarify one thing for me – do human beings have beaks? If not, can I leave this scene and go and have some lunch ...?*

Hey, I told you there would be some bizarre stuff in here, but stay with me. It's all inspirational. Just imagine yourself standing at a "scene" for several hours staring continuously at a small, rather insignificant bone, and you will begin to hallucinate *quite* significantly. As such, the only way this chapter will make any sense is if you are in such a hallucinogenic state on a scene watch, or pissed, like me.

Now the other evening I turned up at a "scene" and fuck me, what a scene it was. You could smell it a mile away. I say "a mile" – it was more like thirty feet or so, but "a mile away" is just a saying which, in this case, is quite appropriate, because it fucking stank to high heaven.

I arrived in a car, for once, and had a quick briefing from Sgt Coat and PC Shake who were already there guarding the scene. Like they

PC Michael Pinkstone

needed to fucking guard it. Like some burglar was going to break in through the window and steal a rancid corpse ...

Oh come on, what did you expect? This is me. I have to have a rancid corpse in every book I write – this being the second one – and I hope to God I never write a book for children.[14] Anyway, back to the scene. I took over the scene log from PC Shake and jotted down my name and the time I arrived. At this stage we were maintaining a scene log because it wasn't yet established whether or not the death was suspicious. There had been the usual arguments raging back and forth as to whose remit it was to remove the body – nothing changes eh? – but somehow the specialist search and recovery team had been persuaded to pop down and do the necessaries, which was likely to be the morning. After all, the corpse wasn't exactly going anywhere. And neither would the unlucky bastard "watching" said corpse, namely yours truly.

Fortunately, in this case, the scene was so horrific I was allowed to wait outside in a car and not actually stand there and stare at a dead man with maggots crawling out of the back of his head, but I wouldn't put it past the counsel for the defence in a court of law – if this death were suspicious – to make some spurious claim that while I sat in the car not actually "watching" the scene, then some unscrupulous person could have sneaked in and fucked about with the "evidence".

You know what? If that truly happened I'd shake the fucker's hand. Good on him. See what we have to put up with? See what I mean about a fucked up country? I put it to you, officer, that you did *not* maintain that scene properly; that you did *not* preserve it; and that by your *incompetence*, PC Pinkstone, you allowed an unknown person to enter that scene and contaminate it. Therefore this is no longer a murder trial – it's a discussion about how shit PC Pinkstone is and how fucking shambolic it is that he didn't stand there staring for three hours, unblinking, at a putrefying cadaver. Yes, PC Pinkstone, you truly *are* a bald ginger c**t ...

I suppose I'm lucky though. I've never had to guard a tiny bird skeleton all night, and I've not had to stand for eleven hours next to some uneventful and uninspiring shrubbery, but that's just the luck of the draw. For if you are a frontline officer it's simply pot luck if you get

---

14 As an ex-primary school teacher I may very well end up writing a book for children, so please don't quote me on that line.

This Victorian Playground - Part 2

to watch a scene. Well, it's not really *luck* in the traditional sense – it's just another one of those phrases like "you could smell it a mile away". In either case it's all random and unpredictable. And shit.

Yet despite all of this, I only had to wait a short while longer, because the specialist search team arrived pretty darn promptly, after already having been on duty for eleven hours – so hats off to them. They got suited and booted and entered the room of death, to do what was required. A few minutes later one of the crew came over to me and removed his mask, looking somewhat haggard. 'That was particularly nasty,' he said, with some feeling. I nodded and looked at the bright yellow body bag lying in the front garden, the horrific stench still lingering in the air. He nodded too, and went off to get changed. Sometimes the scene just speaks for itself.

So, my dear fellow frontline officers, and anyone else reading this book, this chapter is dedicated to the ongoing struggle to preserve evidence in the best possible sense, and to promote thorough investigation into criminal offences, and hopefully secure a jolly good conviction at the end of it. Furthermore, it's a bottoms-up to staring at dead pigeons, putrid corpses and mid-sized hydrangea bushes – the *real* side of scene watches and a true indication of what we do when we arrive ... on scene.

P.S. I *really* am quite trolleyed.

8. Suicidal in Custody

Sorry about that last chapter. I've sobered up now. In which case, let me ask you a rather sobering question: *Have you ever tried to harm yourself?*

Well, *have* you? I mean, let's be serious here. It's a serious issue. If you get nicked and you stand before the custody Sergeant at a police station, he will ask you that question. And what you tell him will impinge upon the kind of attention you get at said police station.

If your answer is '*No*', everyone breathes a sigh of relief. If your answer is '*Yes*', then everyone will straighten up a little and the Sergeant will look at you, half nervously, and ask you to specify. If you say something like, 'Well, I scratched my wrists with a butter knife eighteen years ago after the death of my dog Spanky' – you should be OK and the Sergeant will relax, along with the officer who arrested you.

However, if you say, 'Yes, I'm on anti-depressants and have a history of serious suicide attempts, including one the other day when I cut my wrists down to the bone – here, look at the stitches that I will start to pick out in a minute' – you can be guaranteed that you *might* end up on a cell watch. Yet nowadays you don't really have to be too serious about your own demise to warrant police paranoia.

For the police get very nervous around suicidal or depressed people. They make us somewhat twitchy, especially when they are in our care or custody. Either way, if you are suicidal or depressed and you are within six feet of a police officer, it's all their fault. I don't quite know what kind of fault, or why, or the context of what I'm saying, but you can be sure that it's their fault.

This Victorian Playground - Part 2

So if you end up getting arrested and you have such self-loathing tendencies, you will most likely spend your whole time in custody being "watched" by a police officer.[15] This is so you don't kill yourself and put all the blame onto us for not "looking after" you properly. It's called a "death in custody" and it's fairly serious. Kind of up there with the antics of Saddam and Shipman.

Now, not meaning to be a party pooper, or be cruel in any way to people who truly are upset about shitty stuff that's happened to them – but what the fuck does *suicidal* mean anyway?

I've heard of people who have been suicidal for decades. In which case they are not really *suicidal* per se. I'd say they were rather grumpy fuckers, or attention seeking bastards.

It's all a bit anti-human-rights, but this following sketch is one of my reflections I hope one day to see in reality, if not in some kind of film. You may be able to spot the part where it moves from reality to daydream...

The scene is in police custody, and PC Smart has just brought a male prisoner, Mr Harman, before Sergeant Poole:

Right, officer, could you please explain to me while this person is here?

Certainly Sarge. I've arrested this male on suspicion of shoplifting. He was identified by a security guard at Tesco's, on CCTV, as acting suspiciously in the meat aisle. He was observed by the guard to place several large packets of steak into his shoulder bag, whereupon he quickly exited the store, past the tills and made no attempt to pay. He was detained by the guard outside the store and police were called. He did try to run away twice but had to be restrained. He was arrested at 1540 hours to conduct a prompt and effective investigation, to obtain evidence by means of questioning and also because I believe the investigation could be hindered by him trying to disappear if he wasn't arrested immediately. His name is Ricky Harman.

Right, Mr Harman, I've heard what the officer has had to say and I'm going to authorise your detention here at this police station. Whilst

---

15 For effect, you may want to try to strangle yourself with your paper suit every fifteen minutes. This means you are *really* suicidal and we'll definitely have to keep "watching" you.

PC Michael Pinkstone

you are here you have certain rights and entitlements, namely to have someone informed you've been arrested; to speak to a solicitor – free of charge – either in person or on the telephone, and to consult a copy of a book called the Codes of Practice which governs police powers and procedures. Do you wish to exercise any of these rights now?

No.

No? Well, let me remind you that these are continuing rights and you can change your mind later if you so wish, OK?

(Nod)

Now while you are here at the police station you are under our care and we are responsible for your welfare, so I need to ask you some questions, OK?

(Nod)

Are you currently on any medication?

(Head shake)

Do you take drugs?

(Nod)

What drugs are you on?

(Mumbles)

Heroin.

OK, we'll make sure the doctor gets to see you as well.

(Nod)

Do you have any other welfare concerns that we should know about – are you diabetic? Anaemic? Anything like that?

(Head shake)

OK, officer, was he restrained?

Yes – handcuffed back to back, Sarge.

Mr Harman, do you have any injuries?

(Head shake)

No? Well, like I said, we'll still get the doctor to see you anyway. Now as part of my risk assessment I also have to ask you if you have ever tried to harm yourself?

(Head nod)

You have?

(Head nod)

How have you tried to do that?

This Victorian Playground - Part 2

(Mumbles)

Cut myself.

Sorry, you're going to need to speak up. Did you say you cut yourself? Where and how?

(Mr Harman pulls up his sleeves in a careless fashion to reveal several minor scratches on his forearms)

Well, that doesn't look too serious. How long ago did you do that?

'Bout free munfs.

How are you feeling now?

Pretty shit.

Would you say you are feeling suicidal now?

Yeah, a bit.

Have you ever overdosed to the point of collapse or jumped off a bridge?

(Head shake)

Ever laid yourself down in the path of an oncoming train?

(Head shake)

Ever taken poison or fallen onto your sword?

(Bemused head shake)

No? Well, you don't sound fucking suicidal to me. So, let me ask you again: are you feeling suicidal?

Yeah, a bit. I've been suicidal for ages.

Oh, I see. That means you want to die then?

(Shrug)

Don't care.

No, listen to me, fuck-for-brains. Do you want to *die*?

Don't give a fuck mate.

I'm sorry?

Don't give a fuck.

That would be, 'Don't give a fuck, *Sergeant*.'

(Shrug)

In which case, Mr Harman, you'll have no trouble dying now then, will you?

(Slightly confused look)

Well, frankly Mr Harman, if you are suicidal and want to die then we can arrange to do that for you right *now*. All of this is being video- and

PC Michael Pinkstone

sound-recorded because the Government are a bunch of nannies and feel they have to put cameras in every nook and cranny of police custody suites, so everything we are saying and doing is open to scrutiny. This also means that everything *you* are saying and doing is also open to scrutiny. I suppose these cameras have got to have a fucking use. So, you have been recorded, on video, saying that you don't care if you die ...

(Pause)

In which case, officer, would you please take Mr Harman out to the yard and kill him.

(Very scared look)

Wh ... what?

(Shouting)

Officer Smart! Get this fucker out of my sight and fucking kill him! He wants to fucking die and is incapable of doing it himself, now go and fucking do it for him!

(Extreme look of panic on Mr Harman's face as officer Smart comes towards him, reaching for his baton ...)

(Meanwhile the Sergeant is now screaming ...)

HURRY THE FUCK UP, SMART! I HAVEN'T GOT ALL FUCKING DAY! TAKE THIS MAN OUTSIDE AND *FUCKING DISPOSE OF HIM NOW!!!*

(Mr Harman backs against the wall and wets himself)

No! No! Please! I don't want to die, I don't want to die!

(Sergeant Poole looks at him calmly and coldly)

So, Mr Harman, let me ask you again ... *are* you suicidal?

(Small whimper)

... No

(Gathers papers together in a business-like manner)

Excellent, let's do property then, shall we ...?

Now, I suppose that this small interchange may breach some form of human rights somewhere, but it really is about time that we stopped pandering to people in police custody – people who claim to be "suicidal", when what is really wrong with them is ... nothing. They are usually either drugged-up attention-seeking fuckwits or the kind of people that *need* to be locked in a cell for the safety and security of everyone else.

This Victorian Playground - Part 2

I am sounding as harsh as possible here because police spend *ages* wasting time "watching" people in custody playing up and acting up, pretending that they are either about to kill themselves or trying to kill themselves, or would indeed kill themselves if they weren't being "watched" with their cell door open and didn't have their own dedicated police officer at their beck and call for several hours.

Because the police are so desperately and completely blame-conscious about everything – and because any form of injury or death in police custody is such a horrific thing to happen – then any slight whimper from a detained person about perhaps feeling "slightly down" will allow them all the time and attention they need – and most likely an open cell.

The bottom line is that people take the piss – and do it regularly. Every police officer in this country will have had to "watch" some supposedly suicidal pillock for hours and hours (sometimes through *closed* glass doors!) because they know the system and play up for the cameras. Yet the kinds of people that come through our doors on a regular basis are the kinds of people that need to be shoved in a cell with the door slammed behind them. If they claim to be "suicidal" then let them fucking get on with it.

I make no apologies whatsoever for this chapter. The bottom line is that we have to toughen up from the bottom up. We have to stop being so fucking weak and risk-averse. Is a cell not a safe and secure place? What is there in a cell that could kill you in a few hours, that a lifetime of other, real dangers couldn't accomplish? In which case, if someone dies in a police cell, it would most likely be their own fucking fault …

All we have to do is take a small step backwards from these kinds of people and say, 'OK, get on with it. Want to die? Go for it.' Because believe me, we wouldn't end up with any deaths in custody as a result of a Sergeant saying that.

I know part of our role is the preservation of life, but sometimes the best way to preserve life is to just let it get on with it.

Sometimes care and compassion simply has to be tough.

9. Something and Nothing

One of the more bizarre things I have witnessed in my fairly short but fairly piquant existence, was in the Middle East, when I was happily, and safely, driving my car at about 80 kmh on the outside lane of a large, three-lane highway – the outside lane being the "slow" one – and I happened to glance to my left as I was doing so. A glance that turned into a prolonged look of amazement.

Now the weather at the time was particularly warm as you can imagine. The kind of "warm" that makes you duck inside shops to cool down and drink several litres of water a day, but you still piss treacle. The kind of warm that hits you like a giant hairdryer on full heat when you step off the plane for the first time, and every breath you take is like breathing in the blast of an oven when you open it with your head too close to the door. The kind of warm that makes you tap the temperature reading inside your car as if it's faulty – well, you would tap it if it read 55 degrees Celsius. And that's just how hot it is *outside*. You still have to wait for the air-conditioning to kick in inside the car.

However, despite the glorious heat, I was driving in the middle of a rather spectacular and extensive sandstorm, which was making visibility somewhat grainy to say the least. As such I was perhaps driving a few kmh slower than usual – safety first and all that. Nevertheless the inclement atmosphere did not seem to be dampening the furious driving of many of the road users and especially not the flat-bed truck that tore up beside me.

At the wheel was a Saudi chap in traditional garb, and although he had a windscreen to protect him, he still had almost the whole of his face

This Victorian Playground - Part 2

covered with his headdress, with perhaps the tiniest slit for his eyes to peer through. He was hunched over the wheel of his battered vehicle, calmly powering along at about 140 kmh through the atmospheric alluvium, in the fast lane, without a seatbelt on – and carrying the most extraordinary load I have ever borne witness to on the back of a moving truck. In fact, the most extraordinary load that has perhaps *ever* been on the back of a moving truck.

If this was in Britain – or any other country that actually had some driving standards – and caught on camera, it would have made it onto every police reality TV programme *ever* – probably for years and years. The kind of clip that makes you say, 'Oh, I've seen this *loads* of times!' But you'd watch it again anyway because it's fucking unbelievable *and* hilarious, in a fucked up kind of way. It would also most likely have made the national news, if only for a brief moment, yet perhaps have got many people tutting in disgust and writing in to complain to someone, somewhere, for something to be done.

For on the back of the truck was a giant pineapple. And when I say "giant pineapple" – I mean *giant* pineapple. I think, in fact, it was actually an ornamental local tree of some kind, but in reality it was a ten foot tall pineapple, with a bulk proportionate to its height.

Of course, being some kind of decorative courtyard tree/fantastic enormous tropical fruit, it would have been situated in some kind of sturdy pot of some description. After all, it would need situating somewhere secure for transit, and a large clay pot – perhaps with its own pleasant decorations – would have been ideal.

But no. It wasn't situated in anything at all. It was upright, on its own, in the middle of the truck. Now have you ever tried to "stand" a pineapple up on its base without it falling over?

Pretty damn hard thing to do. In this case, even harder. A mammoth prickly fruit travelling in excess of 80 mph on the back of a ramshackle truck in the middle of a sandstorm, driven by a grizzled Saudi with zero visibility through his headdress and practically zero visibility through the windscreen anyway ... not really a recipe for stability.

But the pineapple was not really alone ... Oh no. That would have been very dangerous and irresponsible. It had assistance. Or "assistants" – it had five little assistants assisting it. Five little Bangladeshi men in

PC Michael Pinkstone

blue boiler suits were lashed to the giant pineapple – with thick ropes around their waists, and each was leaning back, off the edges of the truck, trying to counterbalance the darn thing and keep it upright.

I blinked. And stared. This surely was some kind of a dare? Or a stunt. Where was the cameraman? As the truck moved steadily past me I could see this enormous fucking fruit wobbling crazily on the back, and five little workers valiantly tied to it, each pulling on their ropes or releasing the tension enough to somehow – God knows how – prevent it from toppling over. One chap – the one leaning off the back of the truck – was, I swear, inclined so far he was almost horizontal – his head a few feet away from a lot of tarmac and a lot less skin.

It truly was the most extraordinary sight I have ever seen on a motorway, and I will never forget the yells, screams and panicked instructions audible above the noise of the traffic and the sound-muffling nature of a harsh sandstorm, as the five little heroes continued into the dusky distance, desperate to stay alive whilst protecting a gigantic fruit and earning a few pitiful dinars in the process. Yet others have devoted their lives for less.

* * *

I wonder what each of those brave little souls was going through. What journey they had all been on to end up right there. What hassle they had endured to arrive at that precise moment in time, and whether in fact they survived that particular journey.

If you were to go back in time thirty years and ask one of them – perhaps when he was aged about six, 'What do you want to do when you're grown up?' I wonder what he would say.

Well sir, one day, in about three decades, I want to live in a country that isn't my home because I can't afford to live at home. I want to be treated like utter shit, paid a pittance and effectively live a life of slavery. I wanted to be looked upon as the scum of the earth – in fact, live right at the bottom of the food chain amongst the rest of the downtrodden and maligned individuals of all different countries – countries that aren't able to provide enough employment or welfare to safeguard even their most basic rights or the rights of their families.

This Victorian Playground - Part 2

Then, once I've been there for a while, having stood in as many queues as you can imagine just to earn this right, I'd like to work for some kind of garden centre as a porter – a basic but busy role, and one which I'll do for about fifteen years and, in that whole time, earn one fiftieth of what a local would earn in a week. Then, one day, I want to stand on the back of a flat-bed truck in the middle of a sandstorm, being driven by a crazy Saudi along a motorway – who can't see a darn thing anyway – travelling way in excess of the speed limit and in contravention of any road safety rules that have ever existed, anywhere, in any nation, fastened to a huge tropical fruit by a length of rope, whilst leaning off the edge to stop it from falling over and, as such, be a few feet or a small pothole away from certain death, or at the very least the loss of most of my motor functions or effective use of my brain. Or both. I don't really want, or need, any human rights whatsoever and would gladly offer my soul for this opportunity, and more.

***

This chapter is called "Something and Nothing" for two reasons:

1. We are very good at saying things like '*I want something done about it!*'
2. We are very good at implementing lots of ways of *not* doing something about it.

We are a nation of people who make demands for "something" to be done about stuff. I want something done! Something needs to be done about it! Why doesn't someone do something about that? Something has gotta be done.

If I had a pound – actually, scrap that – if I had *10p* for every time I have heard someone (including myself) suggest something along the lines of wanting something to be done about something else, I would be a pretty wealthy guy by now. For we Brits are experts on demanding that ever elusive "*something*".

It can take many forms and come under many guises. For example, we could be walking down the street and see a large hole in the road.

PC Michael Pinkstone

'Gosh, something needs to be done about that.'

Or, we could be walking down the street and see a load of adolescents acting in a very anti-social manner (e.g. kicking an innocent person in the head and other such "kid stuff") and think, 'The police really need to do something about those youths …'

In another situation we could witness a variety of things (based on personal experiences) and think, 'Something really needs to be done about the immigration problem.'

On other occasions we might hear a work colleague or a friend moaning about some kind of wrong or injustice or personal affair, and give them comprehensive advice along the lines of, 'Yeah mate, you really need to do something about that.'

It's all about *something*. It's an all embracing word. So, dear Reader, what the hell *is* this "something"?

Well, I guess it all boils down to context. It also boils down to someone else doing things for us. Shifting the blame. Shifting the focus. Making it someone else's problem. However, the main point here is that we, as Brits, have a genuine skill of recognising that something needs to be done about certain things. We're not that stupid. And for the most part we have a genuine desire to do the "right thing". We want to solve those problems.

In many cases, of course, we would not possess the skills or have the responsibility for sorting out the problems. Yet when it comes to our daily lives we need to take far more responsibility for that "something" than we do at the moment.

So the next time you hear someone say – or find yourself saying – 'Something needs to be done about that' – just think of what *you* can do about it. For we Brits have become extremely good at *saying* the something and doing the *nothing*. Our concern does not usually result in a decisive response.

We have also become very short-sighted and focused on the minor and the trivial. It's much easier to set our sights on the short-term and the irrelevant. It gives us a sense of self-importance and justifies a whole load of pointless bureaucracy, which looks good on paper.

As such, we are paranoid, and organisationally obfuscated beyond all sense of reasoning or reckoning. This we know already.

This Victorian Playground - Part 2

This was the remit of *Part I*. However, because this is *Part II*, we need to take the argument slightly further and look at where we have arrived. And, sadly, we haven't arrived in a particularly promising place. For I believe that we have become *institutionally incapable* of resolving problems because of this state of affairs. So while we may recognise the issues, we are incapable of dealing with them effectively, because we implement hundreds of ways of not actually dealing with them.

Fuck *institutional racism*. It's the very least of anyone's problems because it *isn't* (and *wasn't*) ever a fucking problem. It was a calculated plot to subjugate the police. I would say our *real* problem is this institutional inability to solve social or organisational predicaments because we have a remit of passing the buck, not accepting responsibility and, whilst recognising that "something needs to be done" – *nothing ever gets done*. Let's be blunt here. Nothing ever fucking gets done! Our mindset doesn't allow it. And, most pressingly, we have become extremely scared of tackling any kind of problem in case we get blamed for doing it "wrong". So, in truth, nothing ever gets done. This nation does not solve its problems – it tiptoes around the edges of them, tutting and dreaming up policies to deal with them, but never ends up actually *doing* anything to sort them out properly. And God forbid if you should actually *do* something ...

Not long ago I saw a news report about a coastguard who had risked his life to save a teenage girl. Basically he had climbed halfway down a treacherous cliff to grab hold of the stranded female, before they were both winched to safety. Afterwards he was quite rightly hailed as a hero and received well-deserved acclaim for his actions.

However, this is Britain, and because he'd taken action and actually *done* something – he got into trouble. Unfortunately his bosses slammed him for breaching some Health and Safety policies. Apparently he should have waited for something or other. Waited for procedure to be followed. Waited for her to die, perhaps?

The other day at work was no exception to this British rule of applying policies at the expense of actual preservation of life. My colleague, PC Trooper (the one who is "18% racist") and I were making our merry way back towards the station one evening when the controller called up

PC Michael Pinkstone

to say that someone had reported a house fire in a nearby street – with persons trapped!

Now I knew full well what kind of uniform I was wearing. And it wasn't fire-proof. I knew that fire was hot, and that it burns. I knew that gas ignites and that there could have been a variety of other dangers too. I also knew full well that the fire service were on the way and that this was their remit. However, at times like these, the police also turn up. We set up cordons. We move people back. We report on the location – any casualties, hazards, dangers etc. We get there as soon as possible and preserve life. If we get there first, God forbid, one of us may actually need to do something to save someone.

So I pressed the blue light button, turned on the sirens, and began to drive towards the scene. I wouldn't consider myself to be a hero, but I would do my best to save someone if the situation called for it. Of course, the best way to deal with such situations is to actually *get* there.

But no. This is Britain, don't forget. We weren't *allowed* to go to the scene. Let me repeat that, please. We weren't *allowed* to go to the scene.

The controller, who was following some kind of procedure, requested that only *one* unit make to the scene and "give updates". They had to arrive, observe, and pass relevant information according to a particular method.

Now, I entirely agree with this. Sorry to butt in with this detached and procedural sentiment, but we need to consider this mentality from both angles: from the point of view of the guys and gals actually *doing* the work, as well as the point of view of the policy-makers and bureaucrats sitting in comfortable chairs.

For example, if I was driving down a motorway and saw a chemical tanker crash, and a lethal, noxious substance start leaking out onto other crashed cars, I wouldn't pile into the melee and start dragging people to safety, whether I was in uniform or not. Instead, I'd get on the radio, or the phone, and stand well back from the scene, whilst relating as much relevant information as possible, so that the right people could be informed and various crisis policies implemented. It sounds mean and people might stare at me, especially if I was in uniform, and scream at me to assist. But I simply couldn't. Some situations would require me to observe and pass relevant information, no matter how desperate the cries of the people who needed help.

This Victorian Playground - Part 2

You see, we really don't want *dead* heroes. That's what the coastguard's bosses said after he saved that girl's life. And it's a rather valid point, I suppose. So I guess these policies we have really do exist for a reason and sometimes they are essential.

But somehow, somewhere, we have become strangled by them, to the point of utter bafflement. We don't want dead heroes? I certainly don't fancy dying in the very near future, but seeing as death is going to come for me at some point, I think I'd rather die a hero than anything else.

If I saw a man wielding a samurai sword in the middle of the street with no-one else around, I wouldn't go anywhere near him. I'd wait for "Level 1 Taser Authorisation", or something along those lines. However, if he was about to chop up some poor innocent bystander, I may find myself charging towards him with my baton drawn and a blood-curdling scream erupting from my lips. If I didn't, I would have to spend the rest of my life grateful that I wasn't a "dead hero", and thank fuck it was someone else that got maimed instead of me. Then the family of the victim would look at me in my uniform – the vows I made still echoing around my mind – and wonder why the hell I didn't do *something.* But I guess I could tell them that the policy prevented me from saving life and limb, and therefore absolve all organisational guilt. So long as my arse was covered in a legal sense.

Yes, these policies. These lovely little policies. We truly are burdened by so many of them that things are coming to a grinding halt! For the most part they sound brilliant in theory, but in practice can be fucking horrendous.

We have implemented them for so many things that don't require them, we are now so overwhelmed by them, that we can hardly move or breathe. Over the past several years, owing to our entirely risk-averse, blame-conscious, fear-of-being-sued, fucked up, precious mentality, we have moved further and further away from action, and replaced it almost completely with *inaction.*

We apply policies to *everything*. And it's not just the police who are burdened by this approach. The fire service, too, are just as encumbered, as are many other organisations.

We have become so completely policy-driven, that the actual circumstances of any particular incident have almost become irrelevant,

PC Michael Pinkstone

which is yet another example of the decontextualisation of life itself in the world of the police. And, sadly, more often than not, our policies equate to nothing more than doing fuck all. But at least we can't be blamed, sued, or maligned if we follow them! Talk about a vicious circle ...

So back to the house fire. I agreed with the importance of a unit giving updates, but I would not have prevented other units from assisting. For like most of the police officers listening to the radio on that particular night, desperate to do our job and ensure the safety and welfare of people in that street, I found myself swearing and screaming in frustration at the utter absurdity of *not being allowed* to go. Yet again – and oh my goodness have I gone on about this a lot – common sense and context were rejected in favour of doing things by the book.

* * *

And it's this mentality that has also fucked up the police regarding problems that might not be considered life-threatening or a crisis. House fires and extremely serious incidents aside, we apply policies to everything, irrespective of what has transpired. It's the same kind of mentality that treats everyone as a victim if they have been recorded as a victim (just read *Part I* again if you fancy ...!). It's the same kind of mentality that treats *every* "domestic incident" as a potentially serious oh-my-God-someone-is-going-to-die kind of scenario. It's the same kind of mentality that means police officers are encouraged to arrest ordinary citizens for sending two text messages. It's the kind of mentality that, while desperate to do the "right thing", actually ends up doing either the *wrong* thing, or ends up doing *nothing*.

In light of this, Britain has become almost entirely unable to sort any of its problems out with any degree of competence whatsoever. From the top to the bottom and from the bottom to the top – in all walks of life and in all contexts, whether schools, businesses, agencies, the police, whatever – we are wallowing in the mire of utter inaction. For all of our plans, policies, arse-covering strategies, procedures – you name it – lead to absolutely nothing being done to suitably resolve problems whatsoever. And even when we *think* we've solved a problem – we usually create more problems in the process. This is because we never really address

This Victorian Playground - Part 2

the real issues behind anything. We just spend most of our time sorting out the aftermath of us trying to sort out the aftermath of our last attempt at solving the aftermath of a problem. And so on.

Seeing as there is a policy and procedure in place for absolutely everything – quite often those policies are not sufficient to tackle the pertinent issues in the first place. Yet we still press blindly ahead and stick with them, especially if someone has got a tick in the promotional box for implementing them. Often they create associated problems, which then inspire further policies to resolve. The sub-problems then become blown out of all proportion and spawn even more mini-policies and after several days, weeks, months and even years, we've completely lost sight of the original problem because we're far too busy trying to sort out the mess that all the extra policies have created.

Please allow me to quote something from *Part 1:*

> *... We stood, holding pieces of paper and mobile phones, all pointing in opposite directions at other people ... If someone asked a question we could look at our policies and check our procedures, but if that failed, what then? What if the answer wasn't in front of our noses? What if our action plans and computer system databases didn't provide the exact solution to the problem? That's right – more policies and procedures. More action plans. We couldn't really move because we were lost, and we had no idea which way was which anyway, so we stayed put and implemented policies on the spot. We began to contradict each other because the left hand didn't know what the right hand was doing. All too often our procedures undercut each other or counteracted each other. When that happened – what then? Nothing. People became lost in the system. Lost in the inner machinations of organisational incompetence. Passed from pillar to post. Transferred and re-routed and led on a bewildering trail, often right back to where they started. If someone asked a question we could look at our policies and check our procedures, but if that failed, what then? What if the answer wasn't in front of our noses? What if our action plans and computer system databases didn't provide the exact solution*

PC Michael Pinkstone

> *to the problem? That's right – more policies and procedures. More action plans. We couldn't really move because we were lost, and we had no idea which way was which anyway, so we stayed put and implemented policies on the spot ... All too often our procedures undercut each other or counteracted each other. When that happened – what then? Nothing. People became lost in the system. Lost in the inner machinations of organisational incompetence. Passed from pillar to post. Transferred and re-routed and led on a bewildering trail, often right back to where they started ...*

Please forgive me for such a lengthy quote – especially one of my own! – but I feel it sums up exactly where we are right at this very minute.

For I'm sure you've gone into work at some point in your life and found some defect somewhere, or some fault with the "system", or any other organisational glitch and thought, 'Hmm, something needs to be done about that ...' Yet no matter how hard you try to sort it out yourself, or establish whose problem it is, far too often you find that it's actually no-one's remit to sort it out! The problem could be as minor as a broken computer or something more complex like a policy that doesn't seem to be very effective (in fact, entirely damaging) but there is nothing that can be done about it. For once things are in place – especially policies – they seem to take on a life of their own, yet even the most trivial and tangible things can be impossible to address, owing to our institutional inability.

I once turned up at work (it would be unfair of me to say where) and discovered that a particular computer desk was broken. So I informed my boss who informed her boss. He informed someone else who informed someone else. Policies were examined and procedures were scrutinised. Lots of emails were sent and angry words exchanged because nothing was being done. The problem was then eventually referred to the caretaker who wasn't actually in charge of things like that and he ended up telling my boss this, who then told me. This took four weeks. All the while, the computer was sitting on a broken desk that not only looked awful (for it was in a shop) but, as far as I know, never actually got mended.

In more recent years, in the police, I have been party to some of the most frustrating procedures on the face of the planet. In *Part I* I mentioned

This Victorian Playground - Part 2

the "Escalation Policy" in relation to domestic incidents. The utter irony of this particular policy was that the only thing it escalated was police officer stress levels. It did *not* protect victims any more than a lace curtain would make safe condoms. Yet we persisted with it to the point of, at times, utter chaos. We were being institutionally inept.

Thus it seems that we spend a great deal of our time dreaming up so many ways to cover our arses, and spending precious hours making sure everything is "in place", that we don't actually do anything at all. Either that or what we do end up doing is so utterly bizarre or useless that we might as well not have bothered. Take this scenario for instance:

Not long ago we received a call from a distressed male stating that his father had taken his son out in the car without his permission. In other words, Grandpa had popped his six-year-old grandson in the back seat and gone out for a little ride, which dad didn't agree with. A few minutes later the chap called us back again with some more information.

The mitigating circumstances were that the caller was very upset, stating that his parents had "kicked him out" of the house and that there were domestic problems between him and his family, because he was a drug addict. The usual blah, blah, blah.

Now the incident was initially graded as a "Fear for Personal Welfare" (which in itself was completely over the top) but this soon got frantically shifted to 'Domestic' when those further details from the caller were obtained at 1.19 pm. Keep this time in mind. The call was logged on the computer system – as per the recording standards you should already be aware of! – and police response was graded as "urgent". In other words, we had to get there pretty quickly. However, we didn't go anywhere for a while.

So what exactly were we responding to? What was our role? What would you do? From my point of view, it was pretty clear that the first few pages of the Log spelled out that this was simply a minor domestic incident that could have been resolved either with words of advice over the phone or, more suitably, a quick visit by officers to the address just to assist in some small way – nothing too intrusive or overbearing. And certainly not anything that would eat up lots of valuable time and resources. In light of this, therefore, how did we handle the information we had been given? What was our response?

PC Michael Pinkstone

Well, here's a list of choices that we *could* have made:

1. Go round to the house straight away and talk to the person who called us and try to find out exactly what had happened and deal with it efficiently, effectively and without wasting too much time or paper.
2. Tell the caller that this really wasn't a police matter and advise him to get a grip.
3. Treat the call as an extremely serious domestic incident – and Fear for Personal Welfare of a six-year-old child – and apply the "Kidnapping Policy".

Now. Take a deep breath, because that's what I'm doing, and guess which choice we made? (Please bear in mind that this is a true story and I have not left anything out or added anything in regard to the initial call to us.)

Yes, that's right. We decided that it was a kidnapping and very soon the Log was being flung off to the farthest corners of the universe so that very important people could view it, panic, and update it with lots of utterly peculiar things for people to do, or not do, as the case may be.

Of course, it would be rather unprofessional of me to spill the beans on our Kidnapping Policy, but I think it's quite appropriate to inform you of a few things that were decided as being agreeable courses of action for the police to take. As such, ten minutes after Grandpa had left the house with his kidnapped grandson, the Log was updated as follows (by someone who clearly left their common sense and perspective at the door when they were promoted …)

1. Treat as a kidnapping.
2. Raise the security level to something a shade of puce below critical.
3. Do not go round to the house unless authorised to do so by the Senior Investigating Officer (who was presumably sent a text whilst out playing golf).
4. Do not contact the caller again unless authorised to do so by the same Senior Officer.

This Victorian Playground - Part 2

5. Send all the information to an intelligence department to check Domestic Violence history, while still not going anywhere or talking to anyone.
6. Do not, under any circumstances, go near Grandpa's car and for God's sake don't try and stop it. Just look at it and say, 'I've seen it.' Then tell someone in the control room and they will pass this information to someone else, who will pass it to someone else and twenty minutes later no further decisions will have been made.
7. Recall vaguely what the caller said to you on the phone earlier – something about an address in Southall – but you can't clarify what he said because you're not allowed to speak to him again for the moment, as per point 4.
8. Make every supervisor in every control room aware of the incident so that the Log at least looks like we've done something to find the poor little bugger.
9. Double-check all of the above and await updates from the Senior Investigating Officer who will give some further advice in a short while ...

So there I sat in the station reading the Log, along with my crewmate for the day, and Sergeant Knife walks in. The job was already over half an hour old and no-one had been dispatched to do anything yet. Far too much panicking and political policy-applying behind the scenes to actually *do* something. Paranoia in practical application is quite time-consuming, I'll have you know. Especially where the police are concerned.

'They're treating this domestic as a kidnapping!' I still find it somewhat incredible that I sounded surprised. After all, was I really expecting any sense of proportion?

'What?' Sergeant Knife looked at the Log. 'Fucking hell.'

'Is it just me?' I said with a frown. 'But is the Kidnapping Policy basically a recipe for not doing anything at all?'

'Yes,' replied Inspector Scary, who happened to be in the office at the time. 'It's a way of avoiding action almost entirely!'

'That's just insane.' I sounded surprised again. Some things are just too odd for words.

PC Michael Pinkstone

'Just go round there and speak to the fucking muppet.' Sergeant Knife didn't mince his words. 'Once the SIO has authorised it, of course.'

So I sat there looking at the Log for another few minutes and finally the Senior Investigating Officer decided that it was perhaps a good idea after all to go round to the house and speak to the caller, which should have been the case from the word go. But who am I to apply fucking common sense to policing?

Thus PC Blessing and I made our merry way to the house and spoke to Grandpa, who was a lovely fellow, and established that the grandson was fine (he'd been taken back to his mum) and that the caller was an obnoxious, drugged-up, fucked up, skanky little sod who, by all accounts, had blown all of his chances and had refused point-blank to come off the gear, despite years of endless patience and assistance from his parents.

The only fear for fucking welfare was the fact that the little boy had such a scum for a father, but you wouldn't see that on any Kidnapping Policy. What a fucking debacle.

And the scariest thing about all of this was the fact that if this job was a *real* kidnapping – with evil Grandpa taking his grandson off to some remote place, presumably to ransom him for a large sum of money – it is perhaps quite interesting to note that the first unit was not dispatched until shortly before 2 pm – nearly *forty* minutes later. So if you report a kidnapping, don't expect the police to turn up until they've faffed about for ages with some ridiculous policies beforehand … just in case the kidnapping turns out to be genuine. For that's the only reason why we have these policies in the first place. At least, then, we can't be criticised if it all goes tits-up!

* * *

It is, therefore, with a sense of head-shaking, shoulder-shrugging resignation that I propose that all of the above melee represents Britain at the moment. It is, quite simply, complete and utter organisational incompetence. And, as a knock-on effect, complete and utter social incompetence. Overseen by – you've guessed it – complete and utter political incompetence. A disjointed, and often bizarre, commotion of crap and anxious inaction.

This Victorian Playground - Part 2

Now multiply all these kinds of problems by millions – and replace them with just about every scenario you can think of – and you will sum up exactly where this nation is at the moment. We are stuck in a rut. We are completely and utterly fucking *useless.* We are something and nothing.

So if this chapter has left you scratching your head in some confusion, and you feel that the paragraphs don't really tally up very well, or it doesn't really make much sense, and leaves you feeling somewhat bewildered – enough to make you want to turn the page to the next chapter as soon as possible ... welcome to Britain. It's what we do best. We scratch our heads, observe the problems (which we have created in the first place), get a bit flustered – and do fuck all.

Oh, and by the way, something needs to be done about those little Bangladeshis and their giant fruit.

10. Breaching the Peace

If you spill out from a nightclub at 3.25 am on a Saturday morning and shout out at the top of your voice, 'FUCK THE FEDS, FUCK THE PO-LEECE!' you may find yourself speaking to a police officer, if one is hanging around the vicinity.

You may also find yourself under arrest. In fact, you *should* find yourself under arrest. For people who come out of nightclubs vocalising that kind of mindless slogan are little more than contemptible little shits who need detaining, hosing down with ice-cold water and sent on their way with a stamp on their criminal chart that suggests if they *ever* do anything like that again they'll be locked up for a goodly amount of time. Such breaches of the peace are simply not acceptable.

For the peace in this country can be breached by a lot of people for a lot of different reasons. There are multitudinous contexts in which the Queen's Peace can be violated.

In many cases we simply need to "remove" the offending party and take them elsewhere. Nowadays we're not really allowed to dump people in the middle of nowhere, but I think the police should be permitted to start utilising this old-fashioned method of breaking up a disturbance. We're just too fucking risk-averse at the moment. And *nice*.

However, I'm a big proponent of maintaining the Queen's Peace in a way that is both hard-line and hard-nosed. Sadly we're not allowed to be either these days. Too fucking pink and fluffy. We're also far too keen for *everything* to be some kind of recordable (and preferably detectable) crime instead.

This Victorian Playground - Part 2

Last year I turned up at a pub following reports of a fight. A disturbance! Report of an injured male! An assault! *Bollocks*. Of course, because of the victim culture and CRAPPIES and the NCRS and this fucking goddamned pathetic fucking Government, it's all about facts, figures, aggrieved persons and crime-recording for the sake of it, and a load of other bureaucratic shit – under the guise of being victim-focused – so I wasn't really looking forward to dealing with this. I wished instead that it was simply a breach of the peace …

I walked in through the door and, sitting on the floor by a table was a heavily tattooed male who looked like he'd seen some time inside police cells and inside prison. He was sporting a black eye and looked pretty pissed.

Ah. Unfortunately this definitely wasn't a breach of the peace – not going by today's policing constraints. Here we have an assault. We have an injured party. We have a scene to consider. CCTV. Witnesses. DNA swabs and the seizure of clothing. Victim statements. CRAPPIES updating. Named offenders and detections to be gained. Apparent and illusory "justice" to deliver. Virtual policing. Conveyor belt rectitude. Lots and lots and lots of hours wasted on a single, well-deserved, old-fashioned thump.

Or, we had a (now finished) breach of the peace, depending on how we managed the situation. Fortunately, this had all happened during the early hours of the morning, and the Log had not yet been seen by the crime recorders sitting and staring at their computer screens, so we were perhaps able to deal with it how it *should* be dealt with. One of those very rare occasions nowadays where common sense is allowed to make a small whimper in the background. There were, of course, the wishes of the victim to consider (how very "victim culture"), but he looked like he could be persuaded to make the "right" decision. As it turned out he didn't need any persuading at all, and for that I wanted to shake his hand.

The male staggered to his feet. The landlord came over. My colleagues spoke to the injured male and I spoke to the landlord. Apparently the tattooed male – a regular at the pub – had got a bit lairy and decided to threaten a group of three males with a pool cue. He didn't hit any of them – he just brandished it in their vicinity and made some low-level, slightly slurred threats.

PC Michael Pinkstone

The injured chap, I could hear in the background, was telling my colleagues that he didn't want an ambulance and that he just wanted to go home. He was quite adamant – and we all agreed he was making the right decision!

The landlord then said that one of the males in the group had punched the tattooed male – once – and then they had all walked out. They didn't hit him with anything except their fist and they didn't hit him when he was down. They didn't kick him in the head or stab him with a knife and they didn't scarper like cowards into darkened alleyways with their hoodies pulled over their faces. They didn't brag about it and say, 'Yeah bruv, I is gonna like defend my bredren. No fucka picks on my bred, you know what I mean bruv …' (This is my interpretation of how such people speak these days, because I generally can't understand a fucking word they say – the stupid, ignorant fuckwits.)

Now, I don't advocate violence, but I do advocate common sense and justice. As a police officer it would be highly unprofessional of me to say that what happened in that pub was "good", but a small part of me thought that what had happened was somehow *just*. The tattooed chap had been a cock, got smacked, and went home with a bruise. He'd wake up with a bruise, come back to the pub the following evening – and most likely meet the chap that smacked him – and all would be forgotten.

If only life were that simple. If only people were able to deal with each other within some kind of moral and ethical boundaries, even if it did involve so-called "violence". *Queensberry Rules.* Nowadays there are no rules. People have no concept of when to stop. They don't know how to *fight* with any form of decency.

Of course, many people have never really fought with decency – it just doesn't happen, but I think we've certainly crossed a line somewhere in the past decade or so, perhaps more. We've gone beyond sorting things out "like men" (to coin a phrase) and entered into some fucked up notion of brotherhood that means sucking our teeth and stabbing each other over nothing, instead of having the decency to smack someone once with our fists and leave it at that. We don't shake hands any more after a fight – we kick people in the teeth when they are already half-unconscious on the floor. Or shoot children. Gangsta rap be damned. You scum.

This Victorian Playground - Part 2

Somewhere, somehow, we have lost sight of the Queensberry Rules – of any kind of rules – and have taken breaching the peace beyond the pale. For we don't really breach the peace like we used to – we have pissed all over honour and decency and come up with a very mangled, very corrupting form of "respect", that usually realises itself as horrific, mindless violence, concerning gangs and allegiances of like-minded nasty people.

I suppose we could blame a whole load of things for this state of affairs – this *postmodern nightmare of truly national dimensions ... a melting pot of fucked up values and contorted morals.*

Yet blaming and pointing the finger isn't going to solve the problem. You can't mend the mentality of a nation by simply telling them that they are fucked up. You have to start punishing people. And you can only start to punish people if you believe that what you are doing is just and decent. Unfortunately, we live in a society, overseen by a pathetic administration, that will not allow its police service to help deliver justice. It also prohibits the justice system from delivering justice most of the time.

In reality, if someone spills out of a club on British soil and starts to shout 'FUCK THE PO-LEECE' – or chant another of their favourites, namely 'WE ... ARE ... BNP, WE ARE BNP!' – they need to be squashed. And I mean fucking *squashed*. They don't need talking to. They don't need a Penalty Notice For Disorder. They need to be squashed. Flattened. Thrown without *any* hesitation into the back of a van and driven at high velocity over every speed bump on the way back to the station. They need to be taken into a police station *without* cameras on every wall and incarcerated until they learn the real meaning of how to behave.

We have suffered heinous breaches of the Queen's Peace for far too long in this country. I use the racial "BNP" example for effect and because it's a true story, not because it's the only way that the peace is breached. I also use the 'FUCK THE PO-LEECE' scenario because apparently police officers should "expect" and "tolerate" such behaviour. We are supposed to accept the fact that we'll receive lots of abuse and let people get away with it.

Er, no. Fuck off you spineless fools. I personally don't care if someone calls me a "bald ginger c**t" – not exactly going to lose sleep over that

PC Michael Pinkstone

– but I will *not* accept the bigger picture: namely that a warranted officer of the law who is serving the Queen should have to stand for that kind of nonsense. It's not me I'm worried about – it's the professionalism and dignity of my role that is under threat, and as such, the sovereignty of the nation is under threat as well. An attack on me is an attack on my role and therefore an attack on the Queen. If we let them get away with it then what hope is there?

For example, a few days ago there were reports of a mob attacking a police station. *A mob attacking a police station.* In *this* country. A group of mindless, violent fuckers throwing bottles, chanting, and *ATTACKING A POLICE STATION.*

That kind of behaviour needs to be met with the most determined and hard-nosed reaction possible. Any such breaches of the peace that undermine the safety and security of this country – that fly in the face of our constitution – need to be dealt with using swift, heady and uncompromising justice. Yet we've become so pink and fluffy that scumbags are pissing all over us.

This *cannot* continue. I made a vow to serve the Queen and cause the peace to be kept and preserved, not stand by and watch helplessly while this country falls into rack and ruin at the hands of vicious and indifferent thugs.

Perhaps when the police service is allowed to enforce the law again, things might change for the better. Perhaps when the Government allows officers to do what they vowed to do then things will start to improve. At the moment, though, we are all pretty fucked.

* * *

And, in case you were wondering, that tattooed male staggered out of the pub – having told me it wasn't the first black eye he'd ever had, and it certainly wouldn't be the last – and I haven't seen or heard from him since. The situation took a little over three minutes to resolve.

And the "offender" got away with it – and I was really, really hoping for a detection to boost my figures. That's not true, of course. In reality, I wanted to buy that fucker a pint. At least he knew how to breach the peace properly.

11. The Joys of Summer

Barbecues can be quite lethal affairs. I know this for a fact. I've been to several.[16] The latest one I went to at work involved three Eastern European males who decided that it was best to drink several bottles of vodka, two bottles of Jack Daniels, an inordinate amount of beer ... and then attack each other in a sadistic way usually reserved for scenes in films such as *Gangster No. 1* or *Casino*.

So if you made a film entitled *Barbecue*, you *could* come up with some pretty gory stuff – based on real life. It might not be the best of names for a film, but it would be quite brutal.

Anyway, these chaps thought it would be rather fun to stab each other with a large kitchen knife and then smack each other over the head with a few garden chairs. A spectacular bloodbath, as it turned out.

PC Butch was the first on the scene along with PC Fresh. I was driving there in the van, of course. It had already been a stupid shift and we were due off at midnight. It was already 11-ish, so we weren't going home for a while.

As usual it had been a rather busy day so far. Nothing out of the ordinary there. Earlier on I'd dealt with a few interesting jobs to keep me entertained. I'd also had to split with my crewmate, PC Snipper, because there simply weren't enough of us to go round, so the one or two that remained available were out on their own doing their best, which usually isn't good enough for the public or the senior management

---

16 The last barbecue I went to off duty was round PC Snipper's house. We somehow managed to set fire to the garden table (a green, wobbly affair) and all ended up with minor burns. As in, 'Gosh, molten plastic is fucking *hot*...'

PC Michael Pinkstone

anyway. What abundant joy.

My first task of the day was to take a robbery statement from a non-English-speaking Turkish male who'd had his phone snatched the previous day on the high street, when he was completely wankered.

Somehow I managed to make the whole thing last three pages, and I have *small* writing. One of my hand-written pages is the equivalent of at least two or three for other people. Without mentioning any names, we have some people on shift who have HUGE handwriting and leave at least three finger spaces between words – and then boast that they took a "seven-page statement"!

Er, no. You haven't *really* taken a seven-page statement. You have, in fact, taken a one-page statement and spread it over seven sheets of paper, because your bubble writing is fucking enormous and you leave enough distance between each word for a Sherman tank to be able to drive through. They never listen though – they just go off muttering 'seven-page statement' to themselves.

Now, my statement was three pages, and the equivalent of a thirty-eight-page statement for the above kinds of people, and really didn't say anything at all, except – "I had my phone snatched by an unknown male outside Boots. And I was pissed at the time." However, when you've been in the job a few years you learn how to dramatise events quite substantially, just to make it look like you're making an effort.

So my victim signed everything and I put the statement in my tray to be sent to archives with a printout of a CRAPPIES report as soon as possible, but before that I was diverted to a criminal damage … in progress! Offender on scene! Offender detained by the victim! All units go, go, GO!

Well, I was the only unit and I was on my own, so it was a case of, 'OK PC Pinkstone, I'll show you en route. I'll try and get you backup as soon as a unit comes free …'

I arrived outside an Indian restaurant to find the usual crowd of people. Not that I'd seen any of them before. They were there for the entertainment. After all, that's why police officers exist – to entertain fucking imbeciles who have nothing better to do with their lives. I mean, what the fuck is so interesting about the police anyway? What's

This Victorian Playground - Part 2

wrong with other jobs? I don't go into Tesco's and film the cashiers on my mobile phone whilst asking them silly questions and getting in their way. Neither do I stand there staring at the sales assistants in Top Man while they hang out the clothes as if it's the most exciting thing in the world, telling them inane things and bigging myself up. 'Excuse me, do you have this in a size 36L? Oh, and by the way, my cousin Jim wants to work here. And my uncle is the supervisor of the Top Man in Hounslow.' Believe me, being a police officer has its moments, but it's actually quite mind-numbing most of the time. Especially nowadays. I'm sure it wasn't always quite so crap.

Anyway, en route I had been passed the pertinent information about this particular incident, namely that a chap had found another chap damaging his car, and had subsequently detained him.

Of course, because you should know me well enough by now, and because you've read *Part 1* thoroughly and understood every word of it (which is more than can be said for myself) you will have already anticipated two things. First thing is that the incident was already on CRAPPIES even before I arrived, and I drove there fairly quickly even by my standards.[17] So it was *definitely* a criminal damage to a vehicle and I hadn't even parked my fucking car or spoken to anyone on the scene yet. Have I told you how much I despise the NCRS and how it has fucked up so many things?

The second thing is that the incident itself really deserved nothing more than a couple of minutes of advice and that was that. Ironically enough, that's what I did – gave advice, but I still had a plethora of subsequent emails from crime reviewers demanding ethnicity details of everyone involved, including innocent bystanders; and whether or not the pigeon crapping on the nearby chimney wanted Victim Support; and that I should provide the dates of birth of the chickens who were chilling in the restaurant freezers. Don't bother using your discretion in the police service any more – there's no point. Your time will be wasted by pointless bureaucratic policies whatever manner you have chosen to deal with an incident. You may as well just give up and let

---

[17] It became something of a challenge to try to get to an incident before it got crimed. However, nothing was faster than a civilian following the NCRS to the letter.

PC Michael Pinkstone

the Government win, which is what they want of course. In which case, they can fuck right off.

So I got out of the car and approached the victim. He really wasn't too bothered about seeing me. Surprise surprise. He wasn't grateful. He wasn't upset. He didn't really need me or want me. He was just using me, like so many of the other morons in this country.

He pointed at a very sleek-looking soft-top car. Worth far more than my own humble diesel with 150,000 miles on the clock. I can't afford anything decent. I can barely afford to eat sometimes. Yet I still pretended to be concerned.

'Everything OK, sir?'

'No it's not OK, officer … look.' Well, I looked, but I didn't see anything. '*Look!*' he said again, as if reiterating the same word would enable me to see what I was supposed to be looking at.

I shook my head and looked at him instead. With a tut of exasperation that implied he'd been sent a blind and useless police officer to assist him in his hour of trouble, the male got on one knee and poked his finger aggressively about three millimetres away from … a three millimetre "mark". I call it a *mark* – it was little more than a tiny, weeny little scuff. It could have been a squashed bug for all I knew, and I didn't even care.

He stood up and looked at me triumphantly. 'That's gonna cost me several hundred pounds to repair! I'll have to have the whole bumper re-sprayed.'

I paused, taking this in. Firstly, you called me here with my blue lights flashing for *that*. And secondly it's going to cost *several hundred pounds* to repair? My own car isn't even worth several hundred pounds. The most valuable part of it is the tax disc. It's such an old shitter that it got quite badly damaged in the police station recently and I didn't even realise. The first I heard about it was when I got an email from a colleague stating that he'd seen someone from the court drive into it and then drive away. I went down and inspected the latest damage to my vehicle and, true enough, there were some fresh – and quite significant – gouge marks on the bumper. I hadn't even noticed.

Now it was perhaps a bit unfair of me to treat this lovely car with the same detached sympathies with which I treat my own vehicle, but

This Victorian Playground - Part 2

I really couldn't see what all the fuss was about. That's when the male said, 'We've got him detained inside the restaurant …'

Well, I walked inside and couldn't see anyone detained anywhere. In my experience, when someone is "detained" they kind of look as if they are detained. Either they are incarcerated in some form of locked cell, or they are being squashed by several police officers. And in this restaurant all I could see were about six people chatting lazily on mobile phones – and everyone ignored me. Now there's a fucking surprise.

After about a minute of fruitlessly asking people where the "detained" person was, some random guy pointed and said, 'I think that's him.'

I'm sorry sir, you *think?* Can you imagine a solicitor turning up in police custody to represent a prisoner and then asking the custody Sergeant for a copy of the relevant custody record to peruse – and the Sergeant casually hands over a piece of paper and says, 'Yeah, I think that's the one. He might be in cell number 8. Not sure.'

Believe me, if you've *detained* someone, it's usually a good idea to know who they are and, preferably, *where* they are.

So I walked over to a fairly well-dressed chap and said, 'Hi, can you tell me what's going on because I really haven't got a clue.'

The male looked at me and said, 'Boss, boss.' He then turned away from me and carried on babbling away on his phone in a language I couldn't understand.

At this point I was kind of getting a wee bit annoyed, so I just said out loud, to no-one in particular, 'Could someone please tell me what is going on?'

Fortunately an elderly man took pity on me and led me over to my "victim" and demanded that he tell me what was happening. It turned out that the "offender" had been walking past the restaurant when he had accidentally – or carelessly – kicked a glass bottle, which had then glanced off the bumper of the victim's car.

The offender had then gone into the restaurant, at the behest of the victim, and they were all making various phone calls to try and sort the car out. It turned out that the victim was getting a quote for the minor abrasion to be repaired (apparently several hundred pounds involving a re-sprayed bumper *and* a courtesy car) and the offender was on the phone to his boss to come down and pay for it all on a mutually agreed basis.

PC Michael Pinkstone

I then asked the victim, once he'd got off his fucking mobile phone, why he wanted me there. He said something vague like, 'Oh I just wanted you here in case they didn't pay for the damage.' Then he walked off with his back to me.

At this I said, 'OK,' (to myself) and swallowed down the urge to go outside and baton the living crap out of his BMW, and then say something like, 'Now THAT'S criminal damage, you time-wasting little shit!' But of course, I didn't. Instead I waited for about eleven more people to turn up and jabber away in some other language, before I shook some random people's hands, gave the pigeon a nasty look and fucked off. Victim support my arse.

On my forthcoming days off I received the obligatory emails demanding all the irrelevant information that I hadn't obtained and that I really didn't need to obtain, but that the Government really cares about. I didn't even get the "offender's" name. That's because he *wasn't*. Dear Government, thanks for the NCRS and the removal of my discretion. It's brilliant! I love it!

Anyway, I was on my way back to the station when I was re-deployed to a traffic accident. Apparently some car had struck a lorry, mounted the kerb, and smacked into a lamp-post.

Time to make those blue lights flash and get those sirens a-wailing yet again. So I drove with all the skill I could muster and arrived at the scene in about four minutes flat, which wasn't bad considering I was about half a mile away to start off with. If Miss Daisy could drive she'd kick my arse.

The "scene" was a fairly straight and empty road, with lots of grass on either side and not generally the sort of place you'd expect to see a car wrapped around a lamp-post – but this is Britain, don't forget. Home of the fucking incompetent, speeding driver.

I got out of my car and surveyed the devastation. There was a stationary articulated lorry parked on the road – its rear end all fucked up – and adjacent to it was a small vehicle that had clearly struck the back of the lorry and then careered into said street-lighting apparatus, at quite a significant rate of knots.

Standing by the mangled little Ford was a whole family of six people. My goodness, you can fit a hell of a lot of bodies into a three-

This Victorian Playground - Part 2

door hatchback these days.

If you've been dealing with the public for a while – especially a certain type of people – then you will know that lots of incidents become family affairs very, very quickly. Quite often the first person the "victim" (or, in this case, the driver) would phone would be a family member. These family members then inform other family members and within about five minutes the whole fucking clan is at the scene, all talking at once and getting in the way. What do they think it is, a fucking party?

And this case was no exception. I was standing there staring at four fairly tall teenage males, a middle-aged woman and a slightly older male. All of them were fine except one of the chaps who had a cut in the middle of his forehead and was holding his arm in some discomfort.

I looked at all of them together and said, 'Who was the driver please?'

The injured male said, 'It was me.'

I said, 'OK. So no-one else was with you in the car?'

The middle-aged woman piped up. 'Yes, I was with him.'

She looked extremely uninjured and perky for someone who had just climbed out of a wrecked car, so I glanced at her and said, '*You* were in the car, madam?'

She said, 'Yes, officer.'

I looked at her and then across at the car. The driver's airbag had activated, but there wasn't one on the passenger side. Furthermore the roof above the passenger side was all caved in. Ignoring the obvious anomalies, I then asked the driver his details and established that he only had a provisional licence.

The middle-aged lady then piped up again. 'He's only got a provisional licence, so I was supervising him.'

I looked at her again. 'Where's the L-plates?' I said, with a slight hint of sarcasm in my voice.

The woman paused and put her hand to her chest. 'Oh, sorry, officer. We forgot.'

Damn you lying bastards. With a slightly heavy hand I got my pen out of my pocket. Not so that I could write with it, but so that it could be used for effect. I recalled my teaching days when I used to wander around the classroom holding a whiteboard marker. It somehow made

PC Michael Pinkstone

me feel in charge. That's why children love writing on the board – it makes them feel special and important.

So with pen in hand I looked at the woman with my most stern but kind expression. This means I looked constipated and probably a little bit scary. In a controlled voice I said, 'I'm going to ask you one more time, madam. *Were you in the car?*' And for each of the words I wagged my pen in her direction. There is nothing more intimidating than a police officer with a biro. Believe me, it's our greatest weapon. You can do more with a pen than with anything else.

The woman looked at me and hung her head. 'No,' she said. 'I'm sorry.'

'I'm sorry too,' I said, as I elbowed her in the face and sent her flying backwards onto the floor. I then stamped on her legs and arrested her for attempting to pervert the course of justice. Of course, I didn't do any of those things. I just said, 'Please don't lie to the police, madam – it can actually result in a fair bit of trouble for you. I appreciate that you are trying to protect your son, but sometimes we just have to accept responsibility for our actions.' Aren't I nice?

So after making sure the driver was all taken care of up at the hospital, and after I'd reported him for a variety of naughty traffic offences, I made my way back to the station to try and collate together some of the things that I'd been doing.

For the following couple of hours I dealt with a variety of trivial things, before the call came in. The call saying that someone had been stabbed.

Now we get a lot of calls like this. It wasn't exactly a novel experience to hear the word "stabbed" over the radio. Nowadays your first thought isn't, 'Oh my God, someone's been stabbed!' It's more like, 'Fuck, we haven't got anyone to deal with that!'

However, small mercies happen, and the night shift had been in the station since 10 pm. They couldn't go out and do anything, though, because my shift still had all the cars and were still dealing with stuff. That's because we really don't have enough vehicles. Fortunately we had a couple of vans spare.

So about six of them managed to pile into a Transit and drove at top speed to the scene of the alleged stabbing. PC Butch and PC Fresh,

This Victorian Playground - Part 2

of course, had already got there. They weren't supposed to be dealing with anything after 10 pm, but you can't really justify driving back to the station to pass the car to someone else, who will then make their way to the scene.

To make myself useful I also grabbed an available van and began to drive towards the relevant street. On the way PC Butch gave his update. His voice sounded different on the radio – slightly higher pitched than his usual dulcet tones, and the information he passed was fairly worrying.

'Yeah, we've got a male with a stab wound to his upper chest near his shoulder and another male with a stab wound to his head and another male with a slash wound to his face. We're going to need an ambulance … or two.'

I arrived at exactly the same time as the other van, because I'd actually driven the right way, and hopped out to survey the situation. It was the usual melee of bad English, shouted commands, screaming women, pissed bleeding blokes wandering aimlessly around, and various onlookers enjoying the show.

After establishing who was injured and who needed the most urgent medical attention, we had to locate where the "scene" was. If you walked into the garden like myself and PC Butch did (who was actually in a wee bit of shock, having witnessed blood spurting lavishly from a male) you wouldn't have had too much trouble locating said scene.

The garden looked like it had been set up to *look* like a scene. The kind of scene you would expect to find in a training environment. There was blood *everywhere* and in the midst of it all was a large knife blade that had broken off at the handle.

All the wooden chairs were broken, and also covered in blood, and there were several – in fact, dozens – of empty bottles of alcohol lying scattered around the place. It looked like someone was taking the piss. A broken knife blade? Yeah, right.

It turned out that the three guys had been drinking far too much during their barbecue and decided, randomly, to stab each other to finish off the evening. Most normal folks would say their goodbyes and get in a taxi, or set fire to a table. Not these guys. They got tooled up and tried to maim each other – a feat they achieved without any apparent difficulty.

PC Michael Pinkstone

Now I've been pissed before at a barbecue – in fact, lots of barbecues – but I've never really had the urge to make my merry way to the kitchen drawer and arm myself with an eight-inch bladed weapon and proceed to hack my friends up. I've also never whacked anyone so hard with a wooden chair it splinters everywhere and scars them for life. Perhaps I've been missing out. Perhaps not. This was obviously some bizarre cultural thing that I'd never hope to understand.

And even more bizarrely, the chap who had been stabbed in the head found it all rather funny. At least he was full of the joys of summer. I just wanted to go home and never see any of them ever again. Stupid little shits. What the fuck is *wrong* with people? Joys of summer my arse …

12. What's Wrong with People?

That's a bloody good query and I say it out loud rather a lot. All you have to do is take a look around you, and the question pops into your head almost instantaneously. You then have to emphasise the word "wrong" and say the question out loud, preferably with clenched fists and a wild-eyed expression – perhaps even inserting a profanity for effect – and you have the full shebang: WHAT THE FUCK IS *WRONG* WITH PEOPLE?!

The other day PC Butch and PC Snipper (the "Tubmarine Crew") dealt with an interesting chap at a local watering hole. He'd decided that it would be a valuable use of his time to fuel himself with an abundance of booze and then get aggressive with the other customers. This aggression took the form of smashing a glass bottle in half and brandishing it around the place, making various threats and generally acting in quite an upsetting manner.

When my colleagues arrived on scene they duly dealt with him, adopting the correct attitude that what he had done was particularly unacceptable and most likely against the law. Yet like most of the fucking morons who do things like that, he took great offence at being arrested.

A struggle ensued, with him protesting his innocence and that he'd "done nothing wrong" and that he was being "brutalised" and blah, blah blah … so he got sprayed.[18]

He then spent the next half an hour crying his eyes out because he

---

[18] He didn't get sprayed because he said he was innocent. That's generally not a reason to make people's eyes water. Instead he faced the evil effervescence because he violently resisted arrest *while* he was complaining.

PC Michael Pinkstone

really couldn't understand why he'd been so badly mistreated. Besides, his eyes were watering anyway so he didn't really have much choice. Meanwhile, the people left in the pub were hopefully grateful that none of them had been bottled, slashed or physically abused in some other way. Yet even with CCTV evidence shoved in front of his nose later on, the little shit *still* claimed he was innocent. I mean, what the fuck is *wrong* with people?

How on earth does one's outlook deteriorate so much that you are left with such a warped, crushed and quite frankly singular viewpoint of the world around you?

What leads someone to stand up in a pub, or anywhere for that matter, and decide that abusing and threatening people with a sharp piece of glass is a preferred course of action for a decent citizen of this country? Of course, this wasn't the first time that the gentleman had acted in such a manner. He had a long and glorious previous history of similar behaviour. Perhaps he wasn't so much dropped at birth, as drop-kicked.

Like my porch-jumping pillock from *Part I*, there are certain individuals in this nation who I will never hope to understand. I'd love to think that the reason for their behaviour is drink and drugs (and often a heady combination of both) and that when they've sobered up or come down they are quite "normal", but something tells me that there's slightly more to it than mere substance-related impulse.

Have we always been like this? Have we always had such unsteady and unsavoury characters in our midst? Of course we have. And drink and drugs aren't exactly new. Gin and opium go back a long way, for example!

Yet in very recent times there has been a noticeable and tangible deterioration in mental health. The nation as a whole seems to have gradually been sinking ever deeper into a slough of quite careless, obnoxious and often distasteful conduct.

We don't appear to be particularly stable or balanced, and our lives are following quite windswept paths. We seem to be quite easily buffeted from side to side by all manner of inducements and any firm footing we may find is often undermined by deeper influences beneath the surface.

It's almost as if we've all been walking through a tunnel for the past few decades and, over time, the tunnel itself has got smaller and

This Victorian Playground - Part 2

smaller. In fact, it's cone-shaped, and we started off at the big end. Now we're all traipsing towards the narrow end, but the change has been so subtle and so slight that we haven't really noticed. For it's not as if we've looked around us and thought, 'Gosh, this tunnel is getting a wee bit small' – rather we've become more pissed off because it's getting pretty darn cramped.

So as we move ever forwards we become more affected by people around us due to their much closer proximity. We find ourselves jostling for space and struggling for air. Some of us push others out of the way, while others get their heads down and try to ignore the obvious signs of trouble.

We obviously can't turn back, so we press on. There's no visible light at the end of the tunnel of course, because it's still thousands of miles away. Yet it's getting hotter and closer and more suffocating the further we tread.

Our lives have now taken on new meanings and new levels of intolerance. We start to make unreasonable demands and become upset by trivial, annoying little things. This happens more and more, and over time we become pissed off most of the time. We no longer walk with a spring in our step, or any sense of hope in the future, because all we see is a steadily narrowing tunnel and everyone trying to force their way down it – millions of souls cramming ever further into a space that is getting simply too small to cope.

Sadly we have created this situation. It's not an issue of over-population. It's an issue of attitude and existence. What's wrong with us? Well, we're idiots. That's what's wrong with us.

Some people have simply gone beyond the pale – like the bottle-smashing moron earlier on, yet many of us are not too far away from breaking in a different kind of way. We are slowly but surely reaching elastic limit. Whether we like it or not, things are collapsing.

Stress has taken on a new sense of importance in the past few years. It's become a byword for not being able to cope with the modern pressures of life. In many respects, it implies that things were easier in bygone years. This is bollocks of course. In years gone by things were probably a lot more harsh than they are now, but people got on with it because they had no choice. They made do and they mended. They put up with immense hardship.

PC Michael Pinkstone

Nowadays we've got absolutely no conception of anything, and our lives are influenced and affected by such a myriad of things it would be impossible to try to make much sense of it all. One thing is certain though – it doesn't appear to be getting any better no matter how much we bang on about human rights or equality or diversity. In fact, it's probably got worse. The mental state of this nation is deteriorating, and deteriorating fast.

Which leads us to the beginning of this chapter and the very first paragraph. All around us are people who seem to have gone past the point of no return. People who have lost direction and abandoned any sense of moral or ethical boundaries. People who have quite simply lost the will and given up. Now their lives follow quite twisted and bewildering routes, and the resulting annoyance at being so lost results in erratic, often violent and unacceptable behaviour, either directed at others or, often, themselves. People who appear unable to accept that they are in a completely different place to the rest of us who consider ourselves to be on the straight and narrow (or should I say the straight and narrow*ing*).

So you may not be the sort of human being who smashes up a bottle and brandishes it in the middle of a pub, but you are hopefully the sort of person who looks at that kind of idiot and says, 'What the fuck is *wrong* with those people?!'

We may not have quite reached that broken glass bottle stage ourselves but we all need to be careful. We need to ensure that any resulting behaviour of people who have gone beyond the pale is dealt with immediately. We need to maintain the peace and to promote worthy and gritty concepts of justice. We need to live with honour and decency that upholds basic rights and freedoms (unlike other concepts of "honour" that result in sickening acts of mindless violence) and preserve law and order on the streets.

It's not a pleasant task and sometimes we have to be quite firm. Sometimes people have to be forcefully dealt with. Sometimes they need to be locked up. Sometimes they need to be fined or given strong words of advice.

If we stop doing any of these things we will face quite extreme consequences. And, as some of you may have guessed – we have stopped doing some of these things.

The result is all part of the degeneration of this nation. A general abandonment of ethics and morality. A widespread disassociation of self from real goodness and justice. The more cramped and crowded things get, the more we have distanced ourselves from what is decent, acceptable and reasonable. Thus we are literally – and also paradoxically – getting more and more fucked.

What's *wrong* with us?

13. The H.P.A.

PC Latvia, who wouldn't look incongruent in the Shire, decided yesterday to form his own little club.

The *Hobbit Police Association* is open to anyone who fulfils the necessary criteria: short stature, hairiness (in particular, hairy feet), a certain penchant for food and a love of pipe-weed. In the case of PC Latvia, Lambert and Butler Silver.

Obviously this Association would be open to other people too, but you would clearly look like a right wally if you were tall, skinny and hairless and went to one of their meetings.

In any case we now have seven strands of diversity: *Age, Race, Gender, Religion, Sexuality, Disability* and *Hobbitness.*

Applications are warmly invited from any candidates who meet any of the necessary hobbit criteria and, under the *Positive Action Aren't We Just Nice And Precious Scheme*, you will be guaranteed some form of extra attention because we don't want to be seen to discriminate.

We don't actually give a flying fuck what you look like or what's wrong with you, so long as you are a decent person and can do the job in question. Actually, that's not quite true. We *do* give a flying fuck what you look like and what appears to be wrong with you because we are obsessed with your obvious "diversity" and it doesn't really make much difference whether or not you are a bald ginger c**t, because you'll still get treated with an almost sickening level of esteem.

***

This Victorian Playground - Part 2

Now let's be candid. Let's speak whereof we know. Let's cast aside all wishy-washy, namby-pamby bollocks and be honest, caustic and downright insubordinate.

I wonder if you have ever heard a police officer grumble to you that there isn't a *White Police Association* and, if you suggested starting such a club, it would be seen as a spin-off from the Third Reich?

In reality, people who suggest such things don't really want a White Police Association – they just don't want to appear sidelined because they aren't "diverse" enough. Plus they hate other people being pandered to simply because of some obvious difference.

Now if you didn't expect to find a chapter on race and diversity in this book, you were sadly mistaken. However, it's the *only* chapter. Thank fuck. And the only reason I'm writing it is because one of my ongoing PDR themes (along with the rest of my colleagues) concerns "Respect for Race and Diversity". In other words, I have to "prove" my "respect" on a daily basis.

I have to prove that when I've dealt with someone who is different to myself, I have treated them with respect.

Now I may sound a little bit thick here, but surely *everyone* is different to me? I've never met anyone who is an exact copy of PC Michael Pinkstone. This, of course, is a major relief.

Imagine this for a PDR entry:

On Saturday 25th August 2007 I attended a domestic incident with PC Glasses. We'd received a call from a male called Mr Naseem of 64 Hulworth Crescent stating that he was having problems with his ex-wife.

Upon our arrival at the address, the door was opened by Mr Naseem who turned out to be a carbon copy of myself. It was like looking in a mirror. We stood gaping at each other for several seconds before Mr Naseem fainted with shock and PC Glasses had to revive him with smelling salts.

Once he had come round he was a gibbering wreck. I was speechless. We were *exactly* the same. It was freaky. We had the same scars, the same hairstyle, the same moles, spots, freckles and minor deformities. We were the same colour, the same height, the same shape, the same build – *everything* about us was the same. The more we looked the more we realised that we were not different in any way at all. We were more identical than identical twins.

Obviously our lives had followed different paths – and I wouldn't necessarily call the police stating that my ex-wife was buzzing on my buzzer because I actually *have* a life – but in terms of our outward physical appearance, we were like two peas in a pod – two completely matching peas.

Once PC Glasses and I left the address, we went back to the station to update CRAPPIES for at least half an hour, and finish off the Domestic Risk Assessment Form, owing to the violent nature of the buzzing, and I contemplated making this entry under my Respect for Race and Diversity section in my PDR.

However, I realised almost straight away, that this would be very difficult. It would be like respecting *myself*. What a stupid entry it would be – hardly the kind of *evidence* that the Management are looking for. My Sergeant would suggest that I was taking the piss, which in many respects is true, but not in this case.

This was a very strenuous situation for me because I desperately wanted to appreciate and value and respect Mr Naseem's diversity, but I simply *couldn't*. It wasn't possible! I felt like a nasty racist and even contemplated calling the Integrity Line to dob myself in. I also typed out an email to Professional Standards but fortunately deleted it before I sent it, because it contained an attachment of a comedic photograph that in itself would be a heinous misuse of the communication system, and they'd stick me on. Couple that with my lack of respect for diversity and the only option would be a custodial sentence, the loss of my pension and the execution of four of my family members. At least somebody important could then send an all-user email warning the whole of the service that such behaviour will *not* be tolerated, and that integrity nowadays means being a false, pathetic, pandering, spineless wanker.

So I sat there in the office feeling very down indeed. How could I *not* have any respect for Mr Naseem's diversity? How dare I? Yet I knew that there was nothing about him that was different to me – except his behaviour, but behaviour isn't one of the six strands and therefore didn't count.

My mind was fucked. I was really confused. In the end I decided that the only thing I could do to make myself feel better – and also provide

This Victorian Playground - Part 2

me with *evidence* with which I could "prove" to the Management that I'm not a racist and love diversity – was to deliberately target someone who was different to me. I thought this was a positive thing to do, so I took action.

I allocated myself a job of dealing with a Mr Mbunguaily, who had reported a burglary, and I spent at least two hours longer with him than necessary just to "prove" that I had respect for diversity, and that my police service doesn't discriminate. It also made me feel better about myself and, as such, led to a very sycophantic entry in my PDR – namely this one – which I have put into the "Quality of Service" section.

I've certainly learned from this experience and hope that if I write it up as such – and if I continue to get on well with my Sergeant – that he will rate me *Highly Effective* in my PDR, which will obviously count towards some form of bollocks at some point. It may even lead me to getting more money than some of my *Effective* colleagues, which would be very beneficial and morale-boosting for everyone.

I love working for this police service and truly enjoy operating under this Government, and I despise PC Latvia's sarcasm relating to the *Hobbit Police Association.* I detest this kind of organisational acrimony and will gladly shoot him next time I see him.

After all, we mustn't destroy the precious.

14. Flying the Flag

Not long ago I turned up to a report of a potential burglary along with PC Grin. A female had reported hearing sounds outside her house and she had called us in what turned out to be complete and utter terror. She was in her twenties and staying on her own, and informed us that she'd been burgled a few months before, and that it had left her very insecure and frightened. The poor girl was shaking.

Now when I was a wee lad I used to be very, very scared of the dark. This isn't true any more, but I do have something of an unnatural loathing of moths. There are two reasons for this. The first reason is that when I was about eight I popped downstairs one morning to have some breakfast and as I climbed onto the work surface so that I could reach the cupboard to get a bowl out – a *massive* kamikaze moth flew straight out of the cupboard and hit me square in the middle of the forehead. Suffice to say I dropped the bowl, fell off the work surface and screamed until my tonsils exploded. It scared the living fuck out of me.

The second reason is that when I was about nine I decided to do some recorder practice in my room (the sound of a recorder now makes me break out in a cold sweat) but discovered that my instrument (if you can fucking call it that) was not making any noise whatsoever.

I blew into it and no sound erupted, so I decided to suck as hard as I could. Obvious crude metaphors aside, I felt what can only be described as "an object" hit my epiglottis and start to slide down my throat. I retched immediately into my hand and there, lying on my palm and covered in a thin film of phlegm, was a dead moth.

This Victorian Playground - Part 2

I have no memory of what happened after that, but I think I may have fainted. Whatever the case, it did not make me feel very well at all.

Fear of crime is a major issue. Fear of moths is more serious, but I think we'll stick to the crime side of things.

If we've had something shit happen to us, it affects us. Simple as that. I'm no psychologist, but it wouldn't take someone with a degree in human intelligence to tell you that a female who hears a noise right outside her house in the dead of night is gong to feel anxious – and that it will be heightened by her previous experiences.

Unfortunately the police cannot eradicate the fear of crime. What we can do, however, is try to lock up the baddies who commit crime, especially people like burglars. We can also turn up at your house pretty soon after you call us, but that may or may not happen as quickly as you would like – as you should be aware by now! Now you may wonder why I bang on about burglary a lot – this is for two reasons.

Firstly, it happens a lot. Secondly, I believe that your home is your solace. It is your escape and your haven. No-one should fuck with another person's dwelling. For when people commit burglaries they are not just fucking with possessions, they are fucking with everything that people hold dear. They are fucking with their feelings of safety and security, and treating their emotions with utter contempt.

If people can't feel safe in their homes then we have a very serious problem. It's therefore perhaps a good thing that I'm not a Judge, because anyone charged with burglary and appearing before me in a courtroom would be given very, very short shrift.

However, because I'm not a Judge and because this Government likes to think that evil drug-taking thieving scumbags can be "rehabilitated" and only need to spend a few days in prison, I have to do something else with victims to make them feel more secure. I have to fly the flag in a different kind of way. I don't have a flag of justice – I have … a flag. It's a bit battered and battle-worn, but it's a flag nonetheless.

I have to turn up and pretend that we are doing all we can to make these people feel safe and that the six officers actually outside on the streets are truly making a difference in this town. I turn up and pass a CRAPPIES reference as if it's the most precious thing in the world and is going to make all the difference.

PC Michael Pinkstone

Ah, thank fuck the police are here! They didn't catch the people who did this to me, but they gave me a seven-digit number, phew! Thank goodness for that. Now I know why I pay my taxes.

* * *

It seems that we've got our priorities a wee bit mixed up. Well, the Government has its priorities mixed up. For when we arrive at an incident the *first* thing that people are worried about now (and that would be the people sitting at computers) is whether or not a crime has been committed, so that it can be recorded immediately in line with the current standards. This we know already. I can't go on about it again too much or I may get a little bit tense.

So, if we've arrived somewhere, we'll often be nagged by the controller to inform them if there are any offences. Usually this doesn't make any difference, because even the controllers are undermined by the mochachino-sipping staff sitting miles away on comfy swivel chairs deciding what has already happened.

In which case, the Government is really only concerned with facts, figures and recording stuff. If it's something that can be measured, then measured it will be. But one thing they can't measure is the look on someone's face when the police turn up and their terror turns to utter relief.

These people don't necessarily want a crime reference number. They don't care what their own ethnicity is. They don't give a flying fuck what their date of birth is, because they didn't call us to tell us that information. They just want to feel safe in their own homes.

When they see that marked police vehicle arrive outside their house and one or two uniformed officers step out of it – and they have called us for a genuine reason – there is nothing that compares to how it feels.

These aren't the kinds of people who swear at us on the street and say, 'I pay your fucking wages.' These aren't the people who call us saying that their drunken ex-partner has sent them two text messages. These aren't the people who report their teenage children missing about a day or so *after* they have gone missing because they don't really give a fuck. These are the authentic people. The ones that we all joined to help.

This Victorian Playground - Part 2

Dear Government, I turned up at an address yesterday at 1 am. The female who called us reported a noise in her back garden. It may very well have been a burglar, and they may very well have tried the back door handle. In which case this may very well need a CRAPPIES reference number and something about someone's ethnicity. However, the female wanted nothing more than the police to turn up, preferably as soon as possible after calling us, and make sure everything was safe and sound. She wanted us to check her garden because she was *terrified* of going outside. In the end, dear Government, we didn't take any details from her because we used our discretion for once, but we did stay with her for twenty minutes until she had calmed down. Sadly there is nothing I can give you to put in one of your fucking precious little pie charts, but the female did cry with relief. I've never seen anyone so grateful to see me in all my life. Now *that's* flying the fucking flag you bunch of ignorant fools.

15. Toeing the Party Line

Why is it that when someone in a public capacity has done something obviously wrong, they lie and lie and lie about it on TV, and in the press, and sound like complete idiots when they do so?

They know they are lying. *We* know they are lying. *Everyone* knows they are lying – and yet, for whatever reason, they stick to their story, no matter how incredibly dubious it is.

I was watching a satirical news programme recently about a senator in another country who had done something a little bit saucy to bring attention to himself. This particular person was a wee bit homophobic, and had made various comments in his career that were slightly unkind towards the gay community. This person was male, middle-aged and married, and often in the public eye.

It also turned out that he was gay. Well, not according to him at any rate. Basically he'd been caught with his trousers down, as it were, in a public toilet. The nature of the situation was that an undercover police officer was waiting in an adjacent cubicle in a public toilet block which was known to be a meeting place for homosexual males.

One of the signals that the males passed to each other – to indicate that they were trying to attract like-minded people – was to attach some toilet paper to the underneath of one of their shoes as they sat on the toilet. If a male next to them reached underneath and removed the toilet paper, this was a clear signal of intent.

Now I'd like you to imagine all of those times that you have innocently reached under a toilet cubicle and generously removed some toilet paper that has been stuck to the shoe of the person sitting on the loo next to

This Victorian Playground - Part 2

you. And by "innocently" – I mean that you did it because it would be very embarrassing for that person to walk out with toilet paper attached to their footwear. Imagine the shame!

This, of course, is the story that the senator came up with. He sat there next to his "loving" and "supportive" wife (in the same way that all of those spouses have "lovingly supported" their other halves on television following some kind of affair or spurious scandal) and assured the interviewer of his innocence.

He sat there and lied. And lied and lied and lied. He fucking lied. He knew it. His wife knew it. The interviewer knew it. The producers of the TV show knew it. Anyone watching it knew it. His friends and colleagues knew it. The undercover police officer knew it, especially when he found a stray hand pulling some bog roll from underneath his trainers and then gently caressing his leg.

Yet *still* he persisted with his lie. And he will continue to do so until the day he dies, no doubt.

Now think of all those times you have watched the TV or read the news – in whatever form – and witnessed the clear, uncompromising bollocks spouting forth from the mouths and pens of people desperate to maintain some form of credible image – or vociferously defend themselves – after a dodgy incident they have been involved with. It could be a mishap that they have simply been a part of, or a slightly more personal wrongdoing that concerned only them. Yet they carry on with their lies. And the point I am making here is not so much that people lie – but rather that we *all know* they are lying!

And you know what? It doesn't make any fucking difference! So they might as well carry on lying because it makes no odds whether they tell the truth or not. Nothing usually happens to them as a result. Even if the things are serious, they still get denied. It makes no difference whatsoever. Lying and bullshitting and covering up comes so naturally to people now that we are immune to witnessing it, and usually we don't care anyway. Too much going on in our own lives to worry about it. Plus we've pretty much given up worrying about it because there's nothing we can do about it anyway. In other words, the "truth" is a mere inconvenience and irrelevance. What matters is how everything looks. How it all appears. The facts are completely by-the-by. And we are all

PC Michael Pinkstone

pretty powerless against this immense politically motivated machine of spin and indoctrination; this self-serving fabrication. The implications, of course, are far-reaching. And it doesn't just happen on an individual scale.

If Governments and other world movers and shakers can get away with promoting their extremely doubtful ideologies – by standing up and justifying their behaviour, through careful, yet clearly apparent lying – and we can't really do much about it except point it out through a variety of mediums, then what point is there? Does anything ever happen as a result? If such people or organisations can quite literally get away with murder – how difficult would it be for them to weather the storm of a minor indiscretion? Yes, some political heavyweights crash and burn, but most people bounce back. And the ones who are particularly influential nearly always bounce back. However, the ones whose careers are permanently tarnished after a relatively small misdemeanour, are simply like that coroner who was fired: stooges. Every now and again the Government will get rid of somebody for something quite irrelevant, spouting that SUCH BEHAVIOUR WILL NOT BE TOLERATED, which allows them to deflect attention away from the abominable things that other people are doing, and getting away with. It's all part of their grand plan of getting us to focus on what is totally immaterial.

The victim culture is so insidious, I'm sure it is a concerted effort to distract our attention away from all the really crap stuff that's happening in this world of ours, and make us focus on things that are irrelevant and false. It's a means of subjugating our minds so that the corporate monsters can truly have their wicked way.

I know, let's conduct an investigation into someone sending a text message and then dismiss him, but let's not worry too much about all the really seedy stuff that is happening in the corridors of power – the corporate empire-building, the bribes, the back stabbing, the extremely detrimental world politics. The worldwide distribution of terror to keep us submerged in perpetual fear. The further you climb or the deeper you dig, the worse it gets. That's why the Government would prefer us to be stranded in the mire we are presently in, because the truth – whichever way you look – is pretty fucking awful. Whether you dig deep and discover just how contaminated our minds have become with triviality

This Victorian Playground - Part 2

and paranoia and sycophantic two-stepping, or whether you scramble up and look at the much bigger picture of corporate behaviour and capitalism in all its decadent and destructive glory – every angle presents a rather fucked up picture of the country, and of the world.

In other words, it's best that we just stay consumed by nonsense and not worry ourselves too much with anything particularly meaningful. Instead, let's pretend – or even assume – that people worry about text messages and trivia. Let's pretend that these are the *real* issues. Oh my goodness! An inappropriate text message! We need Martial Law for that! SUCH BEHAVIOUR WILL NOT BE TOLERATED.

So that's right – you go ahead and fire innocent people and keep us all toeing that party line, while behind the scenes the furnaces rage and horrendous political tools of torture and torment are forged.

Sadly, because this has happened time and time and time again – and we have become accustomed to so much shit, over so many years, and everything is all so complicated and disastrous and full of terror – many of us pour ourselves a drink and don't give a shit, even about the truly important stuff. That's because we are more often than not totally consumed with the not-nearly-as-important stuff,[19] such as worrying about whether our language is politically correct enough, or whether we are "allowed" to say or do certain things. We live under a dictatorship, by the way.

So, in essence, although we are overwhelmed by worry about stuff that is utterly nonessential, we don't *really* care about it. We're not really too bothered if someone sends an inappropriate text message – we're just being forced to be bothered. This is the crux of the matter. I'm going to repeat that, as is often customary: *we're being forced to be bothered.*

Every single day we are encouraged to pretend that we care. We are compelled to toe the party line. In many respects, we have no choice, or it's our livelihood on the line. How long, therefore, can this continue before it all implodes? How belong before we all say: fuck that. I'm not going to be a party to that any more. How fucking dare you draw my

---

[19] If I had the time and the energy I'd also go on about popular culture and all the mindless, unavailing shite around nowadays. It's all part of the same issue – keeping our minds under control. If we focus on what doesn't matter, we are bound to be blissfully unaware of the truth.

PC Michael Pinkstone

attention away from the things that are truly concerning? How fucking *dare* you? How fucking *dare* you try and force me to think that sending a fucking text message is a horrendous thing to do? There are things happening in this country, and in this world, that are beyond detestable. Loathsome, despicable things. Things that deserve descriptions such as "accursed". Things that the Government – and other Governments in collaboration – are getting away with. Plus you have the fact that they are incompetent anyway, and even our most basic needs are hardly being met! (But of course they lie and say everything is hunky-dory.)

At the moment though, things haven't fully collapsed. We are sufficiently conquered to be pretty powerless to resist. The Government is winning this game. There isn't widespread anarchy yet. The melting pot hasn't quite dissolved everything.

There are still people who stand up for what is right and just and honourable, of course. But we must do all of this within a climate of fear. Within a climate of submission. Of deference. Within this victim culture, where everyone apparently must be served. In which case, we must continue to toe the party line or *we* will be seen as the bad guys. After all, such behaviour will not be tolerated. I think I'm going to pop downstairs for a quick drink.

* * *

So *why* did my police service fire someone for sending an allegedly racist text message?

Why? Because they not only think people give a fuck, but are encouraged to force us to believe that we *should* give a fuck. They want to maintain a supposedly credible image – credibility through obedience and subservience.

The police have been given rules and regulations and parameters that are so dependent on public image and perception, that they had no choice. They *had* to maintain that image no matter what. They had to uphold their "standards" no matter what. The fact that they dismissed someone for *sending a text message* is irrelevant. This person who had a family, and bills to pay. This person who had worked hard for the police service for many years and was a bloody decent chap. This person who

This Victorian Playground - Part 2

did what thousands of people in the police service do every single day – sent inappropriate text messages.

Of course, this isn't about text messaging (although I think it's a great example, and I *do* have a bit of a bugbear about the darn things, as you may have gathered). It's about this false, pandering, paranoid, desperate attempt to appear right and just and proper and precious, and not have their name tarnished by anything that is naughty or nasty or unbecoming, irrespective of the context. It's a way of distracting us from the raw, gaping, sordid mess this country is in.

It's a way of forcing our eyes away from what is important to what is allegedly important. If you recall from the final chapter of *Part 1*, I discussed that the current definition of racism, as proposed by important people, is wrong. Why? Because it allows them to tell us what is "acceptable" within an excruciatingly tight boundary, with little room for manoeuvre. Any small breach within this suffocating environment, is thus intolerable behaviour. Something about a dictatorship? So would *you* have fired someone for sending a "joke" text message? I hope you wouldn't. But in this current political climate, you may have had to.

For it's all about what happens afterwards – the spin and the political two-stepping. The incident itself is almost entirely by-the-by. An *inappropriate text message*. Who gives a fuck? But we have to maintain our credibility! We have to appear precious! So we lie. And we fire people for it. And our lies are all as obvious as our actions. The senator lied, and we all knew it; and my police service lied, and we all knew it.

My police service lied about *why* what the coroner did was so bad. Because it wasn't that bad. They made it seem like it was the most horrific thing in the world, even though we all knew it wasn't. They blew it out of all proportion in a manner so common nowadays in this fucked up country. They toed the party line – even though most, if not all, of the individual officers concerned in the dismissal, probably didn't want to do what they did. Why? Because they knew that what had happened wasn't that bad. So they lied to themselves. Then they lied to the rest of us saying that SUCH BEHAVIOUR WILL NOT BE TOLERATED. Then they went home and read their own inappropriate texts and dodgy emails, but didn't get fired. They sat there and got rid of someone just to toe the party line. Just to appear to do what was right.

PC Michael Pinkstone

But appear to whom? Appear to fucking whom? Who would really give a fuck either way?

Who would care if that coroner did or didn't do what he did? Who would really care? Why do we make so many mountains out of so many molehills? And do you know what – NO-ONE ASKS THOSE QUESTIONS. It's not allowed. The Government has already won by imposing those rules, encouraging the police to dismiss such nasty people and then telling us all that SUCH BEHAVIOUR WILL NOT BE TOLERATED. So we all gulp and swallow and many of us believe the lies. But no-one asks the question – who gives a fuck if he sent that message? No surveys are sent out. No general consensus is drawn. No objective conclusions are reached. The Government wins, and forces us to keep our heads down and mouths closed. So we don't make a fuss and we don't make any noise and we let them get away with truly reprehensible stuff because we're so busy keeping out of the way. You should be seen and not heard! And if you are heard, SUCH BEHAVIOUR WILL NOT BE TOLERATED!

Who the *fuck* thinks this Government has made this country any better? All they want is for their precious people in their precious little kingdoms to toe the fucking party line – and thus keep them in line, and ultimately keep us in line. The minute we challenge them – they know they can bat it off like that senator, and because they have batted it off for so long, they know that we don't give a fuck, or if we *do* give a fuck, it doesn't appear to make any difference. No matter how many people stand up for what is clearly a shambolic state of affairs – does anything change for the better?

So whether we care or whether we don't, or whether it's important or not – the Government is winning this game. They must maintain the status quo.

But what is this status quo? Is it a situation where everyone believes wholeheartedly in the police, or any other municipal organisation? Do we believe sincerely in the capacity of our Government? Would we really be totally devastated to discover that people working in these organisations are actually human beings who make mistakes? Do we give a fuck either way?

Are we living in a dream world? Do the Government – and certain senior police officers – truly *believe* that the public think that the police is

This Victorian Playground - Part 2

wonderful and shiny and brilliant and effective? Would their perception be damaged so much if it turned out that the coroner wasn't fired but was given a sufficient warning – perhaps docked some pay or something like that? Would they ring in and complain and demand his head on a platter? Would they give a fuck? Again, as stated before, no-one asks these questions! We're not allowed to. It doesn't fit in with the victim culture and it certainly doesn't fit in with the Government's ethos of subjugating us all by smothering us with a pile of nonsense to keep us browbeaten and scurrying around like idiots.

So this is why the police try so desperately hard to maintain this false image, even when they *know* – and I reiterate – *they KNOW* that things are fucked and no-one really cares if things go a bit wrong, and people make mistakes. They simply have to do it, for the Government controls their every move.

Perhaps it comes down to what is newsworthy. 'POLICE CORONER FIRED FOR SENDING RACIST TEXT MESSAGE.' Oooh, what a nasty man. Oooh, how disgraceful. Oooh, let's send an email to every police officer and tell them that SUCH BEHAVIOUR WILL NOT BE TOLERATED. Again.

OK then, how about this for a news headline. "MAVIS WALBURTON (88) BURGLED TWO DAYS IN A ROW BY THE SAME BURGLARS, WHO WERE MIRACULOUSLY CAUGHT BY SOME EXHAUSTED POLICE OFFICERS ON THE SECOND NIGHT, BUT THE GOVERNMENT LET THE FUCKERS GO, SO THEY CAN CARRY ON DOING WHAT THEY WERE DOING BEFORE: FUCKING PEOPLE'S LIVES UP. OH, AND P.S. THEY STAMPED ON MRS WALBURTON FOR GOOD MEASURE."

Of course, we don't get emails about those baddies. SUCH BEHAVIOUR WILL NOT BE TOLERATED. Actually, it *is* tolerated. It's tolerated by the Government time and time and time again. But let's all worry about the trivial stuff instead shall we?

So the most important thing that you can do is just get on with it and hope that you don't get fired for something irrelevant. Keep your head down and do as you are told. Don't rock the boat and don't make a fuss.

And if you're a burglar, or an otherwise scummy piece of shit, don't worry! You can have anything and everything you want.

And if you're a person who makes decisions that are extremely detrimental to society, the climate, the environment – or whatever – then you don't have to worry either, because there's nothing we can do about it. You just carry on.

And if you're a *really* influential person who holds sway over hundreds, perhaps thousands of people, and you make their lives a misery on a daily basis – that's OK. You've been doing it for years and we'll just let you carry on. We may even pay you lots of money and give you lots of weapons to continue being a bastard, if it serves our interests.

And if you lie and lie and lie some more - and we all know it - then have no fear! It doesn't make any difference. You'll soon bounce back and things will be fine.

And if you've sent an entirely immaterial text message - *you're fired.*

You WILL toe the party line.

16. Brotherhood of the Van

We were the Brotherhood of the Van, if only for the evening. Five brave souls with a cast iron will and a carte blanche remit to maintain the Queen's Peace on the streets of shame. With unwavering dedication and unfaltering courage we battled with chivalrous resolve against the calamitous behaviour of the anti-social and mindless fools bringing disorder to the boulevards of *our* manor … And we told a little old lady to *fuck off.*

We arrived in the van, surprisingly. PC Butch, PC Latvia, PC Butter, PC Prison and PC Pinkstone – the *Brotherhood* – for one night only; with fire in our eyes and passion in our souls.

Beneath the orange glare of the street lamps – I say "glare"; they don't really *glare*, as such. Someone once told me that about 60% of the light from a street lamp goes up instead of down – so in approximately 40% visibility we hopped out of the van and surveyed the setting for our drama.

Two people – a male and a female – with bicycles, having a loud, violent and raucous "domestic" in the middle of the street at midnight, waking the locals and causing a scene.

Upon seeing the Brotherhood, the female removed herself awkwardly from the hedge into which she had just been chucked, took her bike, and stomped off down the road. Good decision. Fuck off home and stop making a noise. However, this was a *domestic* so we couldn't really let her go without "checking on her welfare". She was, after all, part of the surrounding shrubbery upon our arrival.

I approached the male, who certainly looked like a scrote.[20] He looked at me and said aggressively, 'It's just a fucking domestic, mate.'

---
20 There is a "scrote gene" by the way.

PC Michael Pinkstone

OK, let's get something straight here, pal. There's no such thing as *'just* a domestic'. *I've* had the training. So I told him so. I looked at his right ear and it was bleeding, and he had blood on the back of his neck. *Just* a domestic ... I was about to say something else to him, which even now I can't remember, when my attention was diverted somewhat.

The female, bicycle-less, and livid, was charging towards us screaming – with the rest of the Brotherhood close behind her. Face blotchy, and apoplectic with rage, with small bits of twig and leaf in her wild, feral hair, she screeched and lurched in my general direction. I placed my palm upon her shoulder and firmly directed her to *calm down*. True English bobby.

Sadly, she didn't calm down. In fact, she got worse. She was beyond the pale. Then the true English bobby really came out of his shell and took control. While the female screamed abuse in my face – flecks of her spittle rebounding off my ruddy cheeks – I returned fire with fire. This was intolerable. I didn't make vows for nothing, you know.

I took hold of her flailing arms in a vice-like grip and shouted at the top of my lungs, 'I HATE IT WHEN THE QUEEN'S PEACE IS BREACHED, NOW SHUT UP ...!'[21] In reality, there may very well have been some choice swear words inserted at various intervals in my outburst, but to be truthful I was so overcome with civic indignation that I barely recall.

This, however, did not make the female any more compliant and she changed gear, which basically meant she shifted into third whilst overtaking and upped the revs to a shade under six thousand. Then the Brotherhood were upon her and she was taken to the floor, kicking, biting, spitting and cursing – using the C-word more times in a sentence than PC Glasses, which is a feat that would, under normal circumstances, earn someone a small reward. In her case, however, she was arrested for breaching the peace and disorderly behaviour. And the new leg restraints worked beautifully.

Yet while this female was being comprehensively squashed, her "boyfriend" (ah, bless) decided to intervene ...

Face to face with a member of the Brotherhood, his taut and bellicose stance did not make PC Latvia crumble. Oh no. Instead this fine

---

21 Irony never felt so good.

This Victorian Playground - Part 2

officer's weather-beaten brow furrowed into a frown; his piercing blue eyes became mere slits.

GO ... *AWAY* ... The command cut through the air like an icy dagger. Like the clear, high notes of a crystal bell.

'What, you gonna fucking make me?' Oh dear. I stood. Tall. Righteous anger ablaze in my breast. Yes, I'm going to fucking *make* you. For you are breaching the Queen's Peace you bald ginger c**t ...

Utilising the classic "Trip, Whack, Swear and Bundle" manoeuvre approved by the Home Office, myself and PC Latvia had this pillock on the floor in an instant. No mess, no fuss. Well, perhaps a bit of mess and a wee bit of fuss. There always is.

PC Butch dived in and "assisted", along with PC Butter, while in the background the shrieking and cursing of the crazy female was somehow getting worse. By this time two other officers had arrived – PC Hoody and PC Rinse. However, I was not really in a position to shake their hands and debrief them with a cup of tea – I was too busy shaking my Captor spray and trying to remember how the fuck I was taught to use it.

For the first time in my policing career I had decided, for various justifiable and proportionate reasons, to spray our ferociously struggling male in the face, and it was about time that PC Butch was shown how to do it properly. For our nasty chap was not really doing as he was told and needed a lesson in the art of 'Arrrgggghhhh, my eyes, my eyes, arrgggghhhh!'

Sadly, my aim wasn't particularly special. I sprayed PC Butch *and* PC Latvia and completely missed the target. Welcome to the Brotherhood. You think we're competent? Fuck that – we just wing it.

Miraculously the male may have caught the outside edge of my blast and put his hands to his face, when PC Butch dived in again, blindly, going for the head-lock, no doubt. I also rejoined the throng, covering the small distance with a single lunge, landing awkwardly on my knee but meeting scrote-flesh with the heel of my fist. The language was getting stronger and more virulent, and the male promised to rip all of our throats out, while simultaneously demanding my number and promising that my career was over. His head met tarmac with perhaps more force than was necessary, but that was accidental.

PC Michael Pinkstone

By now a small, local crowd had gathered. Clearly better than the TV. Mobile phones out and pointing in our direction. Seven officers on two people – police brutality! Must have been fantastic entertainment. Nine people yelling, two of them swearing (well, perhaps slightly more than two) and still we had yet to handcuff horrible man.

This was accomplished shortly afterwards and the van door was opened. The male was dragged to his feet, spitting venom and offering threats of blood-curdling revenge. We were all dead, and all of our families were dead, and all of our homes were destroyed by fire, and our careers finished.

Er, excuse me, sir, but you are the fucking scum that is handcuffed and *you* are the one who is going in the back of the van. *You* are the non-tax-paying, drug-taking, drug-dealing, lowlife filth that gives humanity a bad name. *You* are the oxygen thief. *You* are the waste of a good skin – they could have given it to someone else who'd have done a much better job. You're the piece of shit here, sir, and don't you be forgetting it. Now get in the van.

No ... What do you mean, *no?* It's not an option, fuck-for-brains. It's not a *please sir, oh please. We'd really, really appreciate it if you popped yourself into the back of this little van. Don't worry sir, you can have my number and I'll resign in anticipation of losing my job anyway. After all, sir, you're calling the shots here ...*

We shall fight on the beaches. GET IN THE BACK OF THE FUCKING VAN! *NOW!* With a shove that sent him lurching forwards, the cage door was slammed behind him. He turned, menacing, and began kicking the shit out of the inside of his mini prison. Poor chap, perhaps we should have just let him go. Left him on the street to carry on beating up his "girlfriend" like he was doing before we arrived. Or was he the one being beaten up? Actually, I don't give a fuck whose fault it was. Both were so high on drugs, drink and misplaced morality, that it was irrelevant. And they were sorely breaching the Queen's Peace. The Brotherhood don't like it when that happens.

But back to the female. She's trussed up like a Christmas turkey but making slightly more noise, and looking nowhere near as appetising, and yet she still hasn't resigned herself to the fact that she's been arrested and that she needs to stop screaming. Just let it go, you stupid little cow.

This Victorian Playground - Part 2

Or should we just let *you* go as well?

Ironically enough, that's what a little old lady might have been thinking. For in the midst of the melee, while PC Rinse and other members of the Brotherhood were trying to stop mad diseased cow from causing herself, or anyone else, further harm – a little old lady stepped into "The Zone" and tapped her on the shoulder. Tapped PC Rinse, that is. PC Rinse, who is rolling around with a psycho trying to keep the streets calm and safe, and attempting – futile though it all is – to maintain some form of order in a nation that the Government has abandoned.

Excuse me, officer, but what are you doing to her? I don't think you should be doing that ... Incredible though this sounds, it is perfectly true. And so was the command to *fuck off*. I'm not going to reveal which completely unprofessional officer said such a thing to an old lady, but it was one of us. How disgraceful. Tut tut. That's not integritised at all. I suggest being stuck on for that. I suggest just letting scumbags rule the roost and watching our streets be governed by people who don't give a flying fuck about the Queen's Peace, or anyone's peace for that matter.

Here, have the streets. They're yours. Take them. The Brotherhood will return to the office and stare at a computer all day and not do anything gritty or physical. Too many human rights to consider. Too much risk. Too much blame.

Goodbye peace. Goodbye Britain ... But no. Not for this member. I don't care where you're from and how old you are. If you try and stop me from maintaining this peace, I *will* tell you to *fuck off*. And so would any decent member of the Brotherhood.

Which leads us quite nicely onto...

17. Public Perception

So, what the fuck do you think police officers do? Do you think we beat up people for fun? Do you think we punch and kick and spray decent citizens of this country for a laugh?

If you've never been a copper, it's perhaps quite difficult to understand just what it's like. Just know one thing though – it's a fucking tough job. And sometimes it means telling old ladies to fuck off. I wish it *didn't* mean that, because there is nothing worse than having to be rude to a decent person, but sometimes it's the only way to get through to people. Do you really think we'd risk our careers, especially considering today's sycophantic and falsely integritised environment, by deliberately being rude to you? We have bills to pay and families to support just like everyone else. Oh, and we need food sometimes too. How fucking dare you complain that we are *eating*? Arrrggghh!

I know, try this out for a laugh instead. Try standing at the scene of a serious injury road accident where someone has perhaps been pretty badly maimed, or killed, and you have blocked part of the road with your police car. The lights are flashing and the barrier tape is out. The road is closed. Believe me, it's fucking closed.

So you stand there with your high visibility jacket and hat on – a warranted, uniformed police officer – and you are directing people to drive in another direction or down a nearby road. You've been doing this for an hour or so in the baking heat and all you've had is abuse.

Yes, abuse. You've been sworn at, shouted at and driven at. I'm sorry, shall I repeat that? You've been *driven* at. People have actually

This Victorian Playground - Part 2

tried to drive *through* you, through the barrier tape and past the big fucking signs that say "Police Accident" and "Road Closed".

I'm sorry sir, the road is closed. Please turn around and go the other way. He swears at you and tries to drive through you.

Do you think I'm fucking joking here? Think I'm having a laugh? Unfortunately I'm not. There are some people in Britain who need dangling over the edge of a very high building until they piss and shit themselves. Sadly you can't do that, so you jump out of the way of their car, run up to the window and tell them, in quite a cross voice, that the road is *fucking, fucking, fucking, fucking CLOSED. There's been an accident and a child is dead. You cannot drive down this road. It is closed. It is fucking closed. It's fucking goddamn fucking closed ...*

You may not swear, but you certainly do sound cross. So the lovely gentleman in the car later complains about you. He complains that a warranted officer of the law was "rude" to him when he was just "trying to find out what had happened" (lying bastard) which is often what the rest of the morons want to know, so they stop their car and block everyone else just to ask you.

What's happened, officer? Sir, move on please. Officer, I'm just asking you what's ... MOVE ON SIR, NOW!!!

Then you get another complaint for being "rude". So after a few hours in the boiling heat near the scene of a mangled toddler you've ended up with several complaints for being 'rude' – and all you've actually done is try to tell people that the road is closed, but they still argue with you and swear at you and drive at you anyway. The British public, quite simply, haven't got a fucking clue much of the time.

Please allow me to quote two related things from *Part 1* ...

There's ... a lot of talk about public confidence in the police. There's very little talk about police confidence in the public. We are confident, however, that we can do nothing right and it's always our fault. If you're going to blame anyone, blame the police.

And ...

Scumbags hail from all walks of life and from all corners of society. They may not provide the overwhelming trivia of the less than classy but they provide more than their fair share of criminals, and a very large share of social aloofness resulting in a general lack of respect for anyone

PC Michael Pinkstone

or anything. They are often morally inactive and just as demanding in other ways. No-one is without fault in this world. Not even those up the higher end of the social scale.

In other words, it's always our fault (even if we have to close a road, for example, due to someone else's horrendous driving) and the classes of people most likely to take offence at not being able to drive down such roads are usually middle to upper class males in nice cars. I've been driven at by men in suits and sworn at by men in cars that are worth more than all of the nine cars I've owned added together. The British public really does comprise some fucking idiots and they are not necessarily council fodder, as we would all prefer to believe.

So the next time you approach the scene of an accident and you see a police officer directing traffic – and the road you want to go down is closed – by all means swear to yourself at the inconvenience (after all, we all get cross at such things) but please don't drive at the police officer or demand to know what has happened. If you do either of these things – and the police officer gets cross with you – take it on the chin, fucking grow up and do as you are fucking told. We don't close roads for a laugh. What do you think we are, the fucking Highways Agency?

And if you're a little old lady and you see a police officer rolling around on the floor with someone and it looks brutal – it most likely *is* brutal. In which case, keep out of the way. We don't roll around the floor with people for fun. Believe me, there's always a *very, very* good reason why we use force on people (and we *are* allowed to use force, by the way) so please don't stick your nose in during the struggle to tell us that we shouldn't be doing what we are doing. You may end up getting told, forcefully, to er, *go away* ...

* * *

Public perception is therefore a very tricky thing indeed. Every police service will want its officers to be extremely professional at all times (which in this day and age is actually quite difficult) so that the public perceive them in a good light.

All of this "policing by consent" bollocks also lends itself to a wee bit of paranoia when it comes to officer behaviour on the streets. I would

This Victorian Playground - Part 2

strongly argue that the police service should be a highly professional and distinguished body of people, but it's been so ravaged by political correctness and all the other issues you may have read about elsewhere, that what remains is, ironically enough, pretty darn *un*professional at times. Because we've been gradually de-professionalised (not sure if that's a word, but it fits) and de-skilled and because our discretionary powers have been replaced by political paranoia (and computer systems), they might as well not bother training us any more. If all we do is follow procedures, you may as well have a trained monkey wearing the uniform.

So how the public perceive us, at present, is nothing compared to how we are currently perceiving ourselves. What you think of us is pretty irrelevant to what *we* think of us at the moment, seeing as our profession has been so completely buggered up and has gone to the dogs.

You are basically dealing with more and more police officers who are losing any sense of morale and motivation, so how you perceive them will ultimately be affected by the shit that we are going through in the station, irrespective of what we have to deal with outside. Therefore when you actually see us dealing with stuff, we are already likely to be in a pretty bad fucking mood. If you've read *Part 1*, or any other decent publication about the state of the police service, then you may fully understand why!

To be brutally honest, I really don't give a poo how you perceive me because this job and this country have gone so completely beyond the pale, that it all barely matters anyway. Perhaps if we were allowed to *do* our job – and help salvage society from this morass – then your perception of us may change. Either way, at the moment, it's all pointless. I'm not going to be deliberately rude, of course, and I will do my best to represent my police service as best I can, but that's about all. For I may as well simply not bother. Fortunately true dedication and will-power are keeping us going, while the Government appears to be doing its best to bring everything to a shameful and grinding halt.

Thus, before the wheels come off completely (if they are not already off...) let us conclude this chapter by considering one of my objectives for this book which, in *Part II*, I have deliberately not shared with you so far.

One of my main concerns is to *alter public perception of the police service*. I want to transform how you perceive us! So hopefully, by now,

PC Michael Pinkstone

you will be thinking about the police in a different light. Hopefully you have read enough to realise that the situation is pretty darn serious. And your attitude towards things is essential. Basically, if *your* perception doesn't change too, then we will all remain unconditionally buggered.

18. An NVQ in Ticking Boxes

A good few moons ago I had the pleasure of working in a large bookshop in Cambridge. In the early to mid 90s I worked in the Law, Economics, Management and Education department.

Over the years that I worked there, it was interesting to observe the changes in society – and in organisational behaviour – reflected in the titles of the books, and the jargon they used.

Back then, words such as "Re-engineering", "Downsizing" and "Benchmarking" became popular in management, with dozens of books published with these words in the title. Some of them sold in their thousands.

Another popular area concerned ways to sell yourself via your CV. Lots of books offering lots of advice on making your CV fit the bill. How to make mundane activities and fairly simple skills sound absolutely brilliant on paper. How to turn yourself from a "Cleaner" to a "Domestic Artisan", or something like that. It was a way of making us all sound good, look proficient, and appear qualified – on paper at any rate.

For I propose that Britain looks fairly good on paper. We have this down to a fine art. We love ticking our boxes and assessing ourselves against a set of half-decent criteria – each criterion being a thing you can hardly argue against, as it sounds so great.

We love our CVs to be neat, crisp and well presented. A good use of official-sounding language to dress our skills and achievements up in a way that does us proud. In other words, we bullshit constantly. Yet we take this bullshitting to such administrative extremes.

Everything we do leaves a paper trail. Everything we do leaves a

PC Michael Pinkstone

tick in a box somewhere. Bullet points and flip charts. Brainstorming and spreadsheets. Filing cabinets and standardisation meetings. Assessment targets and detections. It's all the same stuff. It all fits under the same umbrella.

It's a way of looking good on paper. So long as it's all recorded properly, it doesn't really matter what has happened, or hasn't happened. Does that sound familiar to you?

So long as we are accountable and we have our precious forms all ticked and signed and stamped. So long as the online training packages have been completed. Makes no odds if they are fucking awful. They just have to be done so someone can tick something else, to hand it on to someone else, so that someone else can say that this has been accomplished. Wow, aren't we great?

We are quite adept at producing super-looking lists of targets and requirements that we *have* to meet in order to be "competent". Many of these things are understandably essential, especially when it comes to skilled jobs. There is absolutely nothing wrong with real skills being taught and used, and even assessed.

However, in these paranoid and subjective times, we seem to spend far too much time on the assessing, ticking, recording, auditing and monitoring than we do on using the skill in the first place. And, more importantly, we seem to spend far too much time on the assessing, ticking, recording, auditing and monitoring of ethereal skills.

And what is an "ethereal skill"? Well, we shall come to that shortly. The point at the moment is that we are all obsessed with ensuring that our lists of performance-related criteria – in whatever area of work – are all neatly ticked and checked.

Targets for children. Targets for police. Targets for healthcare professionals. Targets for anyone. It makes no difference where we work – we all have targets. We all have performance criteria. We all get assessed – in *everything*. Stuff that should be assessed is assessed and stuff that shouldn't be assessed is assessed. We love to tick a box for bollocks these days.

So long as it all looks good on paper. Just like our CVs. So long as someone can turn around and say, 'Look what we have achieved' – that's the most important part.

This Victorian Playground - Part 2

This Government, perhaps unlike any other in its pure obsession with ticks, are the ones that can turn around and say, 'Look what we have achieved!'

Look, crime has fallen. Look, children's reading standards have gone up (ahem).[22] Look, thousands of people now have to wait less time in a queue at a hospital. Look, aren't we great.

For this is what all the statistics are used for. They are all sent off to the Home Office number-crunchers who spend their time analysing them in order to make national decisions concerning everything.

Then there's the Government think-tanks and research groups. The Home Office-funded inquiries. The papers and suggestions. The dynamic, fluid, ever-changing self-evaluation of running a country. And aren't the Government doing a great job?

It all looks so damn good on paper. Britain, Britain, Britain. Great on paper. Fucking shit in reality. And that's the part the Government simply doesn't understand.

* * *

We've spent so long bullshitting and hamming up our skills and achievements, that we've neglected to notice that things are deteriorating. We are, in fact, becoming quite de-skilled. A terrible and tragic irony. We are becoming obsolete and insufficient. But we're doing it so fucking efficiently! So if I had to sum up Britain in two words it would be thus: *Efficiently ineffective.*

And this is where we come to the phrase "ethereal skills". These are basically skills that we have been assessing ourselves on for a while, that are simply made out of nothing. They are less than insubstantial. For many years we have been acquiring skills and obtaining qualifications that comprise nothing more than hot air.

We assess ourselves on our "Understanding of Diversity", for example. We tick a box to say that we are "Trained in Diversity". We even put it

---

[22] The National Literacy Strategy, which I once taught, has recently been lambasted in the press. Apparently it's done fuck all for children's reading standards. A few days after that, a further news article suggested that we'd wasted millions on reading strategies for children. Fantastic!

PC Michael Pinkstone

in our CVs. Hey, look at me, I'm *Trained in Diversity*.

If I want to, I can go on a course as a police officer. After five days I could put on my CV that I was *Trained in Diversity Training*.

After a few sessions I could then add on my CV: *"Delivered a high standard of diversity input to candidates in line with the current performance indicator mandate'"*.

Or something like that. Something equally fucking bollocks. And that also sums up Britain.[23] It's mind-boggling the state we have got ourselves into.

Furthermore, there are simply so many boxes to tick, that we spend all our time making sure that we've ticked them all, and spend no time whatsoever actually *doing* anything. Where, in bygone years, essential skills were traditionally handed down from father to son (or daughter), we now have a situation where skills are taught simply by ticking a box.

If I watch you do something, and I write it up in such a fashion, I can award you a skill. I can claim that you are competent! (This is the entire premise of an NVQ in policing, by the way ...)

For example, one of your requirements for competency might be to demonstrate an effective understanding of a particular computer system or, in the ethereal skills department, demonstrate that you treat people's diversity with "respect".

I could sit next to you in a police station and watch you load up a computer system and make a few updates. Then I could take you out in a police car and watch you talk to a member of the public – someone who was different to you.

If, by some miracle, you were able to point and click on the screen without making any horrific blunders, and if you didn't kick the shit out of the member of the public for wearing a turban, I can tick several boxes and mark you down as competent in lots of areas.

You could then put on your CV something like, *"Proficient in the use of CRAPPIES and associated systems"*, and, *"Shows respect for race and diversity while interacting with the public"*. (See what I mean about "ethereal"?)

It's all bollocks. And what's more – we all *know* it's bollocks. Yet

---
23 I would also say that Britain is not alone in this charade.

This Victorian Playground - Part 2

we all still have to do it because the Government wants it to be done. Something about life being a stage? We're all playing a fucking game. Welcome to the playground.

If you were to read my CV you would note that I am *"Trained in dealing with incidents of domestic abuse"*.

The word "trained" in this sentence is slightly misleading, however. A better word, perhaps, would be "experienced". For I am certainly quite experienced in dealing with incidents of domestic abuse.

Unfortunately the word "abuse" in that sentence is also quite misleading. 99% of the domestic incidents I have attended at work have been utter shite and should never have involved the use of a police officer's time. Something about a victim culture?

Also, the word "domestic" is slightly misleading. What is a 'domestic'? The definition of this word is a wee bit broad, to say the least. Nowadays it's just a trigger word. Say the word "domestic" to a police officer and they are likely to scream and run away very quickly in the opposite direction.

So I'm *Trained in dealing with incidents of domestic abuse.* I'm also experienced in dealing with them. But being "trained" is even better. And part of my *training* consisted of the completion of an online package.

This basically meant that on a given day at the police station a couple of years ago, most people got sent an angry "red flag" email stating that they had not done the online training package on domestic abuse.

Most of my team were in the same boat, so we all sat down and rushed through the package (which was completely shit) and clicked on random answers and hoped that our score was above 80%. I think by some fortuitous circumstances I managed to get about 83%. Others had to do theirs two or three times, and others just got someone else to do it for them anyway.

So, in effect, I am 83% competent in pointing and clicking on a screen regarding irrelevant information about domestic stuff. I'm also *trained* in listening to people from the Domestic Violence Unit/Public Protection Unit telling me that if I don't make an arrest at a domestic incident, it will be my fault. We will not tolerate it when people are in a relationship. SUCH BEHAVIOUR ...

Nevertheless, I am able to say for the rest of my life that I am *Trained in dealing with incidents of domestic abuse.* And doesn't that sound fantastic? Basically it's all a load of old tripe.

Yet in recent times it is this kind of "skill" that has become the focus. We are desperate to prove that we are competent in subjective things. Either that, or we're so desperate to tick as many boxes as possible, that much of the stuff we are ticking off really doesn't need a box. *Proficient in the use of breathing and associated bodily functions.*

I can't remember the exact number, but when I did my teaching degree, I had to have something along the lines of one hundred and sixty-three ticks on a list to prove that I was competent enough to be a teacher. This isn't an exaggeration, by the way. And each of those criteria was measured under four headings – something like, "Below Par", "Slightly Above Par But Still Shit", "Satisfactory" and "Excellent".

From what I can remember, I had to have a tick in either "Satisfactory" or "Excellent" – for each of the one hundred and sixty-three competencies – in order to pass my degree.

Of course the Government defends such lists and states that they are all part of the drive to raise standards and that kind of crap. In reality, I was being assessed on things such as:

- *Maximised learning opportunities for all children, taking into consideration their educational needs in light of their diversity.*
- *Elicited verbal or written responses to demonstrate effective understanding of core objectives.*
- *Provided a caring and stimulating classroom environment to ensure an optimum educational setting, guaranteeing full value for money.*

Yes, Mr Pinkstone, I have observed you for ten minutes one Thursday afternoon standing in front of a class of thirty-five children, trying your very best to survive, and I can assure you that you are Satisfactory in the above three competencies, and maybe one or two of the other one hundred and sixty still left to go. However, there was a stage when little

This Victorian Playground - Part 2

Timmy spent approximately eighteen seconds staring out of the window and not concentrating on his Numeracy work, so you need to make sure that *every* child is focused on the task at hand to ensure their learning opportunities are as enhanced as possible. (Brings me out in a cold sweat just thinking about my teaching degree again.)

Now take a look at those competencies for a second time. Note words such as "Maximised", "Demonstrated" and "Elicited". Such words are very familiar nowadays. They appear on all sorts of checklists and ticky-box charts. I'm sure they appear in many NVQs, not least in policing. They are decisive and incisive words – clear, crisp and to the point. They cut through the fat and gristle and get to the heart of the matter. I *maximised.* I *demonstrated.* I *elicited.* How can you go wrong if you pop those words down on paper? Sound great, don't they?

Now take a look at those competencies again. Read them through and distil them down to what they really are. They might sound fantastic on paper, but in reality they are either things that you would do automatically, or are so hammed up by the careful use of language that they simply make you twitch. *Elicited verbal or written responses to demonstrate effective understanding of core objectives.* What the fuck would this mean in practice?

'Timmy, what shape is this?' I hold up a piece of blue cardboard in front of the class. 'It's a square, Mr Pinkstone.'

I walk towards him and hold it closer to his little face. 'Not quite, Timmy, but that's a *very* good try. Have another look and see if you can remember what I said earlier about these two *parallel* lines here, and these two *parallel* lines here.' What a great clue, I think to myself.

Timmy stares at the cardboard, not having a fucking clue what I'm talking about. After all, he's only six. And he's thick as shit anyway. 'A diamond!' he says triumphantly.

I sigh inwardly. 'Not quite, Timmy, but again that's a *very* good guess.' Meanwhile, the other thirty-four children who know what shape it is are whispering it so loudly that Timmy can surely hear them. But no. He's not that sophisticated. All of his focus is on my hands and the bloody piece of blue cardboard.

'I'll give you a clue, Timmy. It starts with a "P".' And at this point I start to say, '*P ..., P ..., Pa ..., Par ..., Para ..., Paral ..., Parallel ...,*

135

PC Michael Pinkstone

Paralello ..., Parallelogr ...' Still the little bugger hasn't got it yet. 'Parallelog!' he shouts excitedly.

'Ooh, close!' I say with real enthusiasm. 'Say it slower – *par ... a ... lell ... o ... gra ...*' Timmy stares and then shouts again. 'Parallelogram!'

I say, 'YES!' with a tremendous burst of applause from my little audience. Timmy looks radiant with joy. The fact that I've just pretty much told him the answer is irrelevant. The fact that he doesn't really need to know what a fucking parallelogram is at age six is irrelevant. The fact that no teacher should have to stand in front of, and be responsible for, a class of thirty-five children is irrelevant. The main thing is that I have just *elicited verbal or written responses to demonstrate effective understanding of core objectives.* Good old Timmy. Thank fuck for that. At least *I'm* competent and the Government has got another tick in the box to prove that they are the best and we should all vote for them again. What a load of fucked up shit.

* * *

So it doesn't matter what we're doing – whether it's teaching a class of children, or training to become a police officer, or writing our CV, or filling out our performance reviews – it's all about bullshitting. The targets and competencies are the most important thing in the world. After all, we don't want to be incompetent!

It's a constant battle to ensure that we have measured ourselves against a set of criteria and come out on top. The context is entirely irrelevant. Now *there's* a fucking surprise. Context being irrelevant. Who'd have thought that was possible?

And this Government has determined that we should all be competent in whatever it is we are doing. *Everything* is measured. Absolutely everything. They even measure hot air, as we have already seen. Look at me, I show respect for race and diversity because it is ticked off in my policing NVQ. Wonderful!

They choke everyone and everything with targets – mostly irrelevant ones. So we spend all our time scurrying around trying to meet those targets and achieve the required competencies, but are we really getting any better? Are we really learning important and useful skills? Or are we just blatting around from one set of irrelevant competencies to another without ever really achieving anything, except putting more pointless ticks in more pointless boxes?

Meanwhile the country remains fucked. In fact, it gets worse – even though we are so "competent"! How can this be? Surely we deserve to be credited with some kind of award for all our diligence? Surely all those ticks have led to something quite fantastic? Surely Britain is a great place to live and everyone wants to stay here?

Oh dear. Oh deary, deary me. We may have got our NVQ in ticking boxes but, like most things nowadays, it's just a load of worthless shite. We are victims of our own efficiency and about as effective as a roof-rack on a submarine.

19. The Miscellaneous Pile

It's a big pile, by the way. And by and large, it's a big pile of poo. We deal with a lot of stuff and a lot of it is extremely miscellaneous. As mentioned in *Part I*, not everything ends up on CRAPPIES and not everything is CRAPPIES-related. For the police don't just deal with crime (and CRAPPIES, after all, is a system that records crime, or bollocks …) – we deal with pretty much everything at present.

In many respects, we always have. And in many respects, we should continue to do so. "Policing" is a very broad word. Unfortunately, at the moment, we are somewhat stuck in the mire of mollycoddling alleged victims, but we do try and contend with other stuff too.

Of course, I'm still writing from the perspective of a frontline officer. Therefore I don't have a remit. Well, I do have a remit – I'm a general dogsbody. In which case I spend a lot of time dealing with "missing" people, one of my many "miscellaneous" tasks.

I'm sure you've heard enough stories about deceased people, so I'll try to make sure that none of my missing people end up dead. Which is why we spend fucking ages looking for them in the first place.

Every now and again you get a "real" missing person. Unfortunately they are quite difficult to find these days amidst all the shit. It's a bit like looking for a real victim on CRAPPIES – they are there somewhere. Something akin to looking for a plastic turd in a sewer, which is a slightly modified version of "needle in a haystack". Like it?

Anyway, back to the missing person. There are actually three types of missing people:

This Victorian Playground - Part 2

- Those who *are* missing
- Those who *want* to be missing
- Those who the Government decide are missing

Do the above categories seem familiar to you? Of course they do. It's all about procedure, and looking for a missing person is about following procedure. It's not really about *looking* for them – after all, how can you really *look* for a missing person? I mean, think about it. Two officers in a town of about a quarter of a million people (in a country of tens of millions) allocated to "deal" with a missing person, and in a nine-hour shift we have to "find" them? It isn't possible. That's because most of them aren't really missing, of course.

So what we've done is create a missing-person database that helps us look for them. Actually, it doesn't. Instead it covers our arses if they wind up dead. For that's all we're worried about. If a missing person pops their clogs after they have been reported missing, then the police will get blamed for not "doing more".

Thus in recent months there has been quite a change of focus when it comes to missing persons. The risk assessment is about as comprehensive as a domestic, and the database for recording what we've done to try to locate them is fairly comprehensive too. And each missing person is dealt with as something of a priority, irrespective of – guess what? That's right, my favourite word... *context*.

For as stated above, there are three kinds of missing people. And as you may have presupposed, we spend a hell of a lot of time "looking" for categories two and three. Obviously we spend time looking for category one, but like real victims, they are lumped in with all the other crap.

Most of the missing people I have to look for are teenagers. And because they are teenagers, they are allegedly more at risk than older people. Since when is a gobby fifteen-year-old scrote who has run away from home and is currently at his mate's house either playing Xbox or shagging some other teenage slapper at *risk*? The only risk in this scenario would be the chance of pregnancy. For one thing the scrotes do amazingly well is *breed*.

However, if little Kieran is reported "missing" again, he has to be dealt with by the police irrespective of the circumstances. This means

PC Michael Pinkstone

going round to speak to the person who has reported him missing and then spending the next few hours checking all the places he is likely to be. And he is very, very unlikely to be out in the cold (if it is cold) or in any danger whatsoever. In fact, he may even be out committing crime.

Ah yes – the missing person who is a criminal. Had a few of those in my time. Little Amjad has been reported missing by his parents and you then get a phone call, having spent several hours "looking" for him, from a police station in London saying that they have the lovely little chap in custody for robbery. Ironically enough he wasn't really "missing" in the first place – he was out being a scrote with his cousin, thieving from innocent people at train stations.

Then there's the teenage female missing person. My favourite. (Can you hear me making puking noises?) Again, the only risk with these females is the risk of getting pregnant, because that's why 99.99% of teenage females go missing – because of boys. It's as simple as that.

Fourteen-year-old Charlotte didn't come back after school and it's now 10pm so she's been reported missing. You spend half an hour completing the risk assessment and five minutes searching her house (that's a requirement by the way).

Then you ring all of her friends and go round to all of their houses. By now it's 2.34 am and despite having only seven officers on shift and despite the fact that you *know* Charlotte is with Kieran, you still have to keep "looking". Eventually you have done enough to cover your arse and then update the missing person database back at the station, so at least no-one could criticise you for not "doing your job properly".

Obviously Charlotte comes home eventually, dripping with attitude and defiant to the last. They always do come home, you know. And they're always dripping with attitude and defiant to the last.

There's also a new breed of missing person who we have had to contend with in recent months. And that would be missing "foreign"[24] people who have come to the country and claimed benefits, and got a house, and then seem to disappear. So the council report them as missing when they haven't turned up to collect their well deserved money. The fact that many of these people are thieving little shits is irrelevant.

---

24 It would be unprofessional of me to reveal which particular European country I'm thinking of …

This Victorian Playground - Part 2

We're not allowed to say such things, after all. They haven't come here to work or to contribute – they have come here to take and to steal. Then, amazingly, the police have to spend ages "looking" for them when they have melted away into the shadows, or have simply buggered off back to their home country with a big wad of pound sterling kindly provided by ye olde British taxpayer. Oh I love this country *so* much. In fact, I think I might just go missing myself. Not that anyone would really "look" for me ...

* * *

Another thing to pop into the miscellaneous pile would be the insane people. There's nothing quite like a nutter to enliven your shift. Not all of them are suicidal, like the wrist-slitting hippo from *Part I*, but this doesn't make them any easier to deal with.

Police receive no mental health training by the way. Yet we have a power to detain someone who poses a significant risk of harm to themselves or others, and take them to a place of safety.[25] In other words, we roll around the floor with them for a while and then drag them to the psychiatric ward at the nearest hospital, where we then have to wait four hours for a mental health team to turn up and let them go again. Of all the people I have detained under the Mental Health Act, only *one* has been kept at the psycho unit.

This isn't because my judgement is poor (well, I don't *think* it is) but because mad people are a wee bit like the cousin that nobody likes or wants to see. How the fuck do you really *deal* with a mad person?

Apart from injecting them with a sedative and strapping them to a bed, there isn't much else that can be done. You can't really talk to them because they're fruit loops and you can't really lock them up, unless they are really dangerous, so the best thing is to let them get on with life as best as possible – which means trying to let them integrate into society.

Unfortunately we often have to mop up the consequences of this, like the other day. I arrived at an "incident" with PC Bump following

---

[25] For "someone who poses a significant risk of harm to themselves or others" read "someone who is as mad as box of hatters".

PC Michael Pinkstone

reports of a disturbance on the street wherein a female had been knocking on all the doors and screaming.

The female in question, who later told me in confidence, that the council had provided her with reinforced windows so that she couldn't head-butt them and subsequently shatter them, lived on her own in a house that she had pretty much just trashed.

Not only had she trashed it, but she was sitting there on her upturned sofa, rocking back and forth, cradling a large kitchen knife. Now please bear in mind that a few days after this my police service had to deal with a horrific murder, where a mad person had stabbed to death someone in their kitchen.

So let's be brutally honest here. Mad people are unpredictable and they can be extremely dangerous. Not only dangerous to themselves, but dangerous to others.

However, as police officers, we do not have power to detain someone under the Mental Health Act (MHA) when they are inside their own home. They have to be outside. Some officers "get around" this by dragging people out of their house to "prevent a breach of the peace" and then subsequently detaining them under the relevant nutter section of the MHA. This, of course, isn't exactly, er, recommended.

Sadly, however, it's often the only way. For example, what would you do? What would you do if you turned up at a house where a young female was sitting on a kitchen stool calmly hacking her wrists open with a razor blade while her best friend pleaded with her to stop?

This friend had called the police in desperation because her friend was hell-bent on ending her life in a messy and quite gruesome manner. So there she was, sitting on her three-legged wooden throne, surrounded by a pool of her own freshly spilled blood, with her friend beside herself with emotion right next to her – and there's no legal "power" you can use to "stop" her from doing what she is doing …

What do you do? Do you stand there and watch her? Do you think to yourself, 'Hmm, I don't have a "legal" power to do anything about this situation, so I'm just going to grab myself a bucket of popcorn and enjoy the show …'

Of course you don't. You vaguely recall something about "preservation of life". It's something you've heard somewhere before but you can't quite

This Victorian Playground - Part 2

remember where. So you grab this female and forcefully manhandle her out of the house, making sure the razor blade is removed from her person. You then detain her under the Mental Health Act and get her to a fucking hospital as soon as possible. You may not have acted as, er, recommended – but you've done what needed to be done. Job be damned.

Anyway, fortunately for myself and PC Bump, the female we were dealing with now had decided to come outside in her dressing gown and scream at the top of her voice – without the knife. Thank fuck. So she was immediately detained and popped into the back of the police car, whereupon she promptly took off her glasses and screwed them up and started babbling on about evening primrose oil. Much better than bleeding all over us.

Meanwhile I went into her house to look for some clothes because she was stark bollock naked underneath the dressing gown and yes, she got dressed in the car, despite desperate pleas from PC Bump not to do so. What do you say to a large, mad, naked, bedraggled middle-aged woman sitting next to you in the back of a car talking incessantly about evening primrose oil? Can you think of how to make *that* conversation any more interesting? I fucking can't.

Fortunately, after we had taken her to the psycho ward and installed her in the "place of safety" (bright, horrible room with chairs screwed to the floor), and after she had projectile vomited a cup of tea and talked some more about weird and wonderful things – she was admitted to the ward and PC Bump and I gratefully left the hospital a few hours later. At least the residents on her particular street would have one night of peace anyway.

* * *

Then there's allegedly "suicidal" people – but not the ones in the same category as the female on the stool, or the mad hippo woman from *Part I*. We've covered suicidal in custody and I must say that my sentiments are pretty similar regarding the same kinds of people outside the police station as well.

It's perhaps a foregone conclusion that when you are rushing around town trying desperately to maintain some form of law and order (I mean desperately trying to pander to everyone and cover your arse), and there are several outstanding serious incidents going on and no-one to deal with them – the police will receive a call from a chap called Steve who says he is standing at the bottom of the local multi-storey car park stating that he's "feeling suicidal".

Steve has rung us at least ten times in the past year saying exactly the same thing. He's not alone. We have our suicidal "regulars" and they never do any more than pretend they've taken 200 painkillers or claim they are about to leap to their death from 200 feet.

The thing is, they *never* leap off buildings or lie down in front of trains – or take dozens of painkillers for that matter. For the people who actually do end up comprehensively killing themselves don't usually announce it to anyone, and they very rarely call the police stating what they are about to do.

So when you get a phone call from Steve you know that he's just wasting everyone's fucking time. This isn't a cry for help, it's a cry for attention. Unfortunately he gets both – help *and* attention. We can't let a phone call like that go, you see. The reasons are obvious of course – it would be all our fault if he killed himself and we did nothing to stop him. It would be all our fault even if he scratched himself with a blunt butter knife, but there you go. It's always our fault.

Thus under the all-embracing banner of "Fear for Personal Welfare" we spend an age looking for Steve. Everyone is looking for him, actually. No-one can fucking find him because he's gone home. He wasn't really going to jump off the car park. In fact, he was nowhere near the fucking car park. I don't doubt that he felt a bit "down" but I seriously doubt his ability to end his own life in such a messy way.

It's therefore, potentially, a wee bit unprofessional of me to say that if Steve rang me saying he was about to kill himself, I'd suggest that he made his way to the next policing area and did it there. Try humouring these people for once! Perhaps pandering to people perpetuates the problem. Perhaps they need a firm hand.

And harsh as that may seem – it is, of course, but a foregone conclusion that if any police officer saw a person about to kill themselves, they would rush to their aid immediately and do everything within their power to save them. Ironically enough, we don't really have any legal power to

This Victorian Playground - Part 2

save life – it's just something we do. More often than not, grappling with someone who is attempting to fling themselves off a bridge, or wrestling a razor blade out of someone's bloodied hand (which I have done on several occasions) – leaves us wide open to allegations of assault! We usually detain that person under the Mental Health Act, which gives us a legal power to use some kind of force on them, but that's about it. Unfortunately there isn't a Preservation of Life Act, but that's probably a good thing. It should come naturally.

So while the police should do everything in their power to preserve life (shouldn't we all?), it should *not* be our fault if someone has hurt themselves or killed themselves. We are *not* responsible for things that people do to harm themselves – but we should do our best to help them if they have done so. Sometimes we simply have to pick up the pieces – without blame and without fear of being maligned for "not doing more". It's a harsh fact of life that people simply *have* to take responsibility for their own existence.

20. Hand-Held Mini Metal Detectors

Ah, that's more like it. Now we're talking sense. At long last. Something incisive from the corridors of power. A ray of hope! A beam of sunlight through the clouds! A parting of the Red Sea! A lottery win! Some hand-held mini metal detectors to tackle gun crime!

I'm sorry, could you repeat that please? Yes, of course ... some hand-held mini metal detectors to tackle gun crime!

No, I apologise, I'm really not getting that. Could you repeat your last? Of course! SOME HAND-HELD MINI METAL DETECTORS TO TACKLE GUN CRIME!

You know toothpaste? Well, I hope you do. Ever looked on the side of a tube of modern day toothpaste? Goes something like this:

Fights plaque. Tick!
Freshens breath. Tick!
Whitens teeth. Tick!
Protects enamel. Tick!

You know hand-held mini metal detectors? Well, you might do. Ever bought a hand-held mini metal detector and looked on the box? Well, *I* haven't, but I guess it would say something like this:

Detects metal. Tick!
Discovers hidden treasure. Tick!
Great for beaches. Tick!
Tackles gun crime. Tick!

This Victorian Playground - Part 2

Perhaps I'm labouring the point here. Perhaps not. It's just that I had such high hopes for our "new" prime minister. I didn't really.

So there I am, sitting at the computer, and I'm reading on the interweb that the prime minister is going to issue officers – in four police forces across the country – hand-held mini metal detectors to tackle gun crime, in 2008.

Now I'm really and truly sorry for this, but such a statement deserves the following. Actually, I'm lying – I'm not sorry at all …

* * *

Sergeant Mickle paused from his typing and mopped his brow. It had been a fucking awful day. First of all he'd had to trawl through six PDRs and add his comments, and then he'd had to make a phone call to a "victim" of an assault. This so-called victim turned out to speak hardly any English whatsoever and appeared to have the IQ of a boiled potato anyway. Typical.

Still, Sergeant Mickle updated CRAPPIES as to what he'd done (otherwise he'd get lambasted), and went to take a piss. On the way to the toilet his phone rang. It was PC Guest.

'Yes mate.' Sergeant Mickle was fairly informal with his team.

'Er, Sarge, it's Graham, er, have you got a second?' The voice was tense, nervous. Sergeant Mickle frowned.

'What's up, Graham?' He tried to sound reassuring, but he knew if Graham was worried, then he should be slightly worried too.

There was a short pause. 'Er, Sarge, er, could you come to my location please, er – got a bit of a situation. Haven't called it up on the radio yet. Control knows about it.' PC Guest did indeed sound pretty concerned.

'No probs mate,' Sergeant Mickle responded straight away. 'Can you give me a heads-up?' He walked into the toilet, phone attached to his shoulder, and began to take a well-deserved leak.

'Er, well …' It was unlike PC Guest to sound disconcerted. 'Er, I think we may have a situation developing at the domestic I'm dealing with – perhaps firearms-related. It's complicated. I've already rung the Control Inspector. He's rung the available armed unit, although we

PC Michael Pinkstone

might need more than one. He said I should contact you now and get you down here. They just want it kept clear of the airwaves for the moment as the job may need its own dedicated channel. Just need a supervisor down here asap.'

Sergeant Mickle frowned again. 'Has a Log been created?' And before PC Guest could reply, the radio Controller piped up.

Zulu Tango, Sierra nine-one. Sergeant Mickle responded to his call-sign in the proper fashion. 'Sierra nine-one, go ahead.'

The controller was female. The one with the husky voice. *Sierra nine-one, are you able to view an immediate Log that has just come in – number 1223 of today, over?*

Sergeant Mickle winced. 'Yes, yes,' he replied. 'I'm just on the phone about that one. Taking a look now.'

All copied nine-one. As soon as you can please. And note the update on Page 3 – supervisor to the scene asap.

'Yes, yes.' Sergeant Mickle told PC Guest he'd speak to him in a short while and walked back to his office, where he immediately loaded up the relevant system. Some quick typing brought up the Log on the screen before him. It didn't look joyful.

Miscellaneous Firearms Incident. 84 Mallard Way. Immediate grading. Reported by PC 635 Guest.

He clicked to page 2. Officer reporting that female at location reporting ex-husband has made threats to kill with a firearm. Threat believed to be real as ex-husband legally owns a shotgun, which is currently missing from its secure cupboard in the house, along with ammunition.

Sergeant Mickle sighed involuntarily. He continued reading on to page 3. Female reports that her husband has been acting very strangely for the past few days and is not himself. Believes threat to be real. Threat was made to female's brother, Michael Sandford, who lives at 55 Littleport Spur. Female believes no current threat to herself but fears for her brother, and she can't get hold of him. Supervisor to scene to debrief caller soonest.

By the time he'd got to the end of page 3, the controller was calling up again. 'Nine-one go ahead.' Sergeant Mickle was used to the incredible amount of updating that went on with such an incident. Barely time to absorb anything in this place.

This Victorian Playground - Part 2

Sierra nine-one, from the control room Inspector, could you ensure all units at the scene have personal protective equipment, and to make you aware that the Lima-Victor unit is on the way. Over?

'Nine-one copied, might as well show me en-route.' Sergeant Mickle pulled on his protective vest and grabbed his high-visibility jacket from the door of his office. As he walked down the stairs to the car park he wondered why the hell they weren't bringing this "female" straight to the station to debrief. 'Fuck it,' he muttered as he started the car up and drove out of the station car park.

Meanwhile, several miles away, the Lima-Victor unit was making to the location at high speed, their silver coloured police vehicle a mere blur. The unit consisted of PC Andy Toster and PC Sam Brandon. Both were firearms-trained and had a variety of Home Office-approved weapons on board, which were securely locked away in a designated compartment between the seats. Each weapon needed authorisation for the officers to wear, let alone use. Brandon had transferred from another force where the authorisation levels were different – less paranoid perhaps – but he knew, as well as Toster, that any use of any Home Office-approved weapon was potentially the end of his career. Such was the state of play.

'Sounds like a pile of shit to me.' Toster, the passenger, added the usual comment regarding most jobs the police had to deal with, even if it had grief potential.

'Yep.' Brandon wasn't particularly vocal, but was thinking exactly the same thing. 'Control, Lima-Victor four-four,' he spoke clearly into his personal radio. *Four- four go ahead.* 'ETA six minutes.' *Roger.*

Sergeant Mickle drove quickly but safely. It wasn't about getting there as fast as possible … it was about getting there. Within three minutes he was pulling up outside the door of 84 Mallard Way, parking his car conspicuously outside, right next to PC Guest's car.

The front door was pulled to, and as he approached it, PC Guest opened it wider. 'Hi Sarge, quick word outside.'

Sergeant Mickle stood by the front door and listened intently, getting his notebook and pen out in case he needed it.

'They got you down here because the female inside – her name is Mrs Doreen Lipton, aged fifty-three – is disabled and needs professional help in leaving the house. Er, and by "disabled" I mean she weighs

PC Michael Pinkstone

nearly forty-eight stone and is unable to be moved unless there's a team on hand. Either that or a fucking crane.' PC Guest shook his head and continued.

'I've been here before too, Sarge. Last week in fact. Domestic non-recordable. Husband is a Geoff Lipton, aged fifty-two. Apparently he's gone off the rails recently and has barely been home. Looks like he's taken his gun with him this time.'

Sergeant Mickle made a couple of notes in his book. 'What's the nature of this threat?' he said with a frown. 'What's this about her brother?'

'Well, Geoff phoned her about half an hour ago while I was here dealing with something else, to say that he wasn't feeling himself, and that her brother was going to get it in the head. He's never liked her brother and she really thinks he's going to do something stupid.'

'I understand she hasn't been able to contact her brother at all?' Sergeant Mickle could feel the situation already escalating somewhat, even though he'd dealt with stuff like this before. Threats to kill usually ended up being piles of crap, but you couldn't rule anything out in this world. One thing was for certain – this wasn't going to be a quick job. And his gut feeling was that it would end up being a whole pile of grief, whatever the outcome.

'Nope. No contact by phone or anything. She hasn't spoken to him for a few days anyway, but there's no answer on his house phone and his mobile appears to be switched off. Same for Geoff's mobile now too.'

Sergeant Mickle puffed out his cheeks and stared at his pocket book. 'OK mate, I'll go inside and speak to the female. Could you keep watch on the door until the Lima-Victor unit get here. They won't be long. Oh, do we know if Mr Lipton has access to a vehicle?'

PC Guest looked on the back of his hand. 'Yes,' he said peering closely, 'he's got an old red Volvo, index Tango Victor Oscar, Five Zero Nine X-ray. I phoned control again before you arrived and they have it on the Log.'

Sergeant Mickle tucked his pocket book into his stab vest. 'OK mate, nice one. See you in a second.'

He was barely into the hall when two things happened simultaneously. Firstly, Lima Victor four-four arrived on scene and secondly he heard his call-sign on the radio again.

This Victorian Playground - Part 2

'Go ahead.' He leant against the wall and looked around him. The house was a tidy mid-terrace. He could see down the end of the hallway into the kitchen, and there was a large, arched opening to his left-hand side, that gave access to the lounge. He just about had a view of what looked like the edge of a sofa.

Sierra nine-one, to inform you that Lima Victor three-four are on the way to 55 Littleport Spur. ETA five minutes. They are accompanied by Mike Charlie five-one, who are in a plain vehicle to get eyeball. Awaiting update from the scene regarding description of the firearm and any other relevant information. Received?

Sergeant Mickle blew through his cheeks again. 'Yes, all received. About to make contact with the female now. Update soonest.'

He turned into the lounge and there, languishing on the sofa, was the most enormous woman he had ever seen. She looked like Jabba the Hutt in leggings. Swallowing back the urge to say something inappropriate, Sergeant Mickle sat down on a dining chair and looked as impassively as he could at the gargantuan shapeless lump with a head attached to it displayed in front of him. She was wearing what appeared to be a marquee.

'Hello officer.' It spoke. She had that wheezy, breathless voice that comes with having your internal organs crushed by so much blubber. 'Thank God you're all here. He's gone crazy and I think he's going to kill Michael!'

Sergeant Mickle, who had been doing the job for nearly eleven years, never failed to be amazed at the way people assumed that he knew all the background to their tragedies upon his immediate arrival in their lives. The number of times he'd turned up at a scene to find himself greeted with a comment such as, 'I want him out of my house!' or, 'You fucking coppers haven't done nuffink about them!' or even, 'He's been shagging Chantelle *again* and I'm sick of him – that's not right is it officer, is it? IS IT?'

Such people, he thought to himself, truly didn't know what the police force was all about. They assumed he'd turn up – automatically knowing exactly what was happening, where it was happening, who was shagging who, which kids belonged to which parent, the pet's name, every single address connected with the family and the sordid personal

PC Michael Pinkstone

histories of everyone involved – and be able to make an instant decision based entirely on the desires of the person who'd made the call in the first place, irrespective of any objectivity whatsoever. That was the trouble with being a police *service.*

He nodded at Mrs Doreen Lipton. 'Hello, I'm Sergeant Mickle.' Without waiting for a response, he continued. 'So, madam, I hear your husband may have a firearm. Could you expand on that please?' As soon as the phrase "expand on that" came out of his mouth he recoiled slightly, but he shouldn't have worried. Such plays on words – intentional or not – were lost on 99.9% of people he usually dealt with. Besides, they wouldn't expect such wit or intelligence from an officer of the law. I mean social worker. I mean agony aunt in a uniform.

Doreen nodded, which is to say that her several chins wobbled, in sequence, to create a rippling effect not unlike a Mexican Wave. Sergeant Mickle was transfixed for just a moment. 'Yes,' she said, once her facial flab had stopped undulating. 'He's got a shotgun that he uses for hunting birds. I don't know what make it is, but it's got two barrels and uses those red cartridge things. It's quite long and has a brown handle thing. Sorry I can't be more specific.'

Sergeant Mickle was impressed. It wasn't a bad description. He'd heard a lot worse than that. 'Do you have his certificate to hand?' He wanted to know exactly what kind of gun it was, just so he could update control with precise information. He knew it wasn't a semi-automatic something-or-other, but he did need to specify.

'Sorry officer, I don't think it's there. Your colleague, that nice young man who came here last week, has already looked. The cabinet is empty. He keeps his gun in there, as well as those cartridges and, as far as I know, all of his paperwork. There's nothing in there now.'

Sergeant Mickle got up. 'Whereabouts is the cabinet?' He didn't expect to be shown the way. Doreen raised a flabby arm to point. It was thicker than a telegraph pole. Certainly gave a new angle to the phrase "bingo wings".

'In the back room, officer.' She lowered her arm, which had clearly been an enormous effort to raise, as she sounded even more out of breath.

'Thanks, I'll just go and take a look.' Sergeant Mickle walked past the dining table and through a small door. The back room was a beautiful

This Victorian Playground - Part 2

wood-panelled study lined with books, which threw him slightly. On one wall was mounted a shotgun cabinet. The door was open and it was indeed empty. There was a writing desk behind him that was devoid of anything except an old-fashioned ink pot and pen stand. He tried to open the drawers but they were all locked. A further glance around the room gave him no further clues, so he made a phone call to control to update them on everything that he'd been able to establish so far, and walked back into the lounge. Doreen hadn't moved, surprisingly.

'Nice room that.' Sergeant Mickle's tone was light, but genuine, as he resumed his seat.

Doreen nodded again. 'Yes, officer. I haven't been in there for a while but he spends a lot of time in there. Well, he does when he's home. This past week he's been out for a lot of the time.'

'Does he work?' The Sergeant had his pocket book out again and was making notes.

Mrs Lipton shook her massive head, causing her multiform chins to knock into each other sideways – an effect not unlike Newton's Balls, observed Sergeant Mickle. 'No, he retired last year. He was a bus driver. Did it for thirty-two years.' She added the last bit proudly, if a little wistfully.

Sierra nine-one. 'Excuse me one moment,' said Sergeant Mickle politely. 'Go ahead?'

Nine-one, to update you. Three-four and five-one on scene at 55 Littleport Spur. No sign of a red Volvo. There is a green Mobility vehicle parked on the driveway. Comes back to a Michael Sandford of that address. Could you establish from the female the following information about her brother – his age, if and where he works, whether he drives his car regularly or not and who lives with him; children, etc. Received?

'Control, Alpha Lima one-five-one – can I come in?' The voice was that of PC Guest, who was outside with the armed crew.

Go ahead one-five-one. 'Yes, one-five-one, I have that information. The brother's date of birth is the tenth of May 1959. He's single and unemployed. So far?' *So far.*

'Yes, he's also got, er, a weight problem too, and has home care. He does have a Mobility vehicle but he hardly uses it any more due to failing health. According to the female at this address, his health has got

PC Michael Pinkstone

worse over the past few months and there has been a dramatic weight increase as a result. He can hardly move and is very likely to be inside the house. He has no wife or children. Received?'

That's all received one-five-one. Sierra nine-one did you copy? 'Yes, all copied.' Sergeant Mickle turned back to Mrs Lipton, having made some hurried notes in his pocket book. 'Doreen, I heard earlier that your husband isn't too fond of your brother. Is that correct? Is there anything else you can tell me about their relationship?'

As Doreen launched into a fairly well-rehearsed tale of her familial issues, PC John Bryant and PC Lisa Bell sat in their parked silver police vehicle two streets away from 55 Littleport Spur. They weren't happy bunnies. Five minutes passed with practically no conversation and no updates from anyone in the higher echelons.

'Always the same fucking thing.' PC Bell wasn't impressed. 'Why won't they let us just go and knock on the fucking front door?'

PC Bryant drummed the steering wheel with his fingers. 'I know,' he said with feeling. 'Fucking risk assessment bollocks.'

A car pulled up beside them. It was Mike Charlie five-one in their plain vehicle. Bryant pressed the window button and nodded at his colleagues. PC Matt Winter and Sergeant Andy Knight were the undercover traffic crew and they gave a succinct update.

'No fucking sign of this red Volvo.' Winter shrugged. 'I think we should do a door knock.'

Sergeant Knight nodded while he spoke. 'Gotta wait though, mate. The usual waiting game.' He looked directly at Bryant. 'Still no updates I guess then?'

Bryant shook his head with a look of disgust. 'Nope. But we have all we need. Some crazy old fucker with a shotgun. Got a lard arse of a wife. He's made a threat, over the phone, saying that his wife's brother will get it in the head, and we have to wait here like fucking idiots as usual.'

'By the sounds of it,' added PC Bell, 'both brother and sister are as bad as each other. Perhaps the husband is so fucked off with being married to that fat character from *Blade* that he's lashing out at her family in vengeance. Can't blame the fucker. Who'd want to be married to a shed-sized marshmallow? Be like trying to shag a pile of duvets.'

Lima Victor three-four receiving? 'Aha,' said PC Bryant, 'a decision at last. Shall we do our job or shan't we? Go ahead.'

Three-four, from the control room Inspector. Authority given for a door knock. No weapon authorisation at this time. Standard equipment applies. Lima Victor three-four only to conduct door knock. Received?

Suddenly – and before PC Bryant could respond – a muffled yell cut through the airwaves, shocking everyone who was tuned in. Faces turned to panic and everyone listened intently to find out who was in distress. Nothing of clarity could be heard except angry noises, the sound of a button being pressed over and over, distant shouts and scorching sounds.

'Fuck!' Bryant studied his radio screen, trying to see what number was coming up. The radios displayed the shoulder number of every officer using the system. This particular number was 635. Five seconds of silence. It felt like an eternity.

'635!' shouted Sergeant Knight. 'Who the fuck is 635?' His apparent anger really being frustration at feeling so helpless, and not knowing who was in trouble, or where. Suddenly a different voice cut through the airwaves, this time making more sense. *Assistance! Assistance! Mallard Way! Firearms!*

'Fuck me, that's Phil!' Sergeant Knight shifted into gear and sped off up the road with a squeal of tyres, closely followed by Bryant and Bell. This was a serious situation. A Sergeant calling for assistance. And there were firearms involved. *Fuck.*

Winter's heart raced as his Sergeant powered through the traffic with lights flashing and sirens blazing. Where the fuck were Lima Victor four-four? he thought to himself. Aren't they with Phil Mickle too? *Fuck.* This wasn't good.

* * *

'Well, officer, it's like this. My husband has disliked Michael since the day we started courting.' Doreen appeared to try to shift her position slightly, which had little effect. Her arse took up all three cushions of a large sofa and probably hadn't seen the light of day for a while.

How does she *shit*? Sergeant Mickle had so many questions running through his mind, and none of them were appropriate.

PC Michael Pinkstone

'Basically he blames Michael for my illness.' Doreen said this with a touch of finality and nodded knowingly to herself, her breath coming in wheezes and gasps. 'He blames Michael for my disorder.' She paused, as if for effect. In reality she was pausing to see what the good-looking officer sitting on her dining chair would say, but he just nodded solemnly and told her to carry on. In reality, he was wondering if she had a variety of household items concealed unwittingly in the rolls of her flab. He was imagining one day that she'd lift up a particularly large round of flesh and reveal the first three seasons of *Scrubs* on DVD, that had been missing for a year or so. The possibilities were endless and it was extremely difficult to concentrate on the story at hand.

'Go on, Mrs Lipton,' he said politely. 'You were saying that your husband *blames* your brother. How is this so?'

Doreen rolled her eyes. 'I don't really know *how* he can blame Michael. After all, it's a genetic illness. I simply put on weight without any effort whatsoever. I've always been that way, and so has Michael.'

Without any effort whatsoever? The Sergeant thought this was highly unlikely but it didn't show in his face. Instead, he made some more notes and gestured for Mrs Lipton to carry on.

'Well, in recent weeks Geoff has been going on about my weight a lot more than he used to. I mean, I was quite big when we met and he has always known about my disorder, but for some reason it seems to have been bugging him a lot since he retired.' Doreen sighed, which sounded like a large air bed being aggressively deflated, and patted the arm of the sofa absently. 'Michael had a go at him a few days ago because it was upsetting me and I think it's upset him.'

Sergeant Mickle nodded and continued jotting. 'Has your husband ever been violent towards you or anyone else that you know of? I mean, is being violent totally out of character for him?'

Doreen shrugged. Well, Sergeant Mickle assumed it was a shrug. Most of her minor facial expressions and involuntary body language movements were indiscernible. 'Yes,' she said at last. 'He's never hit me or even threatened me. He's always been a very peaceable character. Even his arguments with Michael have been just hot air. I knew he didn't like him but it was more of a mutual personality clash, or so I thought.' She paused, collecting her thoughts. 'I don't know, officer. He's just

This Victorian Playground - Part 2

been so out of sorts lately that I can't really get my head round it.'

You'd have difficulty getting anything round it, thought Sergeant Mickle to himself, as he made some final notes on page 54 and turned to the next.

As he did so, PC Guest walked in and greeted Doreen again warmly. She smiled wanly. 'I'm just telling him about Geoff and Michael,' she said with a hint of regret. 'I always wondered if this situation would come to a head.' She shook her head again, her jowls responding with a gentle ripple. 'I just don't know what's come into him.' Her voice trailed off dismally and she sat, staring in silence.

PC Guest looked at her kindly. He also turned to his Sergeant out of general politeness. 'Sarge,' he said, with a glance at Doreen. 'The chaps outside have been authorised to do a quick sweep of the estate. They aren't far away. They've also suggested that we, er, check the rest of the house.'

Doreen seemed to come out of some kind of reverie and laughed. 'There's nothing upstairs,' she exclaimed with a laugh. 'Well, there's two bedrooms and a bathroom, but nothing else. The spare bedroom is practically empty and the other bedroom is, well, it's just a bedroom.'

Sergeant Mickle was dying to ask the obvious questions about the sleeping arrangements and, of course, when was the last time she had actually been upstairs, let alone been intimate with her husband, but he didn't have to wonder for too long.

'I haven't been upstairs for two years now,' said Doreen, interrupting Phil Mickle's train of thought. 'I just sleep down here. On this sofa.' She sighed and placed her hands together across her hugely bloated stomach. 'I think Geoff isn't happy.'

* * *

'Where the fuck is Mallard Way again?' Sergeant Andy Knight was yelling as much to himself as to his crewmate. No officer ever wants to hear their friends and colleagues in distress. It's the worst part of their job. So the stress levels were running extremely high, especially as the last twenty seconds had been silent on the radio. No more updates or clues as to what had happened or what was going on. But someone didn't shout 'Assistance' and 'Firearms' for a joke.

PC Michael Pinkstone

Most gun crimes involve the shooting of scumbags by other scumbags, so to hear that a colleague might be in a deadly situation involving a firearm was not pleasing to the ear. Winter shouted directions above the sound of the sirens, and they were only a couple of minutes away ...

* * *

'He sounds like he needs some help,' replied Graham diplomatically. 'And we're here to support you too. I'm sure this situation will be resolved soon. He may just be drunk and saying silly things because he's angry about something.'

'But he doesn't drink!' Doreen was on the verge of tears now. She dabbed at her eyes with a fold of her voluminous clothing. 'I can't believe he'd actually *hurt* Michael.'

'Well,' Graham continued in his role of tactful social guardian. 'That's why we're here, Mrs Lipton – to help you and Michael, and to ensure Geoff doesn't harm anyone, or even himself. We have officers at Michael's house as we speak.' He paused, letting his words have some effect. 'All the same, Doreen,' he continued, 'if it's agreeable with you, we'd just like to check upstairs in case there is anything up there that can assist us in our enquiries.'

In truth, PC Guest was kicking himself. He hadn't checked upstairs anyway, which he really should have done in the first instance, and so was itching to rule out any potential of naughty Geoff hiding in a bedroom wardrobe and playing silly beggars. Stranger things had happened.

Doreen dabbed her eyes again. 'Of course,' she said, her voice cracked and broken. 'Do what you need to do, officers. I just want my Geoff back the way he was.' At this she finally broke, and started to cry softly, her enormous body shaking ever so slightly as her emotions overcame her.

Graham moved instinctively closer to bridge the gap and spoke gently. 'We'll just be a moment. Perhaps give you a chance to gather yourself, eh? After that I'll pop the kettle on. When I was here last week I recall you enjoyed that green tea?'

His words obviously soothed Mrs Lipton, who smiled through her tears and nodded.

This Victorian Playground - Part 2

'OK, we'll be back down in a sec. Just got to cover all the bases. You know how it is in this life.'

Doreen nodded again, a little more firmly. 'I know,' she said with a sniffle. 'You've got to do your job at the end of the day.'

Sergeant Mickle got up and followed PC Guest into the hallway. 'Just want to quickly check the kitchen and garden, mate,' he said, turning left into the kitchen. A swift glance around told him that nothing was amiss. He walked through the kitchen into a utility area with a door on his left leading to the garden, and a larger door leading to what turned out to be a converted toilet.

The room had clearly been extended on one side to make it much more ample, and was tiled from top to bottom, with a drainage hole in the middle. It had an oversized toilet on one side and a large showerhead protruding from the ceiling. Clearly it enabled someone of a hefty build to shower and shit with some degree of efficiency and minimal mess, thought Phil to himself as he closed the door behind him. Geoff had obviously done his best to cater for his slightly plump spouse.

A brief glance outside revealed a small and tidy garden, with panelled fencing on either side and a thick, tall hedge at the end. Beyond this were some school playing fields.

Walking back inside, it came home to both officers that the house was immaculately kept. 'He certainly keeps this place spick and span,' murmured Graham to his Sergeant as they walked through the spotless kitchen, back past the lounge archway, and onto the stairs.

'What a life though, eh?' retorted Sergeant Mickle under his breath as they climbed upwards. Graham nodded and made a noise at the back of his throat.

'You just couldn't do it, could you?' His response made his Sergeant grin as they walked onto a small landing, to be faced with three closed doors.

At the top of the stairs was the bathroom which, like all the other rooms in the house so far, was very clean and shiny. The bath and sink gleamed and the toilet bowl shone as if newly polished. Everything seemed to be neatly in its place, including the little bottles of shampoo and aftershave arranged pleasingly on the shelf underneath the window.

'Busting for a piss,' muttered PC Guest, as his Sergeant left the room. He pushed the door to, and knelt down in front of the toilet to

PC Michael Pinkstone

avoid spraying or spilling. Being well over six feet he had found it much easier to do this, as it negated any chance of weeing either side of the toilet, which was especially worrying in someone else's house.

He finished and washed his hands, making sure he wiped the sink after using it. Something about the fastidiously impeccable state of the bathroom made him think that Geoff would notice the tiniest alteration to how he'd left it.

As he walked out, he turned to his right, and entered the master bedroom. It was quite a large, airy room and looked out onto the street. The double bed was covered in a cream coloured duvet and was neatly made. On one side was a small wooden cabinet, upon which sat a bedside lamp and a pair of reading glasses. To the left of the bed was a wardrobe filled with orderly hanging clothes and tidily folded jumpers and fleeces.

On the other side of the bed, below the window, was a chest of drawers containing underwear and socks and some miscellaneous items in the bottom. There was nothing else in the room to suggest anything out of the ordinary. So far, they had no real clues as to why Geoff was behaving in such a fashion – if, of course, he was behaving in such a fashion at all.

For many cases such as this resulted in the alleged potential offender being confronted by police officers, only to be completely bemused as to what the fuss was all about. '*She said what?*' or '*He said what?*' being a regularly used phrase by a spouse, upon finding out that their other half had made extraordinary allegations against them, and about their mental state. 'I think you'll find that *they* are the ones who you need to be worried about, officer!' being another well-worn reaction.

You just couldn't beat tit-for-tat one-upmanship in relationships gone wrong, thought Sergeant Mickle as he took one last cursory look around the room. If he had a pound for every time someone blew something way out of proportion – husbands and wives trying to get one over on each other, especially when it came to divorce settlements or custody of the children – he wouldn't need to work again! Also, getting someone "Done For Harassment" was a great way to prove victim status nowadays, and ensure the best possible outcome to a messy separation. How much police time was wasted in trying to solve people's domestic

This Victorian Playground - Part 2

problems for them? He sighed inwardly. What a fucking shambles ... He was woken out of his thoughts by PC Guest noisily trying the door to the third room, and finding it was securely locked.

'Fuck.' Graham knocked instinctively on the door. 'Geoff, if you're in there, stop playing silly beggars and come out, mate!' Sergeant Mickle joined his colleague by the door and pressed his hand to the top and the bottom. It felt pretty solid. The lock also seemed pretty tough and the door clearly needed quite a goodly use of force to open without the key.

'We need to open this really.' Sergeant Mickle pushed against the door hard with his shoulder. It gave slightly but needed much more effort.

'I'll just see if Doreen has a key or knows of its whereabouts.' Graham went back downstairs and Sergeant Mickle waited, pondering the situation. As he stood there, his phone rang. It was the Inspector. There was nothing further that either of them could think of, so the Inspector informed the Sergeant that he was shortly about to authorise a door knock at Littleport Spur. 'I agree, Boss,' said Sergeant Mickle over the phone. 'There's not a lot else we can do at present. The mobile phones appear to be switched off so we can't trace them that way. The only trouble, of course, is the fact that we can't take Doreen or Michael with us, without some form of specialist help. It may yet come to that of course.'

The Inspector agreed and told Sergeant Mickle that the next step was to ensure the welfare of Michael Sandford, now that all the available intelligence had been gained and analysed. One step at a time.

As soon as Sergeant Mickle had hung up, Graham came back up the stairs. 'She hasn't got a key.' he said to his skipper. 'In fact, she didn't even know the room had a lock on it. But she doesn't mind if we bust the door in.'

* * *

'No fucking sign of the bastard.' Andy Toster knew it would be like this. 'The fucker is probably round a mate's house getting pissed and winding his missus up.'

Brandon agreed, and nodded grimly. They'd been driving slowly round the immediate area of Mallard Way for nearly ten minutes and there was no sign of life at all. The usual *area search, no trace* scenario.

PC Michael Pinkstone

It was a very quiet residential area, and at 2 pm on a school day, was pretty deserted. 'Well mate, we'll just go back to the house and await updates.' Brandon turned the car around and turned left into Mallard Way. Number 84 was down the far end, around the corner.

* * *

'It's your turn.' Sergeant Mickle patted Graham on the back. 'I did the last one, remember. Nearly broke my fucking ankle in the process!'

Graham sized the door up. A few good kicks should do the trick. He took a step back and kicked the door firmly with his heel, as near to the lock as possible. It shuddered and the wooden frame warped slightly.

He kicked it again, this time a lot harder. The wood around the lock began to splinter and the panelling of the door split. Graham took another step back.

His final kick sent the door flying inwards, bits of the shattered frame following it inside the room.

The first impression was of a dark space, and both officers stepped inside, with Sergeant Mickle following PC Guest. With the door open wide and the two officers finally having full view of the "spare bedroom", a low whistle escaped involuntarily from Graham's lips.

'Oh fuck. Oh *fucking fuck*.' Phil Mickle turned and began to run towards the stairs, his hand reaching towards his radio button. As he did so, he heard a sound like a firework from downstairs somewhere, and the front door blasted inwards simultaneously, pieces of splintered wood landing in the hallway and up the stairs.

He'd only just reached the end of the landing, but dived backwards in desperation onto the floor. There was no doubt what had taken the door off its hinges. In blind panic he felt his fingers reach for his radio button again. Graham was already pressing his, and he was also on the floor. Between them they couldn't manage to relay any message whatsoever.

An angry voice, shouting loud enough to wake the dead, downstairs on the street outside. "DOREEN! YOU FAT FUCKING SLAG! I'M GONNA FUCKING KILL YOU AND ALL THE COPS WHO DARE COME ROUND MY HOUSE!'

This Victorian Playground - Part 2

Another loud blast and part of the doorframe hung loosely from the wall, chunks of plaster and brick flying everywhere. Stray bits of gunshot buried themselves in the walls of the hallway, ripping pictures from their hooks and smashing the glass panels of the kitchen door.

'*Assistance! Assistance! Mallard Way! Firearms!*' Finally Sergeant Mickle managed to get his message over the airwaves, as he crawled desperately over to where Graham had dived, his body half out of the spare bedroom they had entered only moments before.

'He's a fucking nutter!' PC Guest yelled above the noise of the third blast from the shotgun that shredded through the hallway. As he said this, he glanced yet again at the room around him. It was *full* of guns. They were mounted on the walls like trophies. This place wasn't a *spare bedroom* – it was a fucking armoury. This guy was a serious firearm fanatic, and by the look of it, he'd taken a few weapons with him, judging by some empty hooks on the walls.

A fourth blast cut through the air, followed by the sound of squealing tyres. Then a dreadful crashing sound. 'Fuck, FUCK!' Sergeant Mickle crawled along the landing carpet towards the master bedroom. 'Stay there!' he shouted to Graham, who was still prostrated in the doorway of the spare bedroom. Half getting to his feet, Sergeant Mickle made a quick dash into the master bedroom. He dived over the bed, rolling clumsily off the other side and crashing into the chest of drawers beneath the window. He could hear shouts and screams from the street outside and, above the yells, that same angry voice.

'YOU FUCKING COPPER SCUM! I'M GONNA BLOW YOUR FUCKING ARMS AND LEGS OFF. LOOK AT YOU! FUCKING USELESS PRICKS. BRING IT ON, FILTH!'

Phil Mickle grabbed the top of the chest of drawers, and pulled himself with trembling hands slowly up to window level. He couldn't quite see what was happening, so edged himself cautiously to the side, and a little higher, and managed to peer outside through the curtains.

On the opposite side of the road he saw a silver vehicle with a shattered windscreen in someone's front garden. It had gone straight through a low brick wall. Steam was coming from the engine and a few feet away, wearing green combat trousers and holding a shotgun, was a short, stocky, middle-aged man with grey hair. Strapped onto his back were two more guns, lethal-looking and black in colour, and he looked like he had some kind of utility belt on, loaded with what looked like grenades and … *fuck.*

Another blast from the shotgun, aimed directly at the car. Sergeant Mickle couldn't see anyone in the front seat. Both doors were open. Then he saw PC Andy Toster, miraculously alive, cowering behind the back of the car. There was no sign of Brandon anywhere. '*Fuck!*'

The man with the guns – it could only be Geoff – took a couple of paces forwards. He seemed unruffled, and his movements were slow and precise. 'You fucking weasels!' His voice cut through the air like a discordant note, sending more waves of panic through Sergeant Mickle.

The shotgun was smoking and Geoff calmly loaded two more cartridges into it, the others falling to the floor – their contents mostly buried in the police car. Sergeant Mickle could see Toster move back further behind his vehicle. He had nowhere else to hide and it was far too risky to make a dash for it anywhere else.

Geoff lowered his gun and pointed it towards the rear end of the shot-ridden vehicle. 'Come on out, you fucking cowards! Bring it on!'

* * *

As soon as they heard the sounds of disorder over the airwaves, both Brandon and Toster thought that it was coming from Littleport Spur. They had just turned into Mallard Way and Brandon slowed down, staring intently at his radio screen and listening in utter silence. When Phil Mickle shouted for assistance Brandon knew that things had gone tits up.

Mallard Way was curved and Brandon accelerated as hard as he could, screeching round the corner towards the house they had only recently left. As the house hove into view, the car doing at least 50 mph, both officers saw him at the same time, standing in the middle of the road, a shotgun aimed in their direction. He was only metres away.

'What the fuck!' Toster screamed as they roared towards the man with the gun. He dived to his right, trying desperately to get his head below the level of the windscreen. Brandon's arm was knocked, as he braked simultaneously, and the car veered sideways, and not a moment too soon, as a blast from the shotgun caught the top of the windscreen,

This Victorian Playground - Part 2

raining tiny, lethal, razor-sharp bits of glass upon the police officers inside. The car swerved with a screech of tyres into a wall, half mounting it, half destroying it, and came to a rest in the middle of a garden.

Both airbags inflated, reducing the risk of Toster and Brandon impacting dangerously on the dashboard, and they bounced back into their seats, flung about like rag dolls with the sudden change of momentum.

Sounds, panic, smoke. A roaring noise in his ears. Toster released his seatbelt without realising and half toppled out of the car, landing on some neatly cut grass. His head was pounding and his hands were sticky with blood.

To his right, Brandon somehow did the same. He was less dazed. Acting on pure instinct he opened his door and scrambled out, keeping as low as possible. They were sitting ducks in the car. No time to get anything out of it either. They were unarmed, except for their Captor spray. Crawling on his hands and knees round the steaming bonnet, he saw Toster crouched on the ground, stunned and bleeding.

'We need the fucking hand-held mini metal detector!' Toster choked out the words, coughing and wincing in pain. As he did so he began to crawl in desperation towards the back of the car. He knew he'd stashed his metal detector somewhere in his kit bag, which was wedged between the cones in the boot. It was the only way out of this mess. He also knew that Brandon's was broken, and he'd been waiting a couple of weeks for a replacement, so they only had one between them. They'd risk-assessed it, and decided that it was still safe to go out together. Fool! he thought to himself, knowing that this decision could cost them their lives. Suddenly he heard the sound of gunfire and glass shattering over his head, and he ducked, swearing loudly.

Where is that fucker? Toster reached the rear wheel arch, his heart thumping. He poked his head cautiously past the light cluster and there, about ten metres away, in the middle of the road, stood that man with a shotgun. He wasn't moving and seemed to be laden with weapons of some description. *Fuck.* Can't open the boot without getting shot at.

The man shouted something, but Toster was too dazed to hear it properly. He could hear noises in his radio too – the odd siren blast, people saying call signs, static. He moved backwards and the man yelled again. My god, thought Toster to himself, if ever I needed that fucking

PC Michael Pinkstone

hand-held mini metal detector, I need it now. The best bit of kit since the Self-Defined Ethnicity Chart and I can't even fucking get at it.

***

'Mallard Way! Mallard Way! You've fucking gone past it!' Winter swore loudly as his Sergeant screeched to a halt and made a hurried turn in the road. Bryant and Bell didn't miss the turning, and skidded left into the relevant street. They had arrived in less than three minutes and their hearts beat loudly in their chests as they waited to see what kind of chaos they would find.

***

Fuck. Sergeant Mickle could see that Geoff was a man to be reckoned with. Laden with serious firepower and a psychotic resolve, he wasn't going to be easy to bring down. *Fuck*! he thought to himself again as he realised that his hand-held mini metal detector was in the glove box of his car. Hadn't he been encouraged to keep it on his person at all times? Now he realised why they had all been issued them. Now he realised that when the shit was hitting the fan, there was only one thing that would do the business. He'd laughed at them to start with, and had completed the online training package by clicking lazily on whichever answers seemed best at the time, and now, in this life-or-death situation he found himself in, he knew that he'd been a damned fool.

'Have you got your metal detector with you?' he yelled through the doorway to Graham, hoping above all hopes that at least a PC on his team would be armed with something better than a nasty spray and a short metal stick.

'No! It's in the fucking car!' PC Guest's voice was high-pitched, panicky, extremely strained. 'What the fuck is going on outside?'

Sergeant Mickle's heart was racing. His chest was tight and his hands were sweating profusely. 'He's just standing in the middle of the fucking road pointing a gun at Toster and Brandon! He's not moving!'

A noise behind him made Sergeant Mickle jump out of his skin. Graham was crawling into the room, his face white with dread. 'They've

This Victorian Playground - Part 2

crashed the car,' said Sergeant Mickle, not really knowing what he was saying. 'I think they're OK – just hiding behind it.' He paused, holding back the curtain with a shaking hand. 'I hope to fuck they've got their hand-held mini metal detectors with them.'

'They'd have used them by now, surely!' Graham joined his Sergeant at the window. As he did so, Geoff began to move slowly to his left, so that he could see more of the rear end of the prostrate police car, the gun still lowered and ready to fire. Toster and Brandon were nowhere in sight, obviously hidden out of view on the blind side of their vehicle.

'WE NEED A UNIT WITH A HAND-HELD MINI METAL DETECTOR HERE NOW!' Mickle yelled into his radio, his voice reaching fever pitch. Geoff looked up, having heard him. Not seeing anything through the lace curtains, he continued edging gradually to his left to get a better view of his quarry, who were still cowering behind their car, desperately contemplating their options.

* * *

PC Bryant screeched into Mallard Way, losing the back end slightly, but still maintaining course. He had heard Phil Mickle's last update half a minute earlier, and his heart raced. The shit really was hitting the fan! Instinctively he thought of his kit bag too. His hand-held mini metal detector was in there – slightly low on battery power, but it would do. Surely it would be enough to see them through this? Was there any time left?

* * *

'I can see you fuckers!' Geoff had edged around enough to catch a glimpse of Toster and Brandon, pressed up against the side of the car. He knew that they had nowhere to run. and he was taking his time. He was enjoying his moment of glory.

On his back were strapped two automatic assault rifles. Capable of firing multiple rounds. Devastating and highly illegal. He'd never used them before. Only stared lovingly at them, and cleaned them daily with a fanatical dedication, while his fat fucking wife slobbed it on the sofa

PC Michael Pinkstone

downstairs, gorging herself on thousands of calories that she had ordered him to get for her, in the form of junk food. Still, he thought to himself, as he polished and oiled every moving part, it stops her from coming upstairs to my private room. *My* room. *My* kingdom.

He smiled to himself as he edged a little closer to get a better view of his prey. He could see a booted leg, pulled up close towards the body. It wasn't moving. Ah yes! What was that? A head – *two* heads in fact. One more sidestep and he finally got the eyeball he needed, and so far his fire had not been returned. He'd expected a better fight than this. How fucking typical, he thought, as he studied the two men crouched together, clearly unable to come up with any plans whatsoever. There you are, you fucking weasels!

'Hello gentlemen!' His voice was light and conversational. 'I'm going to fucking kill you both.'

* * *

Toster and Brandon were out of options. Their best hope was to negotiate. Neither of them had any available firearm and, more pressingly, neither of them had immediate access to their force-issue hand-held mini metal detectors. The situation was grim, and the best they could hope for was the imminent arrival of their colleagues. At least, then, the odds might swing in their favour. As their breath came in short, frantic gasps, they realised now that it was perhaps too late. '*I'm going to fucking kill you both.*'

Toster looked to his left. There he was, the man with the gun. The man with the *guns*. He was quite short, and well built. His hair was cropped and grey, and his face gave nothing away.

Toster raised both hands involuntarily, palms outwards. It was a sign that he had no weapon, and that he was at the mercy of his assailant. His voice was thick and strained.

'Sir, we are unarmed. We have no weapons.' Toster had no idea if he was saying the "right" thing. His mind was putty.

'Keep both hands exactly where they are, and your fucking colleague too.' Geoff spoke clearly and carefully, savouring this moment. Two police officers at his mercy and no sign of anyone else yet. Still, he contemplated,

This Victorian Playground - Part 2

I'll be able to hear the other fuckers coming a mile off. In fact, he'd already heard the sirens, but they were still a minute or two away. He'd have plenty of time to get his hostages into the house. Perfect.

'Now get up slowly with your hands in the air. Any sudden moves and I'll pump you so full of lead you'll never get through Heathrow security again in your lives.'

PC Brandon and PC Toster got slowly, and awkwardly, to their feet, with their trembling hands raised above their heads. Geoff could see in an instant that they had no weapons on them, except their kit belts containing the Captor spray and short metal sticks. Plus empty holsters for the firearms they were occasionally authorised to use, but not authorised to carry. The sirens were getting closer.

'Very, very slowly,' he said, keeping his composure, 'with your left hands only, undo your kit belts and let them fall to the floor by your feet.' He was standing only a few metres away from them, pointing a loaded shotgun in their direction. There was no-one else around. The few residents who had heard and seen the commotion were in their own homes, frantically calling the police. They weren't venturing outside.

* * *

'Fuck. Oh fuck.' Sergeant Mickle could see that Toster and Brandon had no choice but to comply. He saw Toster raise his hands and then watched as they both stood up slowly and undid their kit belts, which fell to the floor around their ankles.

He could also hear the sound of sirens. They sounded close, but he knew that the noise carried for miles. There was no way of telling exactly how far away his colleagues were. The radio had also been quiet. Everyone tuned into the channel was waiting with bated breath to find out what would happen. Police officers across the area had thrown down whatever they were doing and run to the nearest available car. Some had piled in four or five up. Some were in plain vehicles. Some weren't even in uniform, but they were on the way, and they had their mini metal detectors clutched firmly in their hands. The poo was hitting the blower and they were ready for action. Kitted up to the max and pumping with adrenaline.

PC Michael Pinkstone

Suddenly Geoff turned and looked straight at him. That is to say, he turned and looked at the upstairs window. The top one was open for ventilation and Sergeant Mickle heard the shout quite clearly from across the street.

'ANY FUCKING OFFICERS IN MY HOUSE WILL BE IN THE LOUNGE WITH MY FAT FUCKING USELESS WIFE BY THE TIME I GET IN THERE, OR I'LL BLOW THESE FUCKERS AWAY.'

Sergeant Mickle's heart rate increased even more and he realised he was numb all over. He watched, dazed for a moment, as Geoff appeared to say something to Toster and Brandon, and then saw all three of them walk towards the house across the road, with Geoff at the side of the two officers, pointing the gun directly at them.

'GET DOWNSTAIRS!' he yelled to Graham, who was also watching, clearly terrified, and the pair of them turned and ran out of the room, across the landing, and legged it down the stairs into the lounge.

They ran in and stood, shaking, by the dining table. Doreen was still on the sofa. Could she be anywhere else? Graham looked at her, and she saw that his face was pure horror. She appeared to have shifted position somewhat – perhaps tried to get up, but the effort and the fright had been too much. Graham noticed a pungent smell. Had she crapped herself?

At that moment Andy Toster and Sam Brandon walked into the room, with their hands on their heads. As soon as they entered, they walked towards their colleagues and sat on the floor, still with their hands on their heads. Sergeant Mickle and PC Guest began to lower themselves in the same fashion, when Geoff walked in, still pointing the gun in their direction. He pulled the curtains and shut the lounge door. He then looked at the four police officers sitting in a row in front of him, each with their hands on their heads, and across at his terrified wife, and smiled.

'I guess we made it just in time.' Geoff looked casually at his watch as the sound of the sirens grew extremely loud, followed by the roar of an engine and the screeching of tyres outside the house. Backup had arrived. But were they too late?

* * *

This Victorian Playground - Part 2

Geoff looked directly at Phil Mickle. 'Tell them on the radio that if anyone enters this house, people will die. Do it now.'

Sergeant Mickle put a shaking hand to his radio. With the button pressed he said quickly and frantically, words all stumbling over each other, 'No-one come in the house! No-one come in the house! We're hostages. No-one in the house! Repeat, NO-ONE IS TO COME IN THE HOUSE!' He stopped and looked across at the mad gunman, hoping above all hopes that he hadn't made a blunder.

Geoff smiled again. 'Hostages!' he said. 'I like that. Now you've got their attention, tell them that I am here pointing a gun at you all and I will update them as to my demands later.'

Phil pressed his radio button again and spoke nervously. 'We are being held hostage by a man with a gun. He will update you later with what he wants. Please no contact with me for the moment. I repeat. We are being held hostage by a man with a gun. He will update you later with what he wants. Please no contact with me for the moment.' He put his hand back on his head, not even sure if he'd made any sense. No contact with me for the moment? He didn't even know what he'd meant by that.

'So,' said Geoff casually, after a short pause, looking nonchalantly at the four silently fearful officers before him. 'Have you been inside my special room yet?' He grinned maniacally at them, the gun shaking slightly in his hands as if he was suppressing the urge to laugh. 'That fat bitch,' he glanced to his right, 'has no fucking idea about my room because she ain't been upstairs for nearly two years!' He glared at the distressed lump on the sofa. 'Isn't that right you fat fucking cow?'

Without waiting for a response from anyone, he continued. 'I think you'll find it's a very, very fascinating den of iniquity.' He paused, enjoying every bit of what was happening.

'There's all sorts of, er, *slightly* illegal weapons in there, including these two bad boys.' He gestured to his back, where he had strapped on the two rather lethal-looking guns. Phil Mickle and Graham Guest had no idea what they were, but Toster and Brandon could see that they were some kind of fully automatic assault rifles. Fully loaded and extremely deadly. How the fuck did he get hold of those? Toster could only stare in disbelief at what he was seeing. This guy was a fucking nutter.

PC Michael Pinkstone

Geoff looked at his watch again. 'I think we'll give them a few minutes to stew outside. Why don't we all have a cup of tea?'

* * *

PC Bryant and PC Bell squealed to a halt outside the house. They could see the front door hanging off its hinges and the damaged brickwork surrounding the frame. To their left was an apparently empty police vehicle, stranded in someone's garden – its front end all smashed up, with bricks and bits of mortar scattered all over the pavement behind it.

Absorbing the scene in a couple of seconds left PC Bryant breathless. He couldn't see a soul. His heart thumped as he looked in desperation for any sign of life. The radio was also quiet. What the fuck was going on?

No-one come in the house! No-one come in the house! Bryant jumped out of his skin, as he heard his colleague shouting frantically over the airwaves. He recognised Phil's voice straight away because he had joined up with him, and revved the engine loudly, speeding away from the house, turning quickly in the road to face the front door, about thirty-odd metres away. The next update from his colleague made his blood run cold – a *hostage* situation. They needed some specialist help and they needed it *now*.

* * *

'Nice equipment, this.' Geoff turned one of the police radios over in his hand. 'Think I might keep it for my private collection.' He laughed to himself and threw it onto the floor beside him.

He'd made all the officers take off their radios and push them across the floor towards him. All except Sergeant Mickle, who still wore his clipped to his stab vest.

PC Guest, meanwhile, was in the kitchen, filling up the kettle with shaking hands. *The guy was insane.* How can you reason with someone like that? He'd told Graham, quite calmly, to go into the kitchen and make five cups of tea and a cup of hot chocolate with six sugars in it for his "slightly overweight bride". He'd also told Graham that if he tried

This Victorian Playground - Part 2

any funny business, he'd fire his shotgun into the three officers sitting in front of him.

As he placed the kettle on the side and switched it on, he thought that there could be no peaceful solution to this crisis. They were shit out of options. The best thing to do was to keep him talking. Perhaps find a link. Find something to latch onto. Who knows? It could work. Maybe appeal to something deep inside Geoff's troubled mind and make him see sense.

No. That ain't gonna fucking happen. Graham shook his head and opened the cupboard to get the cups out. He knew where they were as he'd been here before only a week previously. On that occasion things were so different ...

'So, Mrs Lipton. Has your husband ever placed his hands around your neck?' PC Guest ticked each box on the requisite Risk Assessment Form. This bit of paper was a life-saver, so he had been told. He was led to believe that filling it in correctly could mean the difference between life or death for a human being and here he was – completing it with a human being who weighed more than a people-carrier. Nevertheless, quality of service extended to everyone, not just people who could see their own feet.

He barely listened to the answers she gave. She rambled on so much! Most of her responses were vague and noncommittal. What difference does a fucking form make anyway? Still he did what he had to do and got her to sign it. Thank goodness she did that, he thought, as he got a spoon out of the drawer.

Once she'd made her mark he had gone into the kitchen and made a cup of tea for them both. That was last Thursday. Now here he was again making tea for five people and ... a hot chocolate.

Geoff hadn't asked her what she'd wanted. He'd made all the decisions in the lounge a few moments ago. Graham couldn't blame her for not saying a word. The poor thing was terrified out of her skin, which amounted to a hell of a lot of terror.

He lined all the cups up, his mind whirling. Instinctively he opened the drawer by the sink to get a teaspoon out. Never had he made tea under such pressure before. Never had he made *hot chocolate* under such pressure before. He opened a cupboard above the cutlery drawer.

PC Michael Pinkstone

There was the hot chocolate. He removed it and put several spoonfuls into the largest cup. Geoff had insisted that his wife had enough drink to "satisfy her extensive needs". The words were still ringing in his head. The guy had gone beyond redemption.

As he pulled teabags from the container by the kettle he almost leaped out of his skin when he heard Geoff calling from the lounge.

'Officer in the kitchen! Officer in the kitchen! My wife would also like some chocolate sprinkles on her drink. You'll find them in the cupboard in the corner – the one with the photograph on it ... The photograph of, er, better times ...' The voice trailed off, cackling.

PC Guest called out, 'Er, OK,' cringing slightly. He kept his voice as light as possible, not wanting to aggravate what was already an extremely tense situation. He walked to the fridge and got the milk out. Tea first, then hot chocolate and then ... chocolate sprinkles. He shook his head again, hands still shaking at the bizarre horror of his situation.

* * *

'No units to scene! No units to scene! Officers en route to complete road closure of Mallard Way junction with Gravel Drive!' PC Bryant spoke loudly into his radio, hoping that he too was making sense. He could feel the pressure upon him, increasing with every second that passed.

Sergeant Knight, who had followed closely behind Bryant and Bell down Mallard Way, reversed at high speed to at least thirty metres away as well. He didn't want to give the gunman any indication that anyone was about to burst in through the door. Contain the area and wait for the negotiator. Wait for the updates from above. Wait for everyone else to arrive. Although several units were still on the way to assist, this incident would be controlled from one person at the scene, liaising directly with the commanders over the phone. And as he was the most senior ranking officer at the scene at present, he would have to either assume responsibility, or delegate. Owing to the firearms' element, he knew that Bryant and Bell would be more knowledgeable about the correct way to handle the situation.

Within two minutes the squeal of brakes and the mounting of kerbs announced the arrival of several more police vehicles – the officers

This Victorian Playground - Part 2

holding back in Gravel Drive, awaiting orders from above. They were unlikely to be used now that the circumstances were more apparent, but they might be needed for road closures and other forms of public protection. After all, the scene was in the middle of a residential area. They were sure that there were many very frightened citizens in their homes looking tentatively out of their windows. Mallard Way had just become a mini war zone, and now it was home to a hostage crisis. Not something that happened very often!

* * *

PC Graham Guest found a tray and began to load the cups onto it. Five cups with boiling water and tea bags, and another cup with hot chocolate he had made with the powder. Fortunately it was the mix-with-water kind, although he'd added milk to make it smoother. He'd also put six sugars in it as directed. Not that Geoff would be able to tell how many he'd put in, but he'd done it without even thinking.

As he removed the tea bags from each cup with a teaspoon, and put them in the bin situated in the corner, he thought again how bizarre this situation was, realising that his hands were shaking visibly. His mind awhirl, he put a splash of milk in each cup and placed the tin of sugar on the tray as well. He could hear Geoff talking in the other room and the sound of short replies from his colleagues and, for the second time, jumped with fright as Geoff called out again.

'It's one cup with two sugars and the rest without. Oh, and however you take yours as well.'

Graham put two sugars into one of the cups, feeling his heart thumping even more. He suddenly felt all feverish and swooned slightly, putting his hands on the work surface to steady himself. *Keep it together, keep it together*, he muttered to himself, as he picked up the tray.

Feeling the cups rattling on the surface of the tray, he reached the kitchen door, only to realise, with a small rush of panic, that he'd forgotten the chocolate sprinkles. So, as gently as possible, he put the tray back on the side and walked to the cupboard with the photograph tacked onto it. The photo was a standard six by four and was slightly faded, showing a smiling Geoff with his arm around a much thinner Doreen. She was

PC Michael Pinkstone

still extremely big, but was on her feet, outside in a park somewhere, and smiling too. Graham reckoned the photo was about ten years old. He also couldn't remember whether it was here last week. His mind wasn't really working very well at present. *Chocolate sprinkles,* he said to himself, as he opened the door.

* * *

'I think it's about time we gave them another quick update, Sergeant.' Geoff looked casually across at Phil who was still sitting there with his hands on his head, his arms aching uncomfortably. 'Tell them that no-one is currently hurt but if I see any police officer within twenty metres of my house I will execute one of my hostages.'

At this, Doreen made a small, involuntary whimper. Geoff looked at her with utter disdain. 'Yes,' he said again, coldly. 'I will *execute* one of *my* hostages. And you, *wife*, are one of my hostages.' He looked back at Sergeant Mickle and smiled kindly, the change of tone and facial expression making Brandon shudder. This guy was seriously fucked up. How long had be been cracking for?

For a third time Phil pressed his button and spoke into his radio. 'From Sergeant Mickle, update at scene is that the, er, Mr Lipton, would like no police officers within twenty metres of his house please. All officers hold back please. Updates soonest.' Again he looked at Geoff, who nodded encouragingly.

'Nicely done,' said Geoff approvingly. He was sitting on the arm of a chair by the window, his gun resting across his left leg, which was folded across his right. He was completely in control. How long had he waited for this moment? He was born for this day – a day when he would make history and be able to finally put his guns to good use. After all, a gun was made for shooting bullets into flesh, and he would certainly be doing that today. Oh yes. He even felt his eyes mist over at the enormity of it all. He shook his head, as if to clear himself of any emotional thoughts that would hinder his quest, and called out loudly.

'You got an ETA on that tea in there, officer?' He spoke in that slightly higher-pitched voice people used so as not to cause offence. Not that he cared about causing offence. After all, he had a loaded gun

This Victorian Playground - Part 2

pointing at people.

Graham pulled the cupboard door towards him slowly. He was listening to his Sergeant updating on the radio, staring intently for some reason at the screen of his own radio. When Geoff's voice cut through his concentration he felt that now familiar surge of fresh panic.

'Won't be a second!' he called as casually as he could. 'Just getting the sprinkles.'

'Good lad.' Geoff spoke as if he was addressing a son, perhaps unaware that his unruffled behaviour really was quite terrifyingly disturbing.

The shelf he saw first was full of cooking stuff. Little bottles and jars and packets of powders and mixes. He couldn't see the chocolate sprinkles anywhere. *Damn.* He moved some things out the way, feeling his cheeks flush as he knocked a couple of things over and made a noise. Still no sprinkles.

The shelf above contained tinned foods and various boxes of cereal, but nothing that looked remotely like chocolate sprinkles. *Damn.* He was getting quite flustered now.

He knelt down to the lower shelf, which was also full of stuff – mostly boxes of oddments unrelated to cooking. It surely wouldn't be there. Perhaps Geoff was winding him up?

On the floor of the cupboard was an old brown cardboard box with various wires sticking out of it, and he could see the handle of what looked like an old hairdryer. *Fuck.*

He looked again at the middle shelf, feeling like he'd been searching for ever. In reality, he'd only been looking for just under ten seconds, but it felt like an eternity. And suddenly he saw them, nestling behind a jar of peanut butter. *Chocolate sprinkles!* He reached in and picked them up, and ... hang on.

He felt his body tense, and then tingle with adrenaline, and he dropped the sprinkles back where they were. Blood rushed to his head, and he felt a hundred thoughts crowd into the middle of his mind, all clamouring for immediate attention. *Hang on ...*

That's not a hairdryer handle! He knelt down, shaking with suppressed excitement. With a trembling hand he took hold of the black handle and pulled out the object. It was dusty, and a couple of years old – probably broken knowing his luck – and certainly not police issue, but it would

PC Michael Pinkstone

do. It would surely give them a chance. It would be enough to at least create a distraction, perhaps even enough to get them out of the house.

PC Guest stared at the object in his right hand, heart beating madly. His face a picture of furious resolve. A new strength and vigour in his soul – a stark juxtaposition with the nervous tea-making from a few moments before. He stood up, determined. This was the hour of redemption. This was the hour of deliverance. This was the hour when worlds collided and the will to live stamped its desire upon the face of the earth like the impact of a fiery meteor. Who could stand in its path? Who could bear the brunt of its wrath? This was the hour and he was going to be a part of it.

Graham pressed the button with a trembling finger, and a green LED flickered, then fully illuminated. It worked! He held the object aloft and thanked the gods, like an ancient warrior with a mighty sword, standing upon the crest of glorious battle. He was no longer helpless and *this* was the time to act. For in his hand, he held with a grip of iron, his salvation, and the salvation of his colleagues. 'No man can challenge this!' said Graham out loud, not caring if he was heard.

Turning round and striding towards the kitchen door, ignoring the tea and those damn chocolate sprinkles, PC Graham Guest marched into the lounge to face his evil assailant, his right hand thrust in front of him with a confidence brought about by the best online training package he had ever done. He knew it now, and he'd never question it again.

As he came into the room, all heads turned, and hearts fluttered. Geoff instinctively raised his gun, snarling with rage. Doreen screamed, unsure as to why this officer was charging towards her husband with a short black thing in his hand. He would be killed!

'Put down your weapon!' Graham stood in front of Geoff, his body in a textbook stance. A picture of uncompromising gallantry, inspired by the best virtual instruction the police service could offer.

'Put it down!' he said again, tip to tip with a loaded shotgun, held by a crazed man who was half getting up and trying to back away. 'Comply with my request or I will take you down using reasonable force. I have a hand-held mini metal detector!'

* * *

This Victorian Playground - Part 2

Geoff saw him come in but couldn't quite believe what he was seeing. He almost fired his shotgun but realised that he couldn't. His fingers seemed stuck, and what the hell was that being pointed at him? Fuck! A damned mini metal detector!

He knew the police had been issued with them to tackle gun crime, for he kept abreast with all the news and views, but like many people he thought that they were yet again a complete waste of fucking time and money. Another indication of complete Governmental incompetence.

Hand-held mini metal detectors! He'd laughed to himself as he polished his weapons, thinking that the police would be totally out of their depth when he had his moment of glory, but now here he was – facing his *own* mini metal detector, and he could feel the power radiating from it, almost forcing his fingers away from the trigger! How on earth could this happen?!

He tried to stand up, but his body felt rigid. The metal detector was being pointed straight at his chest and the pain was excruciating. *Put down your weapon!* He had no choice! The gun was slipping from his leaden fingers and he tried to back away, the power of the hand-held mini metal detector overcoming him, his breath coming in gasps.

'No!' He was wrestling with greater demons and his mind raged in defiance. This moment had been so long coming and it was slipping away from him. A rush of hot anger coursed through him, and he felt some life back in his fingers. Although this was all happening in terms of seconds, he could feel every nuance; like he was living in slow motion. 'NO!' he cried again, the gun shuddering in his hands. The officer buckled in front of him – he could see his right leg give way, only slightly.

'Come on, Graham, hold the connection!' Brandon was beside him, his hand upon his back. Doing exactly what the training package said. The energy field was at its most effective with two people, but became unstable with three. Andy Toster and Phil Mickle were already on their feet, hearts ablaze with renewed hope. Doreen stared in horrified amazement, shaking with undiscovered emotion.

'NOOOO!' Geoff roared and slipped backwards, the gun still in his hands, but barely. The force of the metal detector was immense and his shotgun was vibrating so much he knew he couldn't hold it for much longer. Damn that officer! Damn him for getting so close with the metal

PC Michael Pinkstone

detector too! He knew it was at its most potent within a few feet, but he thought that this was purely to do with detecting metal. He had no idea it was a weapon all by itself! 'I WON'T SURRENDER!'

Now Brandon could feel it too, the hairs on the back of his neck sticking up as if he was charged with an electrical current. He could sense the pulses even through Graham's stab vest, so god knows what his body must be going through. The size of the gun certainly made a difference to the energy field, and so he channelled his thoughts; his mind must become one with the hand-held mini metal detector. Their foe was strong and heavily armed. This would be a fight to the death.

Suddenly a crackle of blue electricity shot between the metal detector and the gun, and the vibrations intensified, making Graham's face scrunch up with pain.

'Let ... go ... of ... the ... weapon!' He could barely get the words out, as the spark of blue became brighter and the end of his metal detector began to glow.

Geoff staggered back even more, hitting the wall by the lounge door, but somehow remaining upright. The shotgun was still pointing towards the officers, but he had not the strength to fire it. The metal detector was doing its work well. And as the electrical connection crackled and sparked, he could feel his shotgun heating up, burning the palms of his hands. 'ARRRGGGH!' He roared with mad frenzy, feeling his skin blister with tormenting pain. Smoke was rising from beneath him, and through the sizzling, burning heat he could see the outline of the two officers, immovable and resolute.

With a final yell of wrath, the gun was finally wrenched from his scorched fingers and slammed against the far wall, shattering into a million tiny fragments. At the same time, Graham and Brandon were thrown backwards, as if pulled by a powerful magnet, causing them to smack into their colleagues behind them. But Andy Toster and Sergeant Mickle were ready to catch them both. Part B, Section 10(a), of the online training package clear in their minds. Even though they had skimmed through the answers, scoffing at the seeming absurdity of it, they remembered the diagrams well, and stood with their arms out wide to scoop up their colleagues and minimise potential kickback injury. It was

This Victorian Playground - Part 2

textbook stuff, and Graham and Brandon were spared terrible wounds, for they would have surely gone walloping into the dining room table, perhaps even severing limbs.

Geoff was also thrown backwards, but he was already close to the wall. Instead he rebounded off it and fell forwards, moaning in pain, inhaling acrid smoke and seeing nothing but blurry shapes; hearing confident yells and triumphant shouts.

Instinctively he half got to his feet and lurched towards the lounge door and somehow stumbled through it, into the hallway, reaching behind him for another gun. He wasn't going to give up just yet. Behind him came further shouts, as the four police officers, tangled up with each other, realised their quarry was on the move.

Geoff scrambled towards the blasted front door and staggered through it, half pulling on the barrel of one of his guns, coughing and wheezing, and wincing in pain from the burns on his hand.

Behind him, four police officers were all trying to get through the lounge door at once – a mad scramble, heightened by lots of adrenaline and a determination to bring this situation to an end. They had the upper hand but now the pendulum was swinging slightly in the opposite direction.

Geoff managed to get to his feet and ran in a kind of bent-over totter towards the nearest police car. It was parked only a few metres away across the neatly trimmed grass of his front lawn, in front of another police car. He dived between the two vehicles, and not a moment too soon, as a blue bolt of electricity arced through the air and shattered the windscreen of the nearest car.

'Fuck me!' PC Bryant looked at the hand-held mini metal detector in his hand, scarcely believing its power. 'These things are fucking immense!'

He kept his aim from across the street, having seen Geoff stumble from the front door, his clothes smoking. Immediately he'd grabbed his metal detector and leaped out of the car. Even though he was thirty metres away he had a good line of sight and pointed the detector straight at the staggering body and said the required words.

'Comply with my request or I will take you down using reasonable force. I have a hand-held mini metal detector!'

PC Michael Pinkstone

Even as he said the words he wondered why he was saying them, as Geoff couldn't hear him. Those seemingly stupid clear verbal commands – required every time the police used force of any description! But it was what the online training package had demanded. He also knew that without saying the prescribed phrase he could land himself in a world of shit if this ever went to court. Those damn solicitors would certainly make mincemeat of him if he didn't follow procedure to the letter. Context would be treated with indifference by those blood-sucking scum.

But as soon as the words exited his mouth he finally understood their innate capability. They resonated from him with the force of a potent spell, and the electric bolt shot from the end of the metal detector immediately, for one was not complete without the other. No wonder those online packages were treated with such reverence! Those damn political fools were right after all!

'Bring it on, fuck-for-brains!' he said, adopting an American accent for effect, like a schoolchild in the playground, and aimed the detector anew, even though he couldn't see Geoff, who had leaped out of sight between the two police cars. And as he said this, he could feel the hand of his crewmate on his back, enhancing the energy field and making the pair an almost invincible force in this battle of souls.

Geoff hit the pavement at exactly the same moment Andy Toster charged through the front door and rolled onto the grass, followed by Brandon, Graham and Phil Mickle, all of whom landed in textbook style, except for Graham. He'd seen Geoff dive between the police cars, knowing he had a weapon almost immediately accessible, and so tried to roll over like they do in films to prevent being shot, but somehow managed to end up on his back, facing in the wrong direction, and in the process broke his hand-held mini metal detector.

'Bollocks,' he cursed and scrambled behind a low brick wall at the side of the driveway, and saw his three colleagues do exactly the same, as they realised how exposed they were lying in the middle of the garden a few metres away from a man with two very nasty firearms.

They all saw the electric bolt shoot through the sky with a loud *CRACK!* and shatter the windscreen. Sergeant Mickle was the first to respond and pressed his radio button again, as he rolled towards the brick wall, shouting with a mixture of panic and exhilaration:

This Victorian Playground - Part 2

'ALL UNITS TO SCENE! ALL UNITS TO SCENE! NEED UNITS WITH HAND-HELD MINI METAL DETECTORS NOW!'

Then, suddenly, as a burst of automatic gunfire cut through the air, ripping chunks of brick and mortar from the wall inches above his head, he heard another loud *CRACK!* and the sound of more breaking glass, as well as the unmistakable noise of a tyre exploding. '*Fuck!*' he yelled into the melee, this was one hell of a war.

Geoff had managed to retrieve a gun and pointed it wildly in the direction of his house, as he crouched partially hidden between the two cars. He didn't see which direction the bolt of electricity had come from, but knew that those other officers weren't far behind him and he didn't much fancy having that metal detector pointed at his chest again! He could still feel the tightness, and his breath was laboured, not to mention the extreme discomfort of his injured hands.

Pointing his gun over towards the brick wall that divided his driveway from his neighbour's, he thought he saw movement and pulled the trigger. Bullets tore from the end of the barrel at maximum velocity, ripping into the wall and the garage beyond, causing him to lose balance slightly owing to the kickback.

Just as this happened, he sensed the vehicle next to him take another blast of electric current and the rear tyre behind him exploded, along with the rear windscreen shattering – raining fragments of glass all over his prostrate body.

Somewhere in the distance he heard a loud command. 'POLICE ARMED WITH HAND-HELD MINI METAL DETECTOR! PUT DOWN YOUR WEAPONS!'

Damn, these guys were good! He cursed to himself as he adjusted his position slightly, grimacing as the sharp shards of glass dug into his legs. From where he was crouched he had partial eyeball on the front of his house, but couldn't see anyone. He guessed they were all cowering behind the wall. The shout he had heard came from behind him, somewhere to his left. He wasn't quite cornered, but it wouldn't be long before the backup arrived ...

And as that thought penetrated his frantic mind, he heard the roar of several diesel engines powering up the street, and the squeal of brakes. The sounds of doors opening and slamming. Booted feet placed firmly

PC Michael Pinkstone

on the ground and several commands all shouted at once. He knew, with a shudder, that many hand-held mini metal detectors were being pointed in his direction. Only the two police cars stood between him and certain capture. Would he be able to put up the fight he so desperately craved?

Slowly and painfully, pulling the other gun from behind him, he managed to get himself into a kind of sitting position with both weapons in his hands. His back was against the boot of one car and he could just about see the feet of a few officers about twenty metres away, standing there resolute. Another command cut through the air.

'You are completely surrounded. Put down your weapons and stand up with your hands on your head!'

Geoff blew through his cheeks, sweating, bleeding and determined. This was it. For seven long years he had waited for this moment and he wasn't going to surrender now. He was angry and he was armed. These guns were crafted to kill. Death was their emblem. He was one with his weapons, as the police seemed to be one with their hand-held mini metal detectors. There were more of them, but he was just as passionate about his cause. This would be a glorious moment in the history of going out in a blaze of glory.

Getting very slowly into a crouched position, manoeuvring his guns at the same time, he was ready to stand up and fire in all directions, hopefully taking out some of those fucking police scum before they inevitably took him down. He hadn't counted on those damned metal detectors, but he was still ready for the fight.

'PUT DOWN YOUR WEAPONS AND STAND UP SLOWLY WITH YOUR HANDS ON YOUR HEAD!' The voice was that of PC Bryant, who had walked steadily with his colleague towards him since the first moment he had used his metal detector. Now he had halved the distance and was making even more essential gains. Within twenty feet Geoff would hardly be able to fire his guns at all. Within ten feet he was doomed. There was nothing for it.

With a roar of bestial passion, brought about through long years of fanatical solitude and self-delusion, Geoff rose to his feet, bringing his guns up to waist height between the two cars, and he began to fire. Those lethal metal projectiles ripped from the barrels, one after the other at incredible speeds, smashing into windows, cars, walls, and everything

This Victorian Playground - Part 2

that dared to stand in their way.

Police officers dived for cover, yelling in fright. The online training package didn't suggest that this would happen; and even if it did, would it have prepared them for the real heat of battle? Would it have been enough to portray any sense of what it was like to have a bullet tear into your flesh? They had been lied to. Betrayed. Those pieces of plastic were fucking useless after all.

Two went down screaming in agony, one catching a slug in the right shoulder and one in the left arm. Another felt something whistle by his ear as he leaped backwards behind his vehicle, dropping his hand-held mini metal detector at the same time. One wasn't so lucky, catching a bullet in the head and dying instantly. This was no joke. This was life, death, and all the fucked up shit in between.

In all directions the police officers were desperately scrambling for cover, flinging aside their metal detectors and abandoning hope. Despite their superior numbers and awesome online training, they were but humans with bits of plastic in their hands, facing a murderous foe. How could they vocalise their commands to activate the hand-held mini metal detectors when they were being shot at? When they were dying?

PC Bryant and PC Bell also dived frantically for cover. They still weren't close enough for their metal detector to prevent Geoff from firing. Yes, they could have given him a nasty shock from that distance, but not enough to save their lives if the gun was aimed at them. Yes, the size of the metal object determined the power of the electric bolt, but the guns weren't *that* big to risk being in the line of fire. So they crashed helplessly to the ground, thudding painfully onto the harsh concrete of the pavement, hand-held mini metal detector skidding across the floor and out of reach. All officers were now defenceless and unequipped in this momentous struggle. They were nowhere near in command.

In this moment Geoff realised he had almost fully gained the upper hand. Yet again he had taken control. There were no bolts of electricity arcing towards him. There were no more shouted commands to make him quiver and quake. He knew that the hand-held mini metal detectors were no real match for his fearsome weapons. How could he ever have believed this? And how stupid of him to leave a metal detector lying around in his kitchen, but that was just a silly mistake, and it made no

PC Michael Pinkstone

difference now. His foes were being cut down before him and he howled with deranged pleasure at the grief and destruction he was causing. And when the dust had settled he could reload in seconds – several magazines of bullets in his trouser pockets. Those fuckers wouldn't even dare show their heads anyway. Not now. Not after this. They had been shown the error of their ways, and were reeling from his superior firepower – bleeding and falling and helpless. Destroyed in seconds by his rampant ferocity. So he reloaded and fired, watching and cackling as injured bodies tried wretchedly to pull themselves to safety. His hour had arrived!

Yet, as the noisome chorus of automatic gunfire resounded in the air, muffled only slightly by the yells and screams of fourteen police officers in the vicinity – and all around the chaotic din of shattering glass, exploding tyres and crumbling brickwork made you want to cry with utter dread at this, the end of the world – one man stood without fear and without compromise, a glint of vehement wrath in his otherwise kindly brown eyes. He could see the carnage; he beheld the destruction, and he rose to the challenge, while his friends and colleagues died. In this moment, he became what we all want to be – what our hearts will forever urge us to become – and acted upon instincts that training packages could never impart, and shallow speeches never inspire. This was where it was happening, and there was nothing left but the burning fire of real virtue, in all of its unadorned, primal glory; its bald, naked fervour. Some flames will not be extinguished, though buffeted by the cold, harsh winds of blame and betrayal. Hollow political rhetoric aside, he cast off the mantle of alarm, and set his sights on his evil foe – without some useless prop giving him a false aura of security. Unarmed and unprotected, he leaped over the broken wall; booted feet landing firmly on good old British pavement, and charged with a barbarian fury across the street towards the back of the man with the guns.

And while those demons of destruction raged, and waged war through their man-made weapons of evil, one man burst into the fray with a roar of passion like a champion of old.

Sergeant Mickle launched himself through the air, arms outstretched, another cry of unfettered rage erupting from deep within him, and slammed into the madly firing gunman, bringing them both crashing and yelling to the ground, guns still a-blazing. The tarmac cruelly

This Victorian Playground - Part 2

absorbed the impact, smashing Geoff's nose and crushing his wrists underneath him, leaving him dazed and stunned, and unable to fire any more rounds. He wasn't expecting this, and he felt the air squashed out of him; dousing his fire, like a burning ship sinking beneath turbulent waves. The battle was lost!

He felt strong arms behind his back and cold metal pressed against his wrists, and then more bodies, and shouts around him as the uninjured officers also bundled in, some with their batons already drawn, including Graham, Andy and Sam, who had closely followed their Sergeant across the street, when they realised what he was doing. They were not far from the fight. They were in the midst of it too, and they would follow their Sergeant unto whatever end.

And as Geoff's hands were cuffed tightly together, and the reasons for his arrest carefully explained according to SOCAP, he finally knew that he'd fought the Law and the Law had fucking won. They had somehow made do and mended, and it wasn't the hand-held mini metal detectors that had been his demise, or the number of police officers on his street, but the bravery of one man willing to risk all – with the odds stacked against him – and sacrifice his life, to preserve life, on the streets of shame. And because of this – Geoff realised with a jolt as they took him away – his mission of terror was doomed from the start. He couldn't have won. For the courage to do what is right, and the determination to save life and limb, knows no equal. It has no rival. It will conquer all, and will never, ever be overcome.

* * *

This short story is dedicated to the eternal memory of those police officers in Britain who have lost their lives in the uncompromising pursuit of preserving the sanctity of life; and maintaining peace, law and order, and upholding truth, justice and goodness, in the name of the Queen they vowed to serve.

21. Pavlova Politics (and the Man on the Roof)

Modern day British politics is very similar to meringue: sickly-sweet and insubstantial. There's quite simply nothing to it. So long as it looks pleasing though. At least this will help to mask the trembling, quaking – altogether fragile – interior. It's a frivolous display of frills and feathers, perpetuated by a nervous and submissive disposition. The most important thing is appearance. It's all one big show.

It's a macaroon phantasm; a marzipan-covered nightmare. A sticky, licky daydream. A bruised and used apple, covered in toffee, to deceive the kids and bring in the quids. It's what's on the outside that counts.

So we persist with our fanciful policies and ideals, in the hope that they will at least *look* magnificent to the masses: a beautifully created pavlova, decorated with lots of whipped cream and slices of strawberry. A dessert of quite breathtaking splendour and the centrepiece of the pudding trolley.

Everyone looks at it and claps – hey, I'll have a bit of that! Their plates are thrust towards the waiter who cuts into it with a silver knife. Very soon but a few crumbs are left, and several people are licking their lips so as not to miss the last remaining dustings of icing sugar or tiny blobs of cream.

Yet the minute it is consumed – it is forgotten. It hasn't really filled a hole. And very soon the punters demand another one. Another sweet trophy to scoff. Another wonderful-looking contrivance to satisfy them, if only for the briefest of moments.

We have become so used to being fed with sugar-laden and frosted fancies that we are sickly and undernourished. Every word spoken is

This Victorian Playground - Part 2

caramelised or dipped in chocolate – the bitter edge disguised by careful and deliberate culinary skill.

It's all for the better, they say. It's all for our safety. For our children and for our health. For our futures and for our livelihood. For our good. Yet as we have already seen – it is complete nothingness. It is all posturing and parading and political positioning. It all means nothing and it all melts away as soon as you put it to the test. There's no substance and no backbone. A temporary repair. All nutrition and goodness replaced by a quick fix – an energy boost. Enough to keep us going for a short while, until we demand another hit. Another sugar high. Another short term solution.

It is a rather pathetic and syrupy doom, perpetuated by honeyed words and treacly actions. Sticky faces and sticky fingers. Jam spread thickly over stale bread. An indulgence of over-sweetened political promises, leading to nothing more than the social equivalent of tooth decay. What a fucking tragedy.

For beneath the sugar-frosted veneer lies this stark and harsh reality – we *are* decaying. There can be no doubt about that. Britain is slowly and surely disintegrating.

We stand and watch while our country slides ever further into social chaos – bewildered as to why it is all happening. Confused as to the apparent lack of motive behind it all. Dismayed at the obvious signs of collapse.

We walk down littered and filthy streets, plagued by drunken layabouts, violent anti-social scum, and drugged-up wasters. People who gather in clusters and abuse themselves as much as they abuse anyone else, and we are powerless to do anything about it.

Every now and again some bright spark comes up with a useful scheme such as a "dispersal order" or a power to remove alcohol, which merely dissipates the problem or moves it a few streets away, where it soon becomes someone else's problem.

Pleasant, open spaces, where once families gathered or children played, become assembly points for people who drink, piss, inject, swear and hurl insults at anyone who even walks past their little congregation.

Police get called and we have no legal backing to do anything about it. Oh yes, we may get some poxy arrest for a minor public order offence,

PC Michael Pinkstone

and we may pour away half a can of high-strength lager, but we're not really doing anything substantial. We're not really solving anything. We have no powers to do so.

Everything has to be kept so nice and sweet and precious. It has to be dainty and frilly and lacy. No chance of grabbing these people by the scruff of the neck and demanding that they change *now,* or face being removed. Indefinitely.

No, we are fucking useless. We don't deliver justice. We don't enforce the law. We don't deal with people how they should be dealt with. Instead we let them get on with it and even pay them lots of money to do exactly what they want to do – piss their lives away, physically or metaphorically.

We are no longer "hands-on". If anything, we have become a "hands-off" nation. Far too much risk and blame. Far too much chance of getting something a teeny-weeny bit 'wrong' and getting sued or condemned or fired.

So all we do is step back and watch it all get even more fucked up, and do absolutely nothing about it. To the ruin of all.

* * *

Now, do you want to know why this chapter is also about a man on a roof? Then please read on …

Recently I had the pleasure of being crewed with PC Blank.[26] We make a fine pair of cheerful and upbeat officers, by the way. We are always fully motivated and walk around with beaming smiles and wonderful manners.

Ne'er a swear word passes our lips as we drive around the wonderful streets of our manor, dealing with delightful people doing special things.

Our first port of call was a report of a disturbance in a local park. Apparently there were several males lying around the place drinking, pissing and being generally noisy and abusive.

---

[26] "PC Blank" is a pseudonym for a colleague to whom I have already allocated a pseudonym. I've done this to further protect his identity for reasons that will become clear.

This Victorian Playground - Part 2

Upon our arrival at the scene we discovered that the park was one of those miscellaneous little green areas with a couple of trees and a couple of benches – slap bang in the middle of a residential area. Bordered on one side by a retirement-style housing complex and on the other sides by private flats and homes.

The sort of park that you would expect to see – in bygone days – filled with chatting mothers pushing prams around, while little toddlers played contentedly with wooden toys. The sound of cheerful conversation in the air and the "broom-broom" noise of children's happy absorption.

Nowadays of course, children don't really play like they used to. Instead they watch images flicker in front of their eyes or manhandle toys that do everything for them, leaving little room for creativity or imagination. And their mothers often choose not to take them to such parks any more – and who can blame them?

So as PC Blank and I stepped out of the car we weren't faced with modern society at its best. We were, of course, faced with five drunk males, who took immediate offence at our arrival.

These particular scumbags were black and foreign. I say this because they were, not because I have a specific problem with either of those labels. In a nation afraid to say anything apparently derogatory towards anyone of a different race or colour, we need to start being blunt and honest.

So they were black and foreign. I recognised a couple of them. Unemployed and unconcerned. Not that these two words are synonymous, but when you have dealt with as many wasters as most police officers, you begin to make certain connections that sound a bit harsh.

There they languished – pissed, impertinent and not in the least worried about their behaviour. Yet as soon as we arrived – two white officers in uniform – out came the race card.

'This is just segregation!'

I looked at him and frowned. '*What?*'

He staggered towards me, stinking of booze and his trousers halfway down his arse. 'We're being segregated,' he replied aggressively, making me furrow my brow even more. As his friend joined him, they both lurched away, cursing under their breath and muttering words of victimness and maltreatment.

PC Michael Pinkstone

As PC Blank tried to explain to another male that he wasn't permitted to drink in the town centre "Alcohol Exclusion Zone", I was beckoned over by a nearby elderly gentleman standing just outside the park.

'What are you going to fucking do about them?' he said angrily. I blinked. Did he just say the "F" word to me? He can't say that – he's an *old man!*

I gathered my wits. 'Well, we're just attempting to remove their alcohol from them at present, sir.'

'Can you not just move them on? They are here *every day*. Sometimes until 3 am. Look at them – look at this mess. I've been writing to the council for eight years for them to do something about this problem and you know what happened last week?'

I shook my head. He carried on. 'They sent me a letter saying that if I had a problem then I should call the police and they will do something about it.'

I blinked again. 'It took them *eight years* to tell you that?'

The man ignored this comment and said in a matter-of-fact tone, 'So what are you going to do about them?'

At this point I was joined by PC Blank and for the next few minutes we tried to explain that, at present, there was no dispersal order in place covering the town centre and that if we tried to remove any of the males without any form of legal backing, we could effectively lose our jobs.

The man looked at us and scoffed. '*Fuck off!*'

I blinked for a third time. 'It's true!' I protested. I wasn't cross with him for swearing because I would have told myself exactly the same thing if I was him. His frustration was palpable and I felt every bit of it. For he was me in forty years' time. He represented all of us who feel the same way. I liked him.

'If I manhandle any of these males without using a legal power, I could face a complaint of assault.' The man looked at me and I knew he believed me. He just didn't want to. Neither did I.

'It's a fucking joke,' I said. 'It's this fucking Government. They've fucked up this country. Too pink and fucking fluffy.'[27]

The man nodded. 'I did three years' national service,' he said, with a

---

27 I suppose PC Blank should have "challenged" this "inappropriate" behaviour, which is why I've given him some extra anonymity.

This Victorian Playground - Part 2

dismissive glance over my shoulder at the pissed-up pillocks lying on the floor behind me. 'And now look at this country. What a fucking waste. I did national service for *this*?' Another glance over my shoulder.

I nodded again. 'I don't know what the answer is, sir, I really don't.' PC Blank also looked behind me. 'Shoot them all,' he suggested with heartfelt venom.

'Wouldn't that be nice,' I replied.

Shoot them all. Hold a gun to their heads and watch them wet themselves with terror. Pull the trigger, despite their desperate cries, and watch while their heads explode and their brains splatter everywhere. See their lifeless bodies slump to the ground. Just like a computer game. Mindless and distant.

It's just a phrase, of course. A metaphor. *Shoot them all.* You'd have to be a seriously fucked up person to go beyond the verbal humouring and put a loaded gun to someone's face – and use it. How many times have I said, '*They should all be shot*' and not meant a single word of it?

We all jest and we all jape. Pass me a rope – I need to hang myself. Show me leaping off a bridge. Where's the whisky and painkillers? *Shoot them all.* It's become the conversation-stopper, but not because of its supposed brutality. Rather it's the only thing we can think of to make everything better, even though we don't mean it. A fantasy born out of utter frustration at not being able to do anything else. We can't move them on and we can't lock them up. We can't change them and we can't deport them. So what else is left?

I looked behind me. What pathetic little wretches they were. What sad and sorry fools. What disgusting, pitiful scum. *Shoot them all.* It summed up how we all felt and how powerless we truly were. Not that we really wanted them to die. We just didn't want them doing what they did.

Twenty minutes later PC Blank and I were being told to 'Fuck off' by a pissed middle-aged man inside his own lounge. Fair enough, but pretty annoying seeing as he was the one who had called us in the first place saying that his wife was missing.

She wasn't missing, of course. He was the one who was missing – as in missing the fucking point. Time to sober up, don't you think, sir? *Fuck off.* Well you called us here, sir? *Fuck off.* You sad and sorry piss-head. Your wife has had enough of you and I'm not surprised.

PC Michael Pinkstone

Fuck off. Don't worry, sir, we're leaving. We don't want to spend any more time in your company than is absolutely necessary. *Fuck off.* No, how about you fuck off and get a grip, you worthless piece of shit?

We didn't say anything of the sort to him really. We just looked with sympathy at his poor wife and shut the front door behind us, to a final parting gift of, 'You fucking useless police officers.' Charming gentleman.

* * *

A few hours later the call came in. *Male making off!* A police dog-handler was running after a little thief. Through alleyways and between parked cars. Up streets and down streets. Over walls and into gardens. Then onto a roof.

My colleagues from another shift who were covering the town centre pubs and clubs began to "contain" the area. We love to "contain" things. We contain scenes and we contain people, if we think we know where they are. And we knew where this chap was because we could see him – on the roof of a funeral directors.

So about ten police officers in total got the area contained. They surrounded the building as best they could to make sure that the little shit couldn't get away. The time was about midnight.

Half an hour later and the little baddy had managed to leap from one building to another. He'd jumped right over the head of Acting Sergeant Luton, who was standing twenty feet below him.

Now he was contained on the top of a much bigger building – a warehouse of some description, bordered by a large yard, a multi-storey car park, a service road and the grounds of the funeral directors.

The only escape route was another leap back onto the roof of the funeral directors, for all around the rest of the building was a minimum twenty-foot drop onto concrete … and ten police officers surrounding it completely.

Now, after a few years in the job I have to say that this was the most comprehensive containment I have ever been on, for I joined Acting Sergeant Luton at about half past midnight, and stared up at the top of

This Victorian Playground - Part 2

the warehouse. The situation was in our favour. We could both see the naughty male and he was leaning over the edge smiling at us.

We tried to talk to him but the sound of the helicopter drowned us out. Yes, the helicopter had arrived! Apparently the weather was fine enough for them to take off and now they hovered above the warehouse, pinpointing the male with a powerful beam of light.

Let's just say that he was well and truly contained. This little fucker wasn't getting away. The only problem was how we were going to get him down ...

So we called for the assistance of the fire brigade. Forty-five minutes later they turned up with an appliance. (I'd like to call it a "fire engine" but I don't think that this is the correct terminology.) It had an extendable ladder on the back, but this wasn't deemed "safe".

Instead they opted to call for another appliance – one that had a ladder with a cage on the end of it. Much better solution. Up to this point I was in full agreement with the decision.

Get another appliance. Get some officers in the cage. Get them on the roof and let them drag that little shit into the cage and get him down from there. No mess, no fuss. If he tries to escape, fuck him. If he jumps off and hurts himself, fuck him.

Pavlova politics. Yes, far too much risk! Far too much blame. Under no circumstances are officers allowed to do anything more than go up in the cage and request that the male joins them. Under no circumstances are they allowed to stray any more than sixteen millimetres from the cage and under no circumstances are they allowed to go hands-on with the male. Under no circumstances whatsoever are they allowed to do their job or put themselves in *any* form of perceived danger, despite the fact that they are the ones actually on the fucking roof and can assess the situation themselves. And under no circumstances whatsoever would it be the fault of the baddy if he jumped off the building and hurt himself. In fact, it's all the fault of the police anyway that he's on the roof. We should never have chased him in the first place.

Ah, herein lies the problem. This is where pavlova politics has debilitated common sense and gritty determination. Fight on the beaches? No, we shan't fight on the beaches and under no circumstances shall we fight on the rooftops.

PC Michael Pinkstone

Fight on the rooftops? Now that sentiment sounds vaguely familiar. So at 2 am the second appliance arrived and two police officers, along with a member of the fire crew, extended themselves up into the air and onto the roof of the warehouse.

All that remained now was to listen to the radio and see who would make what decision.

After about a minute came the first update from one of the officers on the roof. 'He's ignoring us.'

Then came further updates. 'Yeah, he's walking back over to the south side of the building and looking over the edge … Yeah, he's now looking at us and smiling and leaning back over where he first jumped across … I think he's still wanting to escape …'

A short while later came a further update. 'To the officers on the roof – from the fire chief – could you please explain why the fire officer is outside of the cage? He's not allowed out of the cage …'

'Yeah, if I could explain that. The fire officer is only just out of the cage and he's been talking across to the male. I think he's getting somewhere. He's only about a metre away from the cage, received?'

'Under no circumstances is that fire officer allowed out of the cage – please instruct him to get back inside …'

Half an hour later … 'Yeah, I don't think that the male is going to come with us in the cage and the fire service want to know how long they have to wait here …'

An hour later and the fire service have left the scene and the police begin to "scale down" their response.

There's now about six officers surrounding the building and one of the original crew who went up in the cage is now lying on the third floor of the multi-storey car park observing the male. He's still on the roof, of course. And he's still looking to escape.

In a whispered voice, 'He's lying down.' In an even more hushed voice, 'He's taken his T-shirt off … I think he's using it as a pillow …'

By this time PC Blank and I had left the "scene" and had to go to a nearby police station to pick up PC Grin. She'd been on a cell watch making sure that a drunk naked lady didn't kill herself, or simply die. Police cells are such dangerous places.

Meanwhile we could all hear further hushed updates over the radio

This Victorian Playground - Part 2

that the male was still wandering around the roof looking over the edge and considering the potential for getting away.

4 am. Most of my shift are about to go home. Some, however, have just made arrests for criminal damage. That's after a twelve-hour shift. Some of the night turn are still containing the male on the roof and the rest have taken over the cars and are dealing with things like outstanding domestics. *My ex-partner has sent me a nasty text.* I know, let's fill out a Domestic Risk Assessment Form at 4.12 am regarding this horrific incident. It's *violence* after all, and policy dictates that we must, irrespective of the time of night or the context.

4.34 am and I'm on my way home. Phone call from PC Snipper. Er, my car won't start. So I turn round and drive back to the station. 4.53 am. Pick up PC Snipper and start to drive him home. For the first time in my policing career I'd decided to take my radio home with me just so I could listen to the "man on the roof" scenario. He was still up there of course.

5.30 am. PC Snipper is delivered home and I begin to drive back towards my house. By the time I arrive it's getting light. 6 am. The chap is still on the roof and the police response has been scaled down even more. Now there's only four or five officers left on the containment. No dogs, no helicopters, no armed crew, no appliances – just four or five exhausted guys and girls on foot.

6.15 am. I can't be bothered to listen to my radio any more. 6.20 am. By this time the chap has been on the roof for over six hours. I roll over and go to sleep.

* * *

The following day I'm back at work. No rest for the tired. I walk into the office and by and large see Acting Sergeant Luton wandering around. 'What happened to that chap?' I ask with a measure of disdain not directed towards my Sergeant, but towards the prevailing attitude that made the whole situation into such a drawn-out and embarrassing charade.

'Well,' said Acting Sergeant Luton. 'They got him in the end!' I breathe a small sigh of relief. '*But he nearly got away,*' he added.

PC Michael Pinkstone

'He what?' I sound incredulous but not particularly surprised. So Acting Sergeant Luton tells me the rest of the tale. To do so he sits on a desk and makes himself comfortable. Blimey, how long is this going to take? It's a guy on a roof for fuck's sake!

In the end, it turned out that certain important police officers much higher up the ranks than anyone actually at the scene, wanted to call the whole thing off. Scale it down. Scale down the police response. Were there any substantive offences? Was it worth it? Cost versus reward? What are the risks? What might happen to us if he falls off? What might happen to us if an officer gets injured? The possibilities were endless, so as a result the remaining guys and gals who just wanted to do their fucking job came up with a devious and cunning plan. Baldrick himself would have nodded in appreciation.

Now, I'm not going to give away our secrets for catching someone once they have climbed onto a roof (actually, I am), so let's just say that four officers were left at the scene and there were no police vehicles anywhere around either.

A few exhausted colleagues of mine – as if we had enough to spare – were left standing in various strategic points around the warehouse for several hours *waiting for the chap to come down.*

Now, let's be blunt here. Several hours earlier we had a fire engine with a cage at the scene and two armed officers on the roof. I didn't mention the "armed" part earlier. Well, I say "armed". They're not really allowed to use their guns, of course. In fact, their guns were probably in the car. We don't have a "Freeze or I'll shoot!" policing mentality in this country. It's more of a, "Are you going to come with me? No? In that case, I'll let you go then ..." mentality. What a fucking pink and fluffy travesty.

So our "armed" crew on the roof were actually unarmed and thus about as effective as chopsticks with a bowl of soup because they weren't allowed to do anything more than *ask* the guy to come with them. There was even talk at one point of getting a *negotiator* to come to the scene.

A *negotiator*? What *was* this, a terrorist threat? A hostage situation? A Middle East peace crisis? No, this was a guy on a fucking roof who needed to be grabbed, restrained and dumped into the back of a van

This Victorian Playground - Part 2

– the original reason for his chase being that he was a fucking criminal suspect.

If he'd fallen off the roof – his fault. If he'd injured himself in any way – his fault. If he'd resisted arrest whilst still on the roof – take him down. But no, don't be ridiculous. It's always our fault.

I'm not really a gung-ho kind of person and I've already said that I don't particularly like guns, but there really is something to be said for pointing a weapon at someone and saying, 'Get down on your stomach and put your hands behind your head. Any sudden moves and I'll take you down. Understand me?'

With that kind of mentality the situation could have been resolved in about ten seconds from the time the officers stepped out of that fucking cage and got on the roof. This isn't a subversive attempt at suggesting all police officers should be armed – it's a heartfelt cry for this wishy-washy, namby-pamby political mentality to be crushed and rid from us. It's about attitude and existence.

It's about time we started taking the lead and taking decisive action. *Walk towards me slowly with your hands behind your head. Now stop. Get down on your stomach. Do it slowly. Put your hands behind your head. We're going to approach you and handcuff you now. Any sudden moves and I will shoot you.*

Not sure of the exact process because I'm not firearms-trained – but I hope the sentiment is clear. Instead we had to face the truly embarrassing situation of this ...

After about a minute came the first update from one of the officers on the roof. 'He's ignoring us.'

Then came further updates. 'Yeah, he's walking back over to the south side of the building and looking over the edge ...Yeah, he's now looking at us and smiling and leaning back over where he first jumped across... I think he's still wanting to escape ...'

A short while later came a further update. 'To the officers on the roof – from the fire chief – could you please explain why the fire officer is outside of the cage? He's not allowed out of the cage ...'

My good God, it's a shambles what this nation has become. We're just trembling, pathetic, sickly-sweet fools. We're *not allowed* to do anything at all any more. Not even allowed to think things we shouldn't.

PC Michael Pinkstone

I'm shaking my head in despair as I write these very words. Perhaps one day I'll look back at this chapter and be thankful that it changed. Or perhaps it will have got worse. Either way, we're currently in the middle of a pavlova politics nightmare.

Anyway, the guy on the roof. He came down in the end. Came down of his own accord. That's because he thought everyone had gone and in many respects he was right. Nearly everyone *had* gone.

So he jumped down and tried to make good his escape. What followed was true Keystone Cops. There was baton-waving and general yelling. Officers running into each other and falling on top of each other. Tripping down steps and all charging in opposite directions. Welcome to the Benny Hill school of policing. Hence my ringtone.

Fortunately, by some miracle, they managed to pin him to the ground and get him trussed up. Highly trained you see. Highly trained in the art of making do and mending as best we can given the current political climate. Our resourcefulness and commitment knows no bounds. And the senior management just wanted to let him go.

It turned out that the man on the roof was not only arrested for the original offence of theft from a motor vehicle (the reason why he was running away in the first place) but was also Wanted twice over – for quite serious offences.

Let him go? Yeah, that sounds about right …

22. Mr Majestic

I arrive in a Transit van, which I seem to do rather a lot. Before me is a scene of utter devastation. It's like the aftermath of a Tourettes sufferers' beer festival. To my left is PC Flower, leaning against a battered pick-up truck and yelling in agony, an extensive trail of snot leaking from his nose and smearing on his neatly creased trousers. To my right is the portly figure of PC Kidney – having what first appears to be an almighty seizure – until I realise he is also screaming in pain, whirling his arms blindly around in a windmill-like motion (the first proper exercise he's done in years) and scattering the local drunks like skittles.

From the nearby Day Centre come howls of anguish and the sound of breaking furniture. Drunken jeers mixing with forceful commands to *stop resisting*. Amidst the hubbub of disorder and chaos a familiar voice yells from an unseen room, 'I'VE FUCKING HAD ENOUGH OF THIS SHIT!' I begin to run towards the Day Centre. This wasn't good. This could only mean one thing, and that was enough to make me sprint. PC Butch was inside. He was cross, and he was fighting. And he'd used his Captor … again. The situation could only get worse …

The scene inside the Day Centre was something akin to a cock-fight. As in, PC Butch was fighting with a right cock on the floor. All around him the town's regular piss-heads and drop-outs were leaning on the walls – cheering, shouting, and raising cans of Special Brew.

My good friend and colleague PC Lan was also there, half kneeling by Mr Majestic's writhing legs – her baton raised in one hand and with the other hand trying to stop him from viciously kicking her. PC Butch had the top half of the body in some kind of grip, most likely a

PC Michael Pinkstone

head-lock knowing him, and all three of them were yelling at the tops of their voices. It was not a sight that brought a smile, although I'm sure it would have made great TV, except, of course, if someone actually got seriously injured.

So I dived, with true heartfelt rage, right in between my two good friends and right on top of somebody who was trying to hurt them. *Please sir, please. Oh just leave them alone sir. Can't we just talk about it? I've got a great new policy if you want to hear about it sir? It's really shiny and glossy and took me ages – oh please come and have a look at it sir ...*

No. We shall fight on the beaches. Or in Day Centres, or anywhere else where the safety and security of this nation is undermined by mindless, violent and evil scum. I don't care if it's one person doing it, or a whole army. We *will* fight. We will fight metaphorically and physically. We will fight with words, wisdom and common sense. Sometimes we will fight with our fists and with our lives. With goodness, decency and courage. Either way, and whatever the context, we are going to goddamn fucking fight. And it's not *fun.*

For this wasn't a *"good scrap"* – this was fucking serious. Every copper in Britain feels some elation after a "good scrap" – but they don't feel elated when they, or any one of their colleagues, gets hurt or dead. For that's all a "good scrap" really is – a *thank fuck* I didn't get broken. And here, in the Day Centre, not only were we surrounded by other nasty scumbags, but there were also two friends of ours outside who had been sprayed in the face with Captor and as such were extremely vulnerable. There were jeers among the local scrotes to attack my colleagues in their unprotected grief. And let's not forget the dangerous maniac struggling violently beneath us three – a man who should have been incarcerated fucking years ago.

I found a spare area of leg and struck it with my knee as hard as I could, as many times as I could. True Home Office-approved pain. PC Lan was pressing her baton down on the back of Mr Majestic's legs too – another approved technique – and PC Butch was trying his hardest to get the arms under control. It wasn't working. In any other country Mr Majestic would most likely have been shot.

To my left I saw two more officers arrive – guys from traffic. Thank fuck. More people. Between the five of us we managed to get Mr Majestic

This Victorian Playground - Part 2

under some form of "control" and he was eventually handcuffed. By this time most of the available officers in the town had arrived. It's called an "assistance shout" which means: *get the fuck here now.* I say "most" – it was actually all of them, with others driving at breakneck speeds from nearby towns to help their colleagues.

Fortunately there were now about eleven officers at the location. No-one anywhere else, of course. Well, I say "no-one". At the police station were at least twenty to thirty police officers, excluding CID and other essential sub-departments, who didn't use radios any more and had no real contact with the outside world. The first they'd get to hear about an officer getting harmed, or killed, would be when they loaded up their emails on a weekday between 8 and 4. Then there would be the dozens of officers at HQ who were more concerned with their little projects than real policing. Days spent wandering casually around those sanitised, distant corridors where everything looks good on paper. We need officers in offices – of course we do, but *that many*?

Fortunately the few remaining survivors who put their radios on and left the station on that particular day were able to make a potentially fucked up situation into a slightly less fucked up situation.

The fact that Mr Majestic attacked PC Butch, and was armed with a knife, is entirely irrelevant I suppose.

We just got lucky that time.

Yet some officers would cry out from the grave that they weren't quite so fortunate. Wouldn't they.

23. No Moon Shift

In this penultimate chapter I hope to further sum up a great deal of what I have written so far in both books – in a manner that leaves little room for sentiment.

Now you may recall from the first Introduction of *Part I* that I aimed to write about "attitude and existence". I hope that so far this has been accomplished. For no matter how much we bang on about policies, procedures, plans and politics – it all comes down to our basic attitude and mentality. And I propose that the mentality of Britain has become so utterly violated, and things have subsequently gone so completely beyond the pale, that we have lost sight of our most elementary tenets of discernment, reason and common sense. And there is no short term fix for this problem. In fact, there may not be a fix at all.

Thus while everything that has been written in my books – or any other book, blog, magazine, journal, newspaper or whatever – may be completely true concerning the way things are so buggered in the police, and in the country – it is the *reasons* behind our demise that need serious addressing. The all-important question thus presents itself: *Why is Britain so fucked up?*

From a police perspective, I personally believe that there are no policies that could *ever* be established to sort things out. It all may have gone too far. Yet people are still working on "improving" the police – by making various suggestions and not addressing the crux of the matter. There is a quest to *improve police performance through operational process redesign*. I guess, though, that the crux of the matter is simply too disturbing to really address, so we don't ever address it! What we do,

This Victorian Playground - Part 2

instead, is worry about making ourselves more efficient and cost-effective. Streamlining our procedures and policies in order to ... er, in order to do what, exactly? That's the part I don't really understand.

We're simply too good at focusing on the wrong things, even though sometimes those things need sorting out. Take unnecessary paperwork for example. I agree with any streamlining decisions to cut ridiculous form-filling down to a minimum, but would it really make a difference? If my Stop and Account form takes me two minutes to complete, as opposed to fifteen, what difference has this made to the country? Efficiency will not lead to improving the fucked up state we find ourselves in.

* * *

Imagine, if you will, creating a monster. You want it to help you around the house. You manufacture it out of various parts and components and, one day, breathe life into it, so it gets up and walks around.

Over the coming weeks and months you train your monster to do different things around the place. You add bits to it and take things away. To start off with, the monster is fucking incompetent. It can't even boil a kettle. But soon, after days of alterations and adaptations and streamlining procedures, your monster can make a cup of tea with fairly minimal fuss.

After a year or so, your monster can complete a variety of tasks in different rooms, including making a full English breakfast and doing the laundry. It's not so good at some things, such as hanging the washing out on the line, but your quest to improve your monster continues. As time goes by, your monster will become better and better and more cost-effective – this is because it eats lots and lots of cheese. So you budget for your monster's appetite by giving it slightly cheaper cheese, and continually improve its ability to complete jobs quickly and efficiently, so that the end result is rather pleasing. The "cheese to work" ratio is much better than it was at the beginning and you smile with satisfaction.

One day a friend visits and comments that your monster is fucking ugly. So you spend a bit of extra cash and tart it up a bit. Now it looks more pleasing to the public, even though it never leaves the house. Its image is, of course, very important.

PC Michael Pinkstone

After three years your monster has got things down to a fine art. However, one January, you read that new rules and regulations have been imposed regarding domestic monsters. You have to spend several hundred pounds teaching it all sorts of irrelevant things to do with Health and Safety, Equality and Diversity. Your monster then has to pass a few bizarre tests in order to demonstrate his competence in various areas. This consumes a lot of time and resources, but you have to do it. There is no choice.

A year after this, there is a public outcry at the use of domestic monsters and it is decided that they should all be granted extra-special rights and not be discriminated against. Laws are passed that prohibit the monster working on Tuesdays and Friday afternoons. Other tasks are also restricted, such as doing the washing and making tea. This is all done to improve overall efficiency and obtain the best value for money and quality of service.

Unfortunately for you, though, your life has taken a dramatic turn for the worse after being hit by a Volvo. Now you need constant care and attention at home, but are unable to receive the level of assistance you need from your monster because it's been crippled by politically motivated restrictions. You make a fuss about it but no-one listens to you. Actually, they *do* listen, but they don't do anything about it. Well, that's not entirely true. They *do* end up doing something about it, which involves implementing some new policies that undercut the old ones, and which makes the whole situation even worse. Now your monster is allowed to do what you require him to do, but he's not allowed to say specific words for fear of causing offence. This is a right old bugger because he needs certain "trigger" words to activate his internal mechanisms, so he has, in effect, been limited even more. The monster policy makers, however, claim that they have made improvements and vociferously defend themselves when challenged. You, meanwhile, haven't had a cup of tea for three weeks.

After months of trying to convince the people behind the scenes that they have fucked up your monster, a report is published that seems to *finally* address the major issues. Surely now your monster will be able to get on with what it was created to do! Surely now things will be better than before! Surely now you can actually have a cup of tea!

Don't make me laugh.

This Victorian Playground - Part 2

* * *

I believe that the gulf between those in their ivory towers and those working on the frontline in this country – whatever their job title – has become so vast, that the people wandering around those sanitised corridors have no conception whatsoever of how awful it all really is. Or, if they have some conception, their concern hardly leads to incisive action.

In the same way that Queen Victoria viewed the horrendous state of parts of industrialised Britain through the window of her royal carriage in the late 1830s, later commenting on the blackened, wretched children huddling together in the sooty effluvium, so the Government today observes the horrific state of things; pays lip service to the tragic demise, and pretends to do something about it. And as we have already seen, that "something" is nothing. Yet they persist with their precious and fanciful ideas!

Do they actually think that a few nice little policies dreamed up in "tripartite committee meetings" (I read that phrase somewhere on a Home Office website) will be able to stem the tide of calamity? Do they honestly hold the conviction that things are getting better and that by making a few performance-related alterations here and there, the situation will continue to improve? Do they think that the foundations are secure and simply need building upon?

I may waffle on at times, but sometimes words fail me. For someone who isn't usually at a loss for something to say or to write, I often find myself speechless.

There they sit in their cool, detached towers, dreaming up plans and procedures that seem so magnificent in theory, but in reality are either thoroughly detrimental, particularly ineffective or uncompromisingly bizarre.

Rather than address the real problems they simply skip merrily around the aftermath of their own incompetence – implementing new ways of undoing the damage caused by their last failed enterprise. Welcome to British politics.

PC Michael Pinkstone

Meanwhile, on the streets – i.e. in the real world – things are just getting worse and worse. As mentioned in *Part I* – no amount of true story-telling or fictionalising can ever really sum it up, hence the fact I'm most likely repeating myself yet again, but until someone in power admits that the situation is indeed quite buggered, I'm going to carry on.

Thus, without any further ado, let us examine a recent shift, which I have decided to entitle "No Moon Shift", primarily because it was an early shift and I couldn't see the moon; but mainly because I couldn't give a fuck what the moon was doing at the time. Far too busy mopping up the social results of being administrated by the crappiest Government you could possibly imagine.

For this was the day of black trash, Asian trash and white trash – a veritable buffet of cultural calamity. This was the day of trivia and tragedy personified. This was the day of Britain at its very worst. This was the day when policing politics made you hang your head in mystification as to how we could have ever got to this stage. This was the No Moon Shift. My little memoir of madness in a country that had gone to the dogs. And, of course, it was a perfectly normal day in the life of your average police officer on the delightful streets of Britain.

* * *

I arrived at work at 6.23 am. It was an early shift. 7 am until 4 pm. Nine hours of joy in a special town. A town scarred and marred by too many illegal or unrestrained immigrants and too many "locals" who didn't work and didn't care. Too many chavs and too many scrotes. A town of clashing cultures and warring gangs. A town I couldn't stand.

'Oh but it's busy and that's good for your PDR,' claim some colleagues. 'You get a lot of experience here,' say others. 'It's like being thrown in at the deep end,' some like to exclaim.

Actually, it's like working in a sewer without a nose peg. It's like walking through the cultural equivalent of a puddle of sick. It's like bashing your head against a pebble-dashed wall. Totally and utterly fucking horrific.

Green and pleasant land? The only green thing about this land – in this particular town – were the cannabis factories. And the pleasant part

This Victorian Playground - Part 2

was finishing work and driving away from all the shit at high speed. At least at home there's a fridge containing cold beer. At least I lived ten miles away from the dump.

No matter what we have been led to believe by lying politicians – there are certain towns and cities in this nation that are simply horrendous. Localities where you can but shake your head in absolute dismay at the virulent social mix and displays of antipathetic behaviour by mindless and asinine fools. Places where the streets are simply not safe and not policed. Places where people have been allowed to get away with living morally repugnant lives, and we all suffer the consequences because the Government are too scared at doing anything incisive about it. Far too many so-called human rights to consider.

Human rights? My arse. My fucking arse. We have absolutely no concept of what that really means – or rather, what it *should* mean. In real terms the issue of human rights means protecting criminals and letting nasty people get away with being nasty – time and time and time again. We can't punish them or deal with them how they should be dealt with because the political attitude won't allow it. And as for the police? Well, we know how fucking useless we are. We're not even allowed to *ask* people anything without filling in a form for twenty minutes afterwards.

So I got kitted up at about 6.35 am – in the same manner that I had done for the past few years. In pretty much the same manner as the rest of my colleagues at the station. In pretty much the same manner as frontline police officers all over the country. Whether their early shift started at 6 am, 7 am or, lucky bastards, 10 am – we all donned pretty much the same gear and walked into similar briefing rooms to read comparable emails on cognate computers.

We logged onto analogous systems and perused equivalent jobs. Checked related crime reports on our own versions of CRAPPIES. Checked them, swore loudly, and said 'hello' to the rest of the team members making their merry way into the room.

I'm lying, of course. They weren't merry at all. PC Glasses looked homicidal as usual and PC Butter had a stinking cold. PC Bump got told straight away that he was on a cell watch – please read Chapter 8 again, just for a laugh – and PC Grin just shook her head in gloom.

PC Michael Pinkstone

PC Snipper sighed and logged on to CRAPPIES for about three seconds before getting his Pocket Notebook out – presumably to write the day, date and a succinct but emotional suicide note, before running like the whippet he is into the path of a juggernaut on the nearby motorway.

PC Rope looked thoroughly morose. She was waiting for a transfer off shift and couldn't wait for the day to arrive. Can't blame her – any form of escape was a grand idea. PC Fresh was typing away furiously on some form of database. It was his birthday the day before. Already long forgotten.

Acting Sergeant Luton arrived and waved. His cheeriness was returned with exhausted glances and half-hearted hand gestures. Sergeant Chelsea also arrived – and spent the next ten minutes hunting high and low for his football coffee mug. He gave up in the end. Can't blame him. He was defeated before he even started anyway.

So there we languished in our newly "refurbished" briefing room. They'd done it to improve morale apparently. Or had they done it because it was a fucking shit pit before? Either way it still looked crap and we still had no motivation.

6.59 am. The usual trudge to the place where we have our little morning meeting. That room adjacent to where the computers are – the one next to the "office". It's like some kind of secret chamber. Makes us feel special. Got some photos of baddies on the wall. They all need to be incarcerated. But no. We spend our lives running around after the same fucking scumbags.

I sit in my usual chair. PC Glasses sits in his. He gets very upset if people steal his seat. Can't blame him. He's been on shift for a year longer than me and my goodness does he need a break. He's a man on the edge. A man close to boiling point. He puts his feet up on the chair in front of him. His regular obtuse pose.

I look around me. *Seven* officers. I do a quick re-count. Maths was always my worst subject. Despite having a grandfather who taught mathematics for the best part of three decades and a father whose maths skills, engineering prowess and technical drawing genius were never in any doubt – there was me having to double-check a number lower than ten.

Seven. Hang on – I thought the Government had increased the number of officers in the past few years. I thought that's what they'd

This Victorian Playground - Part 2

told us. Crime was down and frontline officers were up. Something about priorities.

Bald, lying ginger c**ts. Crime was up and officers were down. That was the truth of it. Not only down in numbers – on the frontline, let me reiterate – but down emotionally and physically as well. Down in every way, shape and form. Down on their luck and looking to go Down Under, some of them.

It was like Exodus without a bearded man with a magic stick. No parting of a sea around here. Just a fuckload of officers fleeing the country without so much as an 'I'll miss you dear Britain'. No, they just couldn't wait to bugger off. *Rivers of blood*. Was that a plague or a speech?

PC Butch got his application form in months ago. Poor chap. He had to have some small hope to cling on to or he might very well have needed sectioning. Even Sergeant Bimmer flirted with the idea. That in itself was highly significant.

I got my Pocket Notebook out. Day and date. Thanks for the memories. Call sign immediate. Motivation lagging; lacking impetus. Writing squiffy and almost illegible. I hardly care. What does it matter? No-one fucking reads these books any more, least of all me. Might as well draw a giant penis on page sixty-six. Unlike me to be so crude.

The briefing starts. Sergeant Chelsea in full swing. That is to say he really hasn't got the effort or the energy. It's like watching yourself. A levelling of the playing field, and we're all certainly playing. It's a game. Has been for ages.

Plenty of burglaries over the weekend. What a surprise. I *wonder* who might be committing those? Could be any number of the dozens of prolific offenders we have on our patch. Little fuckers.

Yes, we know who they are. We even know what they like to eat. We know pretty much everything about the little scrotes and we know we can't do anything about them too. Maybe catch one and put him away for a few months. Wow, what a result. He'll be out soon.

Intelligence required. I never understood that phrase. I was halfway through drawing the shaft when I looked at the briefing screen. Sgt Chelsea was saying something else but I wasn't really listening. *Intelligence required.* I look at the context. It was a photo of one of our

PC Michael Pinkstone

more regular offenders. Mr Rutton. He was into a variety of naughty things, with drugs as his motivation.

We needed intelligence on him. I shook my head and carried on with my sketch. What else did they need to know? Hey, I have a plan. Let me submit a report to the teams behind the scenes. The ones who deal with such sensitive information. Let me give them some "intelligence" on this male. After all, it's *required* ...

Dear intelligence team of shifty-looking officers in plain clothes. You want some information on Mr Rutton? Here you go – he's a fucking criminal. I don't pick up a spade and require more intelligence on the damn thing, do I? I treat it as a spade. Now treat Mr Rutton as a fucking burglar. Tell the Government to lock the bald ginger c**t up until he's going grey and then let him out again. See if he burgles anyone after that. In other words, the system we have at the moment isn't working. It's not fucking working!

What a debacle. They say never work with children or animals. Try working with politicians. It's like a self-harming weekend break with a suicide spa thrown in for free. Cucumbers on your eyes my arse. Awkward phrase, but kind of kinky. Just use hot chilli peppers instead. Fits in with the ethos.

The knob is complete and so is the briefing. I didn't really draw one, of course. That would be unprofessional. I haven't drawn a winky since I was at school. No such immature behaviour any more. So I'd like to think.

I look at the back of my hand. I know the back of my hand like the inside of my notebook. Ironic as they are one and the same. Crewed with PC Geri (short for "geriatric"). Between us we have eighty years on this earth. He has the greater percentage of course, but he's still going strong.

He used to be part of the team but deserted it like a rat fleeing a stinking shit. Or something like that. Either metaphor fits. Again, can't blame the guy. Now he's back from his last escapade being a tutor and he's currently a Neighbourhood Specialist Officer.

Thank you dear Government. You've rolled out neighbourhood policing. What a spectacular idea in theory and what a hideous realisation in practical application. Something familiar about that kind of result.

This Victorian Playground - Part 2

PC Geri is covering on shift because we're so understaffed. That's because many of our staff are either sick, on holiday, leaving the job due to retirement, leaving the job because it's fucked, leaving the country, leaving the country because it's fucked, in other essential departments, in other pointless departments – or on neighbourhood teams.

So when we're understaffed – which is nearly every day – we can't get cover from those who are sick, on holiday, retiring, fucked off elsewhere, fucked off overseas, fucked off overseas in disgust, in decent departments or in "support" units, so we poach *back* from neighbourhoods. A slight irony.

Ah. That's the part the Government really doesn't get. Knock knock. Anyone there? The lights are on but no-one cares about saving electricity these days. So PC Geri is covering shift and not being a Neighbourhood Specialist Officer at all. In fact, he may only get to do his job once every few weeks. That's because he's abstracted elsewhere for other tasks and commitments. Then, when he *does* have a chance to get onto his patch (which is bigger than the asteroid that wiped out our discretion), he'll spend all day apologising to everyone he hasn't had a chance to see, and then spend the next day in a pointless meeting with his "partners". Then he'll have two weeks off, or some Rest Days, cover shift again a few more times and, by golly – retirement. Or death. Whichever comes soonest. Either way he might as well not bother. *Damn.* It all sounded so good on paper …

I get some car keys from the board. This means I'll be driving a diesel Astra with some blue and yellow reflecty things all over it. Inside is a small panel containing several buttons. One I can use to illuminate the blue lights that spin round and round. The other I can use to make my headlights flash. The third is for flaunting the red lights on the top. The final one activates "The Noise". The variations in tone are controlled by the horn on the steering wheel and the driver is PC Geri because I'm eating a bacon baguette. Ooh, how chic.

Can't believe this shit. I go up to the canteen at exactly 7.35 am. PC Snipper orders two poached eggs. PC Grin does the same. We're such lucky swines. We actually *have* a canteen. Many of the others all across the policing area have been closed. Something about money, I guess. Still, when you have seven officers left on shift – who rarely have time

PC Michael Pinkstone

to eat anyway – there is probably very little demand for a canteen. It's swings and roundabouts. You get those in a playground, by the way.

When I started we had twenty-two officers. Not just "on paper" but in the flesh. This meant that with various abstractions here and there we were routinely running with an average of seventeen to eighteen per shift, per day. Sometimes there just weren't the cars. Sometimes I went out on a bike. The locals loved it. I even had a chance to talk to people.

Then, suddenly, the Government decided to get rid of frontline officers and make CRAPPIES, the NCRS, targets, detections, criming, pointless bureaucratic departments, neighbourhood policing – all of this kind of bollocks and more – the most important things in the world. We then faced up to the fact that we had loads less officers actually doing anything substantial, and loads more work as a result. Welcome to being an average PC in Britain. Welcome to the victim culture. What a bummer.

Bacon baguette please, Sarah. Brown with no spread. Dairy intolerant, you see. I have cheese and whine. Nasty affliction. Shame when you actually enjoy Brie and Stilton on digestive biscuits.

7.39 am. I hear my call sign at exactly the same time my breakfast is prepared. How fucking typical. But I'm a dedicated officer of the law and nothing will stand between me and dealing with shit, so off I go.

I walk with my little brown bag containing my morning feast to the car downstairs. PC Geri is already there. The boot is open. The bags are placed inside. My bag weighs a tonne. Strange that. Strange because I only ever use my coat, hat and about three forms. I've given up on the rest of the paperwork. Stop and Account? Don't be ridiculous. 'Hello sir, I'd just like you to stand there for twenty minutes while I fill out this form because I started this sentence with "Hello sir".' Bizarre, but kind of true.

So I have no idea why my bag is this heavy but I do not have the inclination to find out. In any case, I have to go to a domestic. It's happening *now*. It's in *progress*. There's mention of a knife. All systems go, go, GO! Or did I mean all units? Well, there's one unit going – that's me and PC Geri. However, it really is *all systems go* as well. Computer systems that is.

Fuck reality. Fuck context. Fuck the sound of the diesel engine and the brilliance of the flashing lights. Fuck the road users not paying any

This Victorian Playground - Part 2

heed to the bright, noisy car trying to get past them. Fuck, fuck, fuck. That's me in the car, of course. I'm the back-up siren.

Move out of the fucking way you fucking moron! PC Geri, who is an endlessly patient man, suggests that I transfer departments to somewhere less stressful. Bless him, he thinks I'm actually stressed. No. I've gone way beyond that. I've entered a parallel universe. My brain is no longer connected to anything. It's all gone zah-zah. Oh just fucking move. Middle-aged Asian woman in a metallic green Nissan Micra?

Please don't be alarmed. That wasn't a racist comment. It was prejudice based on lots and lots and lots of fact. And lots of experience. Therefore it wasn't nasty. Let's start being honest, and we can do it in a fun kind of way.

Yes madam – you need to move. Well, out of the way would be a start. How about today? Do you need a written invitation? Good God, answers on a fucking postcard please. Fucking MOVE!

She moved, finally. Took some persuasion. I'd nearly finished my baguette by the time she realised that she was behind the wheel of a car, and that by moving various limbs in a specifically co-ordinated pattern, the car would achieve locomotive qualities in a reasonably informed direction.

7.45 am. Still en-route. The car is full of crumbs and each swear word is accompanied by flecks of crusty bread. You can't beat eating your breakfast on the hoof. Or in a car, whichever is the more convenient at the time.

You would have thought that other units would be racing to their cars as well. Sadly not. They were already committed with prisoners – handed over from the night shift.

Handover. It's underlined in red. Like detections. Are they real words? Not sure. Whatever the case, they mean real grief. So myself and PC Geri are pretty much the only crew available and we're still on the way. The morning traffic is appalling and PC Snipper decides to break free from his allotted task and assist. After all, we were potentially in danger.

Nearly there. Updates please. The controller speaks. Passes names and places. Descriptions of events and offenders. We have an aggrieved and we have a baddy. It's logged. It's graded. It's already on CRAPPIES before we turn right at the lights.

PC Michael Pinkstone

Number what? Number 189. Ah, I recognise that number. Name? Ah, I recognise that name. Something about a pimp and a crack house. Something about prostitutes and cocaine. Something about context? Nah, don't be stupid.

We're driving at top speed through heavy traffic during breakfast to deal with the scum of the earth. We knew this anyway – even *before* we knew, if that makes any sense. It's not called intuition. It's called experience, seasoned with cynicism and spiced with local knowledge.

PC Snipper and PC Grin are already on the way. The controller speaks again. We're looking for a female called Yolanda who has been threatened by her ex-partner with a knife. She's outside. She's inside. She's seen the knife. She hasn't seen the knife. She's not making much sense. You should read the Log. Doesn't make much sense either. You should consider the context. Don't make me chuckle.

Female is wearing a red top. Yes, yes. We've located the female. She's marching up the road with a suitcase. She's black with dreadlocks. She turns to face us.

Yolan ... oh my God ... da? Sharp intake of breath. She's certainly not a looker. Face like an ingrowing toenail. She walks up to the car and I get out.

I stare at her nose. Sorry, I just can't help it. A crusted-over cigarette burn or something like that. And the rest of her neck is terribly and terrifyingly scarred and scorched. Old wounds – not fresh. I don't ask her how she came by such injuries, but I guess she fell asleep whilst high on drugs and got set on fire by her cigarette, crack pipe or spliff – or maybe all three. She woke up when the flames reached her neck. Jamaican accent.

'Go and have a word wiv him. I want my tings. He got some white girl. I tell her nu'ting. He want me in bed – tree in a bed. Dat's not right.' Teeth suck.

Takes me a short while to adjust to her accent before saying anything. 'Hi, I'm PC Pinkstone from the station. What's your name, madam?' I believe that introductions are best practice.

'Yolanda ... I want my tings. He got some white girl. I tell her nu'ting. He want me in bed – tree in a bed. Dat's not right.' Teeth suck.

'So, Yolanda – why have you called us?' I think she may have just told me, but I can't really understand her. Besides, I hate the word "ting".

This Victorian Playground - Part 2

Teeth suck. 'He got white girl. Some white trash. I want my tings.'

I stare at the nose again. Bit of a pause. 'Sorry, why have you called us?'

'I want my tings.'

'Your tings?' I cringe somewhat. Saying that word was like sucking on a slice of lemon.

'I want my tings.'

Slight frown. 'I'm sorry, why have you called us?'

'He got white girl. I want my tings.'

I sigh inwardly. She just doesn't get it. 'I'm sorry, why have you called us?'

'Go and have a word wiv him! Go arks him for my tings!'

I hate the word "arks" as well. Made me want to slap her thoroughly. 'What do you want me to *ask* him?' There was no harm in trying to educate her subliminally.

Teeth suck. 'He got no right to have her in da house. It's his dad's house. He died last week. I came up for the funeral.' Teeth suck. 'He got no right to treat me like dat.'

I hated teeth-sucking too. My fists clenched involuntarily. 'Like what?'

'He come down the road chasing me wiv a knife!'

Recalling the updates from earlier, I stared into her bloodshot eyes and said firmly, 'But you said you haven't seen a knife.'

Her hand flicks. I hate that gesture too. It's so fucking dismissive. 'He chase me down! He chase me down! He chase me down!'

PC Geri has joined us. He looks at me. I look at him, and then back at Yolanda. 'I'm sorry, why have you called us?'

'Because I want my tings!'

My will-power has all but ebbed away. If only the phrase "Not a police matter" was still allowed. If only context still had some part to play. 'What things?' I arks, wearily.

'My necklace.'

'Your necklace?' I look at her neck, thinking that an item of jewellery was the least of her problems.

'My gold and white silver necklace with the lion's head!' Of course, how silly of me not to know that already.

PC Michael Pinkstone

'Whose necklace is it?' I knew what she was going to say.

Teeth suck. Short pause. 'I bought it for heem! But now I want it back! I want my tings!'

I don't think she realised that by saying "tings" she was indicating a plurality of items, so I just wanted to clarify that small point. 'Anything else Yolanda?' I'm sure I sounded genuinely interested in her plight.

'No. Just my necklace. I WANT MY TINGS! GO GET MY TINGS!' At this point she shouts in my face and starts to push past me.

'Just calm down Yol—'

'I WANT MY TINGS!'

'… anda. Just, wait, no, you can't go back in the—'

'I'M GOING TO TRASH THE HOUSE! I WANT MY TINGS!' PC Geri stands in her way too. I walk away. Can't help it.

I knock on the door. Number 189. 'I want my tings' resounding in both ears. PC Geri trying to make sense of it all. He's doing much better than CRAPPIES. For the system has already decided what's happened, how it's happened, where it's happened, when it's happened and what the fuck we should do about it. Thank goodness for a crime-recording standard.

I want my tings! Oh will you just shut the fuck off! PC Snipper taught me that one. Amazingly enough I hear his voice on the airwaves. 'Does PC Pinkstone require any assistance?' That's a negative.

'Does PC Pinkstone require us to remain in the area or would he like us to cancel … *tings* … cancel?' I press my button and speak. 'Thanks to that unit but it certainly is a complete load of cancel cancel.'

The door opens. Hello drug-dealing, drug-taking pimp. Having a nice morning? Teeth suck. *Tings!* Oh for fuck … *tings* … sake. It's like verbal fucking hiccups. I notice that he's wearing a gold and white silver necklace with a lion's head. It's fucking hideous.

He looks over my shoulder. 'Just get her out of my sight, officer – she threatened to trash my house!'

'Has she already done it?' I reply, as I look over his shoulder. What a shit pit. He looks at me and frowns. 'Never mind,' say I.

PC Geri has got his Pocket Note Book out. *I want my tings.* I want my sanity. Yolanda – I think it's best if you just leave. *I want my tings.* Yol … (insert something to do with tings) … anda. Will you please just

This Victorian Playground - Part 2

listen to me for one mo ... *tings* ... ment? I just ... *tings* ... push ... get back, Yolan ... *tings* ... if you carry on like this ... *tings* ... you're going to be arrested for a breach of the peace because you are sorely breaching it now ... *TINGS!*

YOLANDA THIS IS YOUR FINAL WARNING! Even PC Geri has had enough.

I'M NOT GOING TIL I'VE GOT MY TINGS! Someone pass me a fucking rope. RIGHT, LET'S GET YOU OUT OF HERE. GET IN THE CAR!

'You know what,' she says. 'Keep the fucking necklace!' She strides towards the car, hurling abuse at the window of number 189. 'Keep my tings! I don't care! YOU FUCKING PIMP!' Meanwhile, young schoolchildren are walking past, staring and listening. What a special moment.

She finally clambers into the back seat, muttering curses under her breath. We take her to the nearest train station. She smiles and says, 'Thank you.'

I say, 'You're welcome. Take care.' I didn't mean it.

We drive away, breathing sighs of relief. PC Geri looks at me. The problems have only just begun of course. 'I can't wait to see how you're going to write that one off,' he smiles.

I look at him. 'Just wait,' I say.

'Ah,' he says. 'How can you justify not filling in a Domestic Risk Assessment Form with her and not do anything about the knife?'

Thank you, dear Government. Do you have any idea whatsoever? I'd love to see a politician negotiating *The Return of the Ting.* What a grand fucking finale that would be.

The radio crackles. 'It's on CRAPPIES,' says the controller. 'Can you update the Log when you get back to the station?' says the controller. 'It's been graded as *Domestic Violence,*' says the controller.

PC Geri looks at me again. 'Be calm,' he soothes.

We're en-route back to base when we are re-deployed. Urgent Fear for Personal Welfare. I guess the Log will just have to wait. Those ticky boxes too.

Female calling us regarding her daughter who called her stating she'd taken an overdose at 4 am. Ambulance arrived at 4.10 am to discover

PC Michael Pinkstone

an extremely abusive female who told them to 'Fuck off' (which they quite rightly did) and for the past four hours the mother has not been able to contact her daughter. She's called Sally.

Could we go and check on this female's welfare? Our options consist of:

1. Yes
2. Yes
3. Yes

There are no other options. She has become our responsibility. Her life has been placed in our hands. She has been reported as potentially in danger and she now has her own *Fear for Personal Welfare* Log. If she dies, it's our fault. If she stubs her toe, it's our fault. Whatever happens in her life from this moment in time will be our fault. She'd better not be fucking dead or injured in any way whatsoever, or questions will be asked. *Serious* questions. Inquiries will be held. Witches will be burned at the stake, along with all the police officers who didn't do their "job".

Preservation of life? What about promotion of personal responsibility and the fact that people are accountable for themselves? But no. We *have* to attend. In fact, if we don't get there soon – and she is dead – we might as well join her. In truth, we don't mind attending one little bit. We *want* to preserve life. We *want* to go there and make sure she is OK. But all of this is irrelevant.

So we drive to the "scene". Knock on the door. No answer. Knock on the door again. No answer. Fuck. Knock louder. No answer. Even louder. No answer. Knock on all the windows. No ans ... the door opens!

Thank goodness, she's alive! Hello, Sally?

No, I'm Vicky. Sally's on the floor in her room.

I walk inside with PC Geri. Sally is indeed on the floor in her room. 'Fuck off,' she says. 'Shut my fucking door,' she moans. 'I've only just fallen over,' she mutters. 'Now fuck off.'

Er, sorry Sally, but we can't. We have now assumed responsibility for your whole existence whether you like it or not. We certainly don't like it but we don't have a choice. Not that we don't want to help you – of course we do. We love getting told to "fuck off" by pissed, obnoxious,

This Victorian Playground - Part 2

drugged-up, mental little bitches. It's very special. We vowed to preserve that kind of life, after all.

She crawls onto her sofa and hides under a pink cardigan. 'I hate my life. I don't want to be here any more.'

My goodness, Sally. I hate your life too and I don't want to fucking be here any more either. We are in complete agreement. Shall we celebrate it by examining the various tablets you've ingested, and move some of these empty liquor bottles out of the way?

'We've called an ambulance, Sally.' PC Geri is calm and kind.

'I don't want to be here any more. They took my daughter off me. She's three.' She starts to cry. The tears are real and her body shakes with uncontrolled grief.

My heart wrenches just a tiny bit, and the cynical, sarcastic hot air dissipates. It always does when I deal with true emotion. It doesn't come from the training. I look at her more closely. She's about twenty-five and quite attractive. Her make-up is well applied and she is wearing very nice clothes. She isn't skanky or manky. If you saw her on the street you wouldn't think she was the emotional equivalent of diarrhoea. I want to help her with every fibre of my being, but I am powerless.

They'll get you checked over, we say. Try to keep calm and talk to us, Sally. We want to make sure you're OK. We do, of course. *It's our job.*

The ambulance crew arrive. They try to deal with her but she just gets abusive again. They retreat outside the room and talk to us. This isn't a criticism. 'She needs to go to hospital,' they say. 'Needs to be checked over properly.'

When a paramedic tells me this, I have to agree. No choice. PC Geri says, 'Let's drag her outside.' The paramedic concurs. None of us have a legal power to do what we do, but we're here to preserve life after all. What a fuck-up.

So PC Geri and I drag her from her bedroom and carry her outside, kicking and screaming, whereupon she is plonked onto a stretcher. She resists all forms of hands-on and continues to be more obnoxious than you can possibly imagine.

Truth is, she didn't really need to go to hospital. Not that I disagreed with the paramedics. We just had a fair bit of arse to cover, in particular our

PC Michael Pinkstone

own. If she collapsed and died, it would be our fault. Not because we didn't do enough. Not because we didn't care, but because we were *called*.

There was a Log. Simple as that. It wasn't about saving life any more than it was about fried chicken. It was about concealing our butts in a manner that left little room for blame or criticism.

If it was about saving life, we wouldn't have even knocked on the door. We'd have kicked the fucking thing in straight away and dragged her out straight away. Ambulance would already be on scene with us and injecting her with a powerful sedative straight away and taking her straight to hospital. There she would undergo thorough tests and have her welfare checked on constantly by highly trained staff using highly technical equipment. Now *that's* Urgent Fear for Personal Welfare …

But no. It's not really about saving life or limb. It's about justifying what we do when someone has reported something to us. That's the bottom line. All blame lies with the police. We are responsible for everyone and everything.

We couldn't walk away. So we ended up doing something that we had no legal power to do, but had no other option. Perhaps I should be arrested for assault? CRAPPIES eat your fucking heart out. Thank you, Government.

* * *

Back at the office. I've updated the Logs. I think my arse is covered. Well, I hope it is. Yolanda is on CRAPPIES as a victim – for the rest of her life – but I didn't do a Risk Assessment Form. Oops.

This means in a decade's time, when she is dead – murdered at the hands of the chap with her ting – I am going to have to stand up in court and justify why I didn't take some form of "positive action". Can't tell you how much I hate that phrase. I even hate the word *domestic* now.

Domestic in progress! What the fuck is that supposed to mean? Domestic in progress? What's in progress? A domestic? *Life* in progress! *Existence* in progress! *Relationship* in progress – all units go, go GO!

I simply can't get my head around it. *Domestic in progress!* Domestic *what* exactly? *What*? Tell me – *what*? I don't get it. *Domestic in progress!* Am I the only person who finds this phrase completely bizarre? Help!

This Victorian Playground - Part 2

Police! I'm having a domestic! What's happened sir? Er, nothing – I'm married. That's a domestic isn't it? *Marriage in progress!* Isn't that some form of domestic incident? A "non-recordable"?

Non-incident in progress! Nothing is happening in progress! All units make to the scene – whatever isn't happening is happening now! It's a non-incident, non-recordable, non-domestic in progress, but we'll record what hasn't happened as a domestic incident anyway. Just in case.

ARRRGGGGGHHHHHHHHHHHHHHH! FOR FUCK'S FUCKING SAKE! WHAT THE FUCK HAS HAPPENED TO THIS COUNTRY? DOMESTIC IN FUCKING PROGRESS? FUCKING FUCKING FUCKING HELL.

I request that the Logs are closed. Then my phone rings. Got to go to another station to speak to someone. Can't speak over the phone – it has to be in person. Have to take some paperwork over there.

The other station is eight miles away. That's about a sixteen-mile round trip. Just to drop off some pointless paperwork regarding a pointless job.

PC Geri goes off to the nearby court. He's dealing with a nasty man, relating to an ongoing domestic. Most of them are. Ongoing, that is.

I get in the car. Billy No Mates. The controller pipes up – tries to send me elsewhere – to an outstanding domestic. One of many. I say, 'You want to send me to a domestic?'

She says, 'Yes.'

I say, 'Outstanding!'

Not really. I tell her I'm committed. There's a brief pause. She says, 'Er, OK.' Then she calls the Sergeant. He says, 'Go ahead.' She tells him that she's got no officers left. He says, 'I know. I don't have a box of them under my desk.' She laughs.

Then the Inspector calls up over the radio to 'take note'. Not because of the laughing part, but because Inspector Eyebrows is fairly realistic. A decent chap. So he calls up over the radio to 'note' that there's simply not enough frontline staff to deal with stuff. He's done an awful lot of "noting" in recent times. He knows that things are all fucked up, but what can he do? Two pips in the system is like two peas in a puddle – overwhelmed.

PC Michael Pinkstone

So there's no-one left to deal with anything. I start to drive towards the other station to deal with my urgent enquiry. Some chap is in prison and there's an urgent case review to do with something or the other. I've already been around the houses trying to sort it all out. Might as well not bother. Might as well just let him go. They'll probably do that anyway.

Twenty minutes later and I arrive at the nearby station. Twenty seconds for the gates to open. Two hours to find a parking space. That's a slight exaggeration but the sentiment is realistic.

I walk inside. 'Hello PC Glasses! What are you doing here?'

PC Glasses swears, as usual. 'Been here all morning,' he says.

'What for?' I reply with heartfelt interest.

'So some guy can get NFA'd[28] for Domestic Common Assault.'

'What joy,' I said – with real conviction.

'Yeah,' replies PC Glasses. 'We nicked him this morning *by arrangement* for having had an argument with his wife. He handed himself in. Spent an hour and a half bringing him here and booking him in. Spent an hour interviewing him and taking him back downstairs. Spent an hour and a half writing a CPS report and getting advice. Spent three seconds being told that there was no evidence, which we knew when we arrested him four hours ago. But we had to fucking nick him or we'd have got into trouble ourselves.'

My eyes roll in my head. Then they glance at the wall to my right. Cardiac arrest? No, it's just our yearly crime figures. Laminated. July looked pretty good, judging by the trough. August was worse – bit of a peak. I remember the emails. Felt special to be alive.

'Anyway mate, I'll see you later.' PC Glasses returns to custody. Needs to spend half an hour booking his man *out*. I guess by the time he's finished he'll be ready to go home. Not just emotionally ready, but actually ready.

I go upstairs and deposit my paperwork. Something to do with the CPS. Way beyond my understanding, so back downstairs I go. Into the car park and into the path of PC Jug driving an unmarked Corsa. We say "unmarked" – most of them are knackered.

He gets out and we chat for a couple of minutes. PC Jug is from my team, so we know each other well. He's coming back to shift soon,

---

28 No Further Action.

This Victorian Playground - Part 2

having spent some time abstracted elsewhere. Yes! One more person! Going to make so much difference!

I leave him parking his car and get back into mine. I'm calling it a "car" but it was fondly known as the "Cub Van". So I guess I should call it a van really. Time to go back to my home station and perhaps locate my crewmate. Twenty-five minutes later and I'm pulling up in the yard. Parked the van and got out. Contacted PC Geri – he's still committed.

I go upstairs and log back onto a computer. CRAPPIES bits and bobs. Real policing. PC Droll is sitting in front of me also doing some real policing. He's not from my shift but is doing funny hours as he's in court tomorrow. It's midday, sunny and all is well. A lovely green and pleasant land.

Suddenly, I hear a disturbing sound on the radio. Someone shouting the name of a car park, accompanied by the sound of the panic button. *Fuck.* It's an assistance shout. PC Lost. She's new and on an "attachment" to a neighbourhood team. It's fucking lunchtime and the sun is shining and a colleague is out there yelling the name of a car park – and it sounds manky.

PC Droll and I run to the yard. Steps are taken two at a time. I leap the last four. Into the van. The radio has gone quiet, except for the sound of the panic alarm. We know where we're going because my colleague had the presence of mind to call out her location. A car park – just around the corner.

Other units are making to the scene. They drop what they are doing and run to their cars. Statement paper left in situ. Pens abandoned. CRAPPIES forsaken. Well, only for the frontline staff. I can't blame everyone who works behind the scenes but there are some departments who do fuck all. They have a bureaucratic role. So it's down to the guys and gals who are left. The ones who still pound these streets of shame.

The van bursts into life. The gates take *ages* to open. Come on! Come on! We screech around the corner and drive to the end of the road. It's a right, right, right – through the traffic and towards the scene.

I hear jumbled sounds on the radio. Other units have got there first. Was that an "All in order"? I don't know, so I keep on driving. Into a car park and into the melee.

It's the usual scene, especially in this part of the country and, more

PC Michael Pinkstone

specifically, in this part of our patch. An awkward multicultural melting pot in a pebble-dashed shanty town.

Now, where the hell is my colleague? Ah, that would be him over there, surrounded by Asian males. A small selection of born and bred Brits, and many others who are otherwise defined. There's more cultural people in the car park too – a group of Eastern Europeans drinking in the shade. Whatever this place is called – it doesn't end in *shire*.

There's about thirty people in all. My colleague, PC Kidney, is dragging some handcuffed Asian male towards the Cub Van. Knew I arrived for a reason. Sergeant War is also there. PC Lost is looking a wee bit exhausted. I think the situation has calmed down somewhat, although the handcuffed male is kicking off. Spitting words and struggling. He makes demands. He gets shoved inside the cage.

All around me are the now familiar faces of my countrymen. Somewhat distant and perhaps a bit annoyed. After all, we've arrested one of them and he's in handcuffs. Most of them are in "traditional" clothes. Many of them don't speak English, and never will. They look at me as if I'm the stranger.

This is their little kingdom around here. It's their car park. Their shops. It's like a part of somewhere else. It's *in* Britain but it somehow doesn't feel a part of Britain. I've been here before, but when I was overseas. The same faces and the same looks. I don't feel attached to this place any more, and I'm sure they're all just as bewildered as me.

Immigration and integration – and subsequent social consternation. Buzzwords and bywords for ills and wrongs and faults. I blame this and I blame that. Too many of this and too many of that. Whatever we feel, and however we express it – we cannot deny that the problems are here, and they need to be addressed. No wonder the Home Office bury their heads deeply in the sand.

The cage is being kicked from the inside. PC Kidney clambers into the van. So does PC Lost. Everyone else disappears, except the "locals" of course. We're being stared at. Angry and sullen faces. I'm behind the windscreen. Protected and preserved. Nothing is physically thrown, but we are being attacked. It's a mental assault. I can feel the anger. I can sense the hostility.

We back slowly out of the car park. No-one is smiling at us. No-one

This Victorian Playground - Part 2

looks relieved. No-one thanks us for our intervention. *Thank God the police arrived.* None of that. We're being resented. Our presence is not welcome around here.

I turn out of the car park. I see another large group of Eastern Europeans. Slightly darker skin than the ones knocking back cans of imported lager in the shade. A different race entirely. They're squatting in a huddle. It looks furtive and somehow distasteful. Everything about them makes me feel removed from my surroundings. I'm sure they have a part to play – I just haven't worked out what it is yet. They are just stopping off for a quick breather before they arrive at the benefits office. Can't blame them. I'd do the same if I wasn't from here. Doesn't make it any the easier to swallow though. Integration? Mustn't malign them though – that would be intolerant. My God, what a debacle.

Our prisoner is agitated. 'Fucking prick!' He yells this to PC Kidney through the bars.

PC Kidney remains calm. 'You shouldn't have kicked off,' he said.

'Fucking prick,' came the reply.

Back at the station the prisoner is removed from the van. He refuses to be touched. 'I can fucking walk myself,' he rants. I take his arm. 'Get the fuck off me you prick.' I help him inside. His face is red and his eyes are watering. That's because he's been sprayed. PC Kidney had done this, and rightly so.

The male is pacing around the holding area. He's fired up, pissed off and lashing out. Well, he's lashing out verbally because he's still in cuffs. *Calm down.* We try to keep him still. 'I've got no fucking respect for the police!' He tells us what we already know. After all, he's probably innocent. Aren't they all?

He gets booked in to custody. Defiant to the last. Looks of animosity and hatred in all directions. He hasn't accepted his fate.

Ah, and what fate would that be exactly? A jolly good ticking off? A tickle with a pink and fluffy duster? Some extra-special grovelling because he's from a "minority"?

So I stand there in custody and listen to PC Kidney as he explains why this male has been arrested. Goes through all the points. Got to make sure it fulfils all the necessary criteria. After all, this male has been

PC Michael Pinkstone

detained against his will and taken to a place he doesn't want to go by people he hates. This needs some pretty serious justification.

PC Kidney begins his story. 'Well, Sarge, I was on duty in Bell Street Car Park with PC Lost. We saw a male driving without a seatbelt on. I approached this male and spoke to him. I then decided to issue him with a ticket for not wearing his seatbelt. This gentleman –' indicates to the prisoner '– then approached me with several other males and demanded to know what I was doing. He told me that it was his dad in the car. He then got aggressive with me and I told him to get back. He squared right up to me and refused to get back. He then kicked off and tried to assault me so I sprayed him with Captor, which was when PC Lost called for assistance. I arrested him under Section 4 of the Public Order Act in order to investigate the offence promptly and effectively and to prevent any harm coming to anyone, especially myself for trying to do my job.'

* * *

Oh, is that it? I thought it would be much more exciting than that. A bloody seatbelt ticket? An aggressive male? Tsk tsk. I think PC Kidney should have perhaps tried *talking* to him. Tried *reasoning* with him. Tried to understand and appreciate the local sensitivities involved. This was, after all, a delicate community issue.

Er, no. Fuck whatever community it was and fuck what ethnicity was involved. PC Kidney was doing his job – irrespective of what people think about the importance of seatbelts – he was doing his fucking job.

And while he was doing his job he was assaulted. A male came up to him and *demanded to know what he was doing.* Let me say that again. He *demanded to know what he was doing.* When this male was told to get back he got aggressive and then he attacked PC Kidney. He then called him a 'fucking prick' because he got arrested and told all of us that he has no respect for the police.

Excuse me, sir, but I have no respect for *you*. My grandfather didn't fight with his life for this country, for his descendants to give up and give in. For his descendants to let people who care *nothing* for Britain take the piss and *attack* police officers. For his descendants to be overshadowed by violent, vicious and mindless fools who have no concept *whatsoever*

This Victorian Playground - Part 2

that their actions are totally and utterly unacceptable.

No sir. *You* are the piece of shit here and don't you forget it. Unfortunately, he won't forget it because he never realised it in the first place, and probably hasn't realised it since. We're all fucking pricks and he has no respect for us.

I go back upstairs. Use the computer again. My little solace. If nothing else, it makes me feel better. There's something about staring at a computer screen these days that's oddly detached and soothing. I might stare and swear at CRAPPIES, but at least I'm *safe*. It's all bluster but at least it's *indoors*. Phew! I could be out there issuing tickets and getting my head kicked in. Thank fuck for "necessary bureaucracy". So I do half an hour of "updates" without speaking to anyone or going outside. Now that's *real* policing.

My watch tells me that it's about 2 pm. I've had my sandwiches (turkey and tomato with plenty of black pepper, in case you were wondering) and things are on an even keel. That is to say CRAPPIES is pretty much up to date.

Suddenly, without warning, I hear a sound on the radio. Another assistance shout. You have to be joking. Does that mean I have to go *outside* again? Fuck me, I was getting used to being behind my desk.

PC Desert is calling up. He's being assaulted on the High Street. I guess that means he needs some help. And if you knew PC Desert, you would also know he's not one to waste words or call up without good reason.

I run to the van. PC Droll behind me. PC Bump too. We climb inside and roar out of the car park. Anyone would think this shit is exciting. We swerve around the corner – the back end a graceful arc – and power our way towards the "scene". I use the words "roar" and "power" – it's called exaggeration. If you've ever driven this Cub Van you'd know that top speed is 55 mph and to achieve that takes the best part of half a century.

So, eventually we make it. The scene is outside the local Job Centre. Why do they call it a *Job* Centre? In this town it's a magnet for piss-heads, drop-outs and layabouts.

Can I tell you a short story? I don't know why I'm asking because I'm going to tell you anyway, but I feel it polite to at least pretend I'm

PC Michael Pinkstone

obtaining your permission.

One day, several years ago, I finished my teaching degree. My body and my mind were fucked and I had no energy, motivation or will-power left. I was, I think, at my lowest ebb ever. I was overweight, unfit, and physically and mentally exhausted. So I decided to take a month or two off.

To this day I don't even know why I wanted to do this. Maybe because I was on the verge of giving up teaching even before I'd started. So I went to the Job Centre and asked to sign on.

The woman looked at me. I looked at her. She carried on looking at me. I stared back. Then she looked at my qualifications and looked back at me again. And that's as far as I got. A whole lot of looking. Followed by a, 'Why are you here, Mr Pinkstone? Can you not get a job?'

I had no answer to that, so I gathered up my papers and went home. Shortly after that I started doing some supply teaching. Oh what a great country this is.

Anyway, that is completely by the by, and I pulled up outside the Job Centre to hear PC Desert on the radio, updating that two people had made off. I could see him and PC Hat manhandling a violent-looking woman into the back of a van, so it was clear that things were pretty much under control – and we drove off to look for the outstanding baddies, but not before a sweaty PC Kidney had joined us in the van. Yes, he'd *run* out of custody and all the way up the street. Big-time respect for a man who weighs more than a bungalow.

Thirty seconds later we can see two people legging it away down a nearby street. They fit the description and we drive after them. PC Kidney, PC Bump and PC Droll leap out of the van and charge after them. Strange thing is – they don't look particularly old. Are they the right people?

There's lots of noise on the radio. Various people calling out various things. CCTV updating. The controller requesting. PC Desert establishing. It would appear that there are actually *three* outstanding baddies – an adult male, a young female and an even younger male.

This confirms my suspicions. The two people we have running away must be the latter. The other male has gone another way.

So I continue to drive and catch up with my three colleagues who in turn have caught up with the male and female. She looks about fourteen.

230

This Victorian Playground - Part 2

He looks about eleven. Are these the ones? At this age? Surely not!

They are both white and speak with an accent I have come to know only too well. Friends from our travelling fraternity. Aren't we polite? Didn't I tell you that this chapter was about all colours of trash? Well, this was the grand finale to my day.

I don't say "trash" because they were travellers. Oh no – that would be harsh. I say "trash" simply because they were. Fucking scums. Local fucking scums. A family who had caused nothing but grief since being bricked up. A family who, in truth, needed evicting and preferably incarcerating on a prison island somewhere. They really were a waste of good oxygen.

The boy was defiant. Arrogant. He sat in the back of the van quite unconcerned. His sister, in the cage, joked that he was being "gay" with us all. PC Desert had their mother in his van. The other chap who had run away turned out to be the father. The whole fucking clan. How pleasant. What a lovely, special family. What wonderful citizens of this country.

The journey back to the police station with our two precious children was, in effect, quite depressing. I've rarely met any persons with a combined age of twenty-five who were as indifferent to being arrested as those two sprogs.

They quite simply didn't give a shit. They weren't bothered. Totally and utterly nonchalant. It was a walk in the park for them. Or, in this case, a nice little trip in a Cub Van. The young lad even threatened to kill PC Kidney. What a wonderful child.

I want my tings! You fucking prick! I'm going to kill you! Oh what a super day in the life of this nation. What a smashing display of diversity in action – a truly magnificent feast of cultural chaos. And the police really had an *impact.* Our involvement was a positive influence.

What's more, at 4 pm, when it was time for me to go home, after having dealt with a few more trivial things – all of these people finally realised the error of their ways, and started behaving in a much more socially responsible manner. Mrs Ting came off the drugs and stopped being fucked up in the head. Mr Handcuffed Angry Asian Man apologised profusely for his actions and now volunteers helping old people in a day centre, and the travelling family began to live decent, honest and hard-working lives. They became model citizens in an otherwise fractured community. A rather pleasant end to this chapter, don't you think?

Oh, before I go – I forgot to mention *why* the family were arrested in the first place (we picked up the father about half an hour later). It was because *all* of them attacked PC Desert on the street. They *attacked* him. Including the children. Then they got released, with the most pathetic of sanctions as their "punishment".

A rather pleasant end to this chapter, don't you think?

24. The Victim Culture Part III

Britain is dancing around on the toilet seat, seemingly oblivious to the slippery, sweaty-arse patches and unidentifiable gritty bits clearly posing a danger. Instead we twist and twirl and pirouette, our pretty, lacy frills billowing in our wake, coming ever closer to the edge. This pink and fluffy dream of ours; this fallacy; this playground fantasy – unhampered by the stark reality of our situation.

Soon, and without warning, we'll simply slip into the bowl; our scream of despair – and surprise, no doubt – met with a deep, cold plunge. Then we'll slide down the U-bend without further hesitation and be lost forever. What a fitting end to a once glorious nation: flushed down the bog like a turd.

Sadly we haven't always been this fucking ignorant.

Well, perhaps some of us have ...

* * *

Charles Darwin. Now there's a name you didn't expect to see staring out at you from this page. It's also a name that many people in certain Victorian ecclesiastical circles didn't want to see staring out from *any* page.

Basically Darwin's theories buggered up a lot of things. They created havoc. They fucked up an entrenched mindset and a fixed exhibition of beliefs that undermined whole generations of established convictions.

Now, while you're possibly reeling from the fact that I've just mentioned U-bends in one paragraph and Darwin in another, try to place

PC Michael Pinkstone

yourself in the shoes of some people who were just happily going about their daily business in Victorian times.

There they were, frilly and lacy. Happy and contented (except the poor buggers working down the mines or in the cotton mills, or anywhere else just as crap). However, you are *not* of those lower echelons of working class minions. You're not a drone. You can afford to live the way you fancy and perhaps own a mill or two. You also go to church and *believe* – well, you believe whatever it is you've believed for years and your father before you. And his father before him, etc. etc.

Years of singing hymns and pretending to be righteous. Years of pent-up sexual frustration relieved through the odd saucy lithograph or a sly glance at an uncovered pianoforte leg when no-one else was looking – either one of these subversive actions was enough to give you something of a thrill.

But, nevertheless, you are a good person. Educated and disciplined. Nothing in excess. Wholesome and stable and completely aghast at inappropriate behaviour. Your little Victorian fantasy is not undermined by the whims and follies of the inferior intellect. You are learned and schooled. Blind and fooled, but not stupid. You know the score, even if you are deceiving yourself.

Then, out of the blue, some balding bastard with huge sideburns comes along and tells you that you're descended from an ape. An *ape*! A fucking *ape*! How dare he?! What a complete and utter *bald ginger c**t!*

Of course, you'd call him this anyway, because it apparently doesn't make any difference what one looks like for them to receive such an insult. My goodness, pass me a fan and let me collapse in a chair with theatrical exhaustion. An *ape?*

This is unheard of! This is simply not happening! Could it be that … could it be … no, surely not. Could it be that … Oh my dear God, an *ape*?

Let's make no bones about it – Darwin caused a formidable stink. He shattered many, many illusions. He pissed all over the church without even trying – its sensitivities and sensibilities repudiated; it's hypocrisies revealed; its belief system revoked.

Yet Darwin wasn't the only proponent of his kind of theory. He wasn't the only person causing grief. However, he did represent a major

This Victorian Playground - Part 2

ball-ache for a lot of people and, for me, became somewhat symbolic of the age of modernity already taking root in Victorian times.

For by the end of the 19th Century great changes were afoot in terms of art, architecture, industry, politics, literature, scientific rational and general attitudes. From the Age of Reason to the the Englightenment, to modernism in all its fractured and discordant forms; to its progeny – or perhaps merely an offshoot – *post-modernity*; the world would never be the same again.

By the time the First World War had ended, society had lost not only a great deal of its innocence, but a great deal of its citizens. Millions of souls destroyed, fighting over scraps of land, seemed to grate rather awkwardly with the progress and change promised by modernist thought, yet was still somehow echoed by the dissonant and somewhat existential concepts evident in some modernist circles.

Whatever the view or take on the world – and whatever the artist, philosopher, theorist, linguist or scientist claimed – it was clear that something pretty darn serious had happened, and the world would never be the same again.

Following the Depression and the rise of Facism in the 30s to the beginning of World War II, it became even more clear that the world was perhaps taking a dramatic turn for the worse. In the years following the war, nations desperately tried to gather their political thoughts and establish themselves in the vacuum of freedom.

Then from the Cold War to the Vietnam War, to ethnic cleansing and natural disasters beamed live to your lounge; from images of horrific social deprivation, to reports of scientific and technological advances so magnificent they make you gasp; from the many shattered and discarded philosophies and abandoned theories; disowned politics and disregarded proposals – it is evident that we have seen and heard it all. Our minds have contemplated everything.

Are there any more Darwins? Will someone come along and propose something so radical it makes us gawp? Is there anything else that can happen – save the complete destruction of the world – that will shock us any more than we are now? For whether we like it or not – indeed, whether we realise it or not – we live in shock. We live in constant disarray. We live in fear, which is often muted, but it is fear nonetheless.

PC Michael Pinkstone

Our lives have become intangible and severed – there is nothing of substance. Nothing of any moral or ethical permanence. Things are all fucked up. Things are weird. If you take a look back at the past 100 or so years, you can only gape at the relentlessness with which mankind has broken through mental and moral barriers and pushed social boundaries to the farthest limits. One surely cannot deny that we live in days of great turbulence and change. Days of teetering collapse.

* * *

This is where we have arrived. We didn't get here in a van, but we might as well have done, because this is where we are and we can't change it. You've piled out of the side door and this is what you're facing. This is the nation you live in; the world you inhabit. It is not the remit of my book to cover in any great depth the issues of modernism, or provide you with a detailed historical or cultural analysis of the past century. If you want that kind of book, buy another one! However, the last few paragraphs were necessary to give us that greater bit of context for the brief remainder of this volume.

After all, this is the world we live in. And this is the society we are part of. As discussed in *Part I*, the victim culture – in all of its irresponsible eminence – could be seen as a natural progression from the "rage culture" I briefly mentioned a couple of times. Yet however we label society, or aspects thereof – and I chose "victim culture" for a number of reasons – the point is that there are certain trends and themes that are pretty evident and I have already attempted to bring some of those to the fore:

We *are* socially irresponsible.
We *are* weak and dependent.
We *are* fractured and divided.

Our society *is* on the brink of mental, emotional and physical overload, hampered by ineffectual policies, with seemingly little political desire to safeguard our economic and historical sustainability.

The police, and other frontline organisations, *are* wading in unnecessary bureaucratic sludge created by a pathetic and wheedling

This Victorian Playground - Part 2

Government, whose policies on a whole raft of issues reek of specious and cringing incompetence.

And above all, the world has *never* been stable ...

Thus the victim culture itself takes on a newer and wider angle. We are victims of the past, as much as we are victims of the present. While we may not be responsible for the sins or follies of our forebears, we are affected by the choices and decisions they made. Thus if we are going to turn to anything or anyone for some form of stability or assurance, who are we going to turn to? We find it very difficult to turn inwards, despite being told to search for the hero inside ourselves.

We find it somewhat impossible to drag ourselves up out of the mire. We are but helpless and hopeless against the calamities and disasters we face on a daily basis. Yet here I am using such strong words: *calamity, disaster*. Since when was the sound of your phone beeping and the receiving of an unwanted text message a *disaster?*

As already stated time and again, we have a desperate need for context. In these uncertain days we live without boundaries; without suitable social confines. We don't really know where we are, what we're doing or why we're doing it. A world split asunder by various controversies, wars, destruction, famine, disease, poverty, global warming, terrorism – this list could go on forever – has made us all victims of fear and horror. And because of this, we have no tangible lifeline to hold on to.

Thus the smallest and most trifling of our problems become blown out of all proportion, because there is no context, and often become the remit of someone else – yes, you guessed it – and the wider social problem becomes self-perpetuating.

Now at this point I could begin to repeat exactly what was written in *Part 1*, but I fear that you may just put the book down in disgust and stomp off to the fridge to get a beer. I know I would. However, it is imperative that we always consider this wider picture; this greater context. Our lives, attitudes and fortunes have been shaped by a myriad of things – many of them tragic and horrific; our destiny built, more often than not, upon spilled blood. We live in shattered, disillusioned and disenchanted times. The wider picture is so incredibly disparate that no-one could possibly draw all the strands together to provide a complete context for discussion. Thus here is the context. It's not pleasant but it surely cannot be denied:

PC Michael Pinkstone

at the moment we're fucked. I'm not sure what philosophical school of thought this pertains to, but I don't suppose it really matters.

It is, therefore, our mentality that needs addressing. We need to re-evaluate our own sense of reason. It is what we do and why we do it that needs our attention. It is the rationale behind our actions and the emotion behind our endeavours that lie at the crux of the matter. It is the actions we take and the choices we make that will define us in an insane world. If those actions and choices are good, decent and honourable then surely this is enough to rebuild some stability and promote public reassurance. Sadly the Government appears to be doing little to encourage worthy human behaviours. Whether or not it intends to be so false and pathetic is irrelevant, as the end result is awful. This victim culture – e.g. Britain at the moment – is in a right old mess. It is therefore up to all of us, individually, to do what is right. If we continue as we are, however, we'll carry on being completely fucked.

And what is *right* depends entirely on who we are and where we are. Yet deep down inside we all have an inkling of right and wrong. There are some intrinsic things that link every human being on the face of the planet. If we could but reach out and grasp at those tiny, fragile lifelines that connect us and unite us, then maybe, just maybe, we'll survive.

* * *

PC Michael Pinkstone

There will be another.

MELROSE BOOKS

If you enjoyed this book you may also like:

This Victorian Playground Part 1:
Policing a Victim Culture in Britain
PC Michael Pinkstone

This Victorian Playground is a combination of treatise, commentary, diatribe and memoir on policing in present-day Britain. It is absorbing, informative, convincing and hugely entertaining.

"I do solemnly and sincerely declare and affirm that I will well and truly serve the Queen in the office of constable, with fairness, integrity, diligence and impartiality, upholding fundamental human rights and according equal respect to all people; and that I will, to the best of my power, cause the peace to be kept and preserved and prevent all offences against people and property; and that while I continue to hold the said office I will to the best of my skill and knowledge discharge all the duties thereof faithfully according to law…"

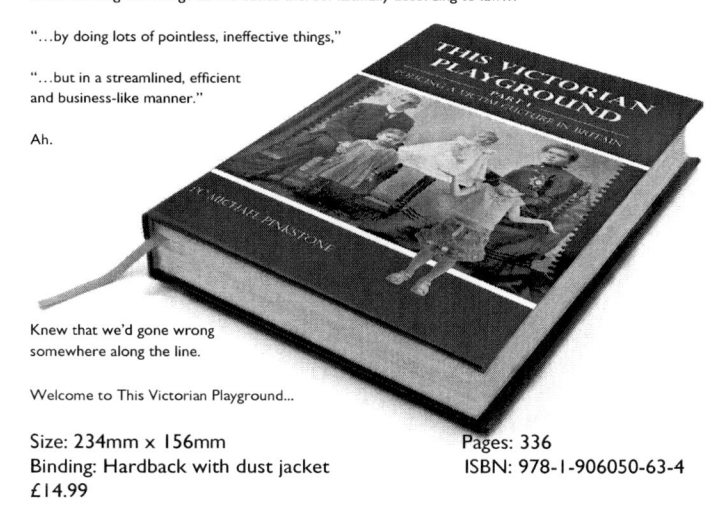

"…by doing lots of pointless, ineffective things,"

"…but in a streamlined, efficient and business-like manner."

Ah.

Knew that we'd gone wrong somewhere along the line.

Welcome to This Victorian Playground…

Size: 234mm x 156mm
Binding: Hardback with dust jacket
£14.99

Pages: 336
ISBN: 978-1-906050-63-4

St Thomas' Place, Ely, Cambridgeshire CB7 4GG, UK
www.melrosebooks.com   sales@melrosebooks.com